THE ADVANCED
SEEKERS' SERIES

THE ADVANCED SEEKERS' SERIES

AN ANTHOLOGY OF ADVAITA BOOKS

(VOLUME ONE)

Copyright © 2011 by Floyd Henderson

Published by Henderson Books
Montgomery,
TX 77256

ISBN: 978-0-578-08496-1

Printed in the United States of America

CONTENTS

A NOTE TO READERS

This anthology of four books by Floyd Henderson contains the volumes that make up what has been called "The Advanced Seekers' Series" for those seeking Realization via the Advaita teachings.

For those who have studied any of the various types of yoga and who have studied either Traditional Advaita Vedanta, Neo-Advaita, Neo-Vedanta, or Pseudo Advaita: the author of this book is a disciple of Sri Nisargadatta Maharaj so he uses the Direct Path Method of teaching along with the Nisarga (Natural) Yoga, all shared in simple, everyday English.

Other anthologies of Henderson's books will be published in the future.

Presently, all of his books are available at
FloydHenderson.com
or
amazon.com
or
amazon.co.uk
or
amazon.de

FOREWORD

When I attended a three-day Advaita Retreat at Floyd Henderson's lakeside "loft" in Texas in 2009, it was the culmination of over two decades of seeking. After that, I was no longer a "seeker."

Prior to traveling to Texas, I had already participated in Floyd's on-line Advaita Classes, which entailed reading all of his books, some of which are anthologized in this volume. Of course, being a "good spiritual giant" at the time, I tried to start the Advaita Classes at the advanced stage. Floyd suggested I start at the beginning, which was - of course - the proper manner.

As a "recovering" Baptist with a primary Type Six Personality, I was an unlikely seeker. Floyd's teacher, Sri Nisargadatta Maharaj, said that only one in ten million seekers would ever Realize. Type Sixes and those suffering from religious or spiritual intoxication are the most unlikely to be in that miniscule percentage.

After several years of praying and taking communion in the Methodist Church, I took up fasting, chanting, and meditating in the Asian tradition. When none of that worked, I tried to mix Methodist worship and Zen meditation. That was very weird and the chaos of dualistic existence did not end.

Fortunately, I came across Maharaj's book, "I AM THAT" at the Zen Center during my meditation phase. Something about it resonated, and in the years that followed, as I continued to seek, Maharaj's message was always returning.

I began to search for "western advaita" on-line. I found Floyd Henderson's website and began to follow his Nisarga (or Natural) Yoga pointers. Today, as a result of studying Advaita and Nisarga Yoga with Floyd, my existence is no longer ruled by dual thought, personality, and emotion. The meaning of the statement "I Am That; I Am" is understood.

The understanding brought about by following the pointers shared by Floyd is that we have become separated from our Original Nature by seven degrees or stages. This separation is brought about by the conditioning, programming, acculturation, and domestication that are inherent in coming of age in a culture characterized by duality. We accumulate concepts, ideas, and beliefs, all dual in nature and all untrue; in other words, we fall under the influence of learned ignorance.

Utilizing the Direct Path Method and offering the Nisarga Yoga, Floyd Henderson reverses the process and takes the protégé step-by-step back through the stages of separation, discarding the learned ignorance in the order in which it was received. This ignorance includes false identifications and spiritual concepts and religious dogma. There is no longer any need for prayer, worship, communion, chanting, or meditation (as it is typically understood). If the pointers are followed, the protégé can realize her or his Original Nature and live naturally, quietly, and peacefully without the chaos of dual thoughts or the drama of emotional intoxication.

I'll let Floyd tell you about the stages, degrees of separation, and pointers in detail by way of the content of the books in this anthology. The pointers in this collection (along with the readiness) are all that are needed to begin following the Nisargan pointers. Get on with it. Read these books, and if possible, do as I did and visit the "loft" on Lake Conroe. According to Maharaj's estimates, there are only 670 on the planet today that are Fully Realized. Relative living is most enjoyable if you happen to be one of those.

Andrew C. McMaster

Florissant, MO

WHO IS FLOYD HENDERSON?

The literary tradition is to preface a book with a biographical snapshot of the author as a person. What can be said then, about the Advaitin Teacher, who has moved beyond personal biography?

To describe the person or the personal (the date of birth, the nationality, the job, the interests, the home, the child, the books read, the path followed) is to describe the attributes that actually take us further away from uncovering the teacher's identity.

The reality is that this "Who Is ..." question itself brings us to deeper and more authentic questions. What is this understanding in which the teacher resides? The state of Realization is not different from teacher to teacher. That Self-Knowledge is unchanging. In this way, there is no difference between a Nisargadatta Maharaj, a Floyd Henderson, or any other Realized teacher.

The Realisation of SELF means the shattering of the shell of separation so that the non-dual nature of Reality is directly known. How can this be different from person to person? Only in the ABSENCE of the person is this nature revealed. In this way, Floyd Henderson invites us to strip away all that is personal, all that is dualistic, all that separates us from this understanding of Oneness – from our True Selves.

The summative statement "I AM THAT; I AM" describes that understanding of SELF in absolute terms as well as its expression in the relative. Floyd Henderson is THAT – just like all human beings; however, Floyd is fixed unshakably in this understanding, so all functioning, relatively speaking, flows directly from this SELF-Knowledge.

In this way, the biographical details (such as, "born" in Louisiana; moved to Texas; worked as a teacher and business owner over several decades before taking early retirement to write; father of a daughter named Ashley; current resident in the community of Walden on Lake Conroe in Texas; years of seeking followed by twenty-five months in the forest dweller stage and experiencing a vision that resulted in the dramatic peripetia or flash of Realization; functioning as a Direct

Path, Nisargan teacher; and author of over forty Advaita books) are the attributes or flavourings which coloured the pure consciousness in the particular shape and form at the relative level.

Yet, these attributes are false ingredients. They cannot provide a true answer to the question "Who is Floyd Henderson?" because he recognizes no who-ness at all ... believes in no "who" that is living "here" at all. He once explained it this way when asked if he was ever bothered by people:

> "... How could persons possibly bother Me? They do not have even the slightest clue about where I truly live. Only a few on the entire planet called "earth" have a clue. Some might enter what is called 'floyd's house' or 'floyd's home,' but that is not where I live; in fact, 'where' I live has nothing to do with a 'where' at all.
>
> In this regard, there is actually only the 'how.' 'How' I abide is as the aware-ness, as the Original Nature, as the natural state which has no boundaries, which has no defining traits, and which does not change. 'How' I abide is without conditions or conditioning, without qualifications, and without limitations.
>
> I can seem to be 'here' one second and 'there' the next, but that is about 'how-ness,' not any actual 'here-ness' or 'there-ness.' I am not confined to a space or form; furthermore, I can enter other spaces and forms, and do so regularly (as might happen the instant You read these words).
>
> Abiding beyond consciousness and beyond beingness and beyond non-being-ness, I can span the globe ... I can span the universe ... I have spanned all universes. Yet such 'while manifested' spannings seldom happen anymore, requiring far more energy than is worth the effort, and it most assuredly need not happen with You.
>
> As for Me, abidance will continue to happen in a whole and unadulterated and unambiguous manner until the consciousness unmanifests. Until that happens, then abidance will happen as Reality is overlaid on the relative without exception. When the consciousness unmanifests, then the drop shall enter the ocean of energy from which it came and will span the Absolute; Awareness shall be, but aware of-ness shall not. Later, other universes might be spanned as well, or might not. Yet all of that is stated, so it, too, cannot be the Truth which You know but do not yet know that You know. Tap into the

source and know Truth, but even then, do not suppose that You will be able to express Truth in words."

Thus, Floyd describes the AM-ness regarding "floyd" as a "composite unity" of an elemental plant food body that is circulating air and that is temporarily housing the manifested consciousness.

The THAT-ness he sees as a field of energy from which the conscious-energy manifests and to which it will return.

As for identification with any WHO-ness, he discarded that when identification with the Nothingness came, followed eventually by not even identifying with Nothing - or anything else.

Louise Sterling
Cape Town, South Africa

EDITOR'S NOTE

Before I found the Advaita teachings, both my seeking and my life were totally disorganized. I had read over two hundred books during my search which began around the age of eleven or twelve. All of the content of those books was very confusing. Why?

While some presented teachings that seemed in the beginning to be of value, in the end they proved useless because none of the pointers were organized in a way to offer in a step-by-step manner the route that had to be followed to move away from identification with the false "I" and return to My Original Nature.

It became clear that - in my case - I required a teacher that could offer such an explanation and that could be available to answer my many questions along the way.

Though my reading left me a supposed "expert" is subjects dealing with the brain and the mind and psychology and psychiatry, there was no understanding at all of the functioning of the totality.

So my searching continued for many more years, moving from one book to the next and from one religion to the next and from one spiritual movement to the next and from one philosophy to the next. I studied Taoism, Christianity, Hinduism, Buddhism - you name it - I studied it.

It is suspected that many may have traveled as arduous a road as the one I traveled, but few likely traveled a more arduous route than the one I traveled during my years of seeking.

The searching in one venue after another continued until an acquaintance shared certain profound pointers that seemed to resonance deeply within me.

I asked what he was talking about ... asked if the pointers he was sharing were associated with any particular philosophy or religion that I could further investigate. He answered, "What I'm sharing is what is called 'a non-dual perspective'."

"What is that?" I asked.

"Basically, the simplest teaching is that everything is one."

That made little sense, but it did seem to reverberate at some spot deep inside me. Eventually, intuition was re-awakened and there was some sort of "psychic consciousness" that began to vibrate when non-duality pointers were being considered.

After being given some labels for further investigation - specifically, "non-duality" and "Advaita" - it soon became clear that I needed to find a capable Advaita teacher.

The irony was that, as I began searching for a teacher, all of the online sites promoting and ranking various teachers were actually reinforcing duality ... ranking this one as "best" and that one as "good" and that other one as "not so adept." Instead of focusing on how we could eliminate our beliefs in hierarchies and separation and judgment, they were promoting all of those.

So I left the listings and began googling "Advaita" and found a blog site where Floyd Henderson was offering daily postings of non-dual pointers.

I began investigating this guy, wondering who he thought he was to be posting pointers about Advaita. He was not even from the Far East. Worse, my investigations uncovered the fact that this guy lived in Texas.

Being yet embroiled in ego, I asked, "Who does this guy living outside of Houston, Texas think he is ... acting like he 'knows it all' about these teachings?" I concluded, "Heck, I live in Texas. I guarantee I already know as much about non-duality as any other person living in Texas. Who from Texas could offer anything about this eastern philosophy?"

Then I clicked the link for the retreats he offered and saw that, of even greater offense, he wanted to charge a fee for retreats where he teaches non-duality. (At the time, it did not register that I was not providing free meals to everyone who entered one of the restaurants in the chain I own.)

[NOTE: What Andy is not revealing here is all of the altruistic and philan-thropic projects and charities which he has funded for years, offering assistance to the downtrodden and suffering.]

A year would pass, and more and more searching continued, but at least once a week, the name "Floyd Henderson" came into the forefront of consciousness.

As much as I tried to ignore the name, it would not leave me, so after a year of continued seeking even after having first found his name and websites, I finally went back to his Advaita blog site, looked at the cost of a retreat with him, and concluded, differently this time, "Well, actually it really is only a nominal fee he is charging, and he does have to pay his bills."

So it came to me, "What if this guy just might have what you've been looking for all of your life?" I determined that I might as well spend a few dollars - a small amount really in comparison to the fortune I had already spent during decades of seeking and searching ... all with no permanent results at all.

Right now, it is giving me cold chills just reflecting on that decision and what happened afterwards. I had reached a point where I felt as if I were going to pop right out of my skin from all of the suffering and misery and anxiety and stress that had characterized my existence.

For me, it had to get so bad that I became willing and ready - ready to give up all of the ideas and beliefs that had served me not at all and to seek the Truth that was obviously beyond all of the concepts I had ever taken to be the truth.

Eventually, I went to a retreat at Floyd's home and left three days later having found that I was not only willing to give up all of those concepts but had become willing to give up this fear-based "andy" that had been at the root of my problems.

Now, I look back and laugh. Before the time spent in Floyd's home, I hated to wake up in the morning. Now, I can't wait to get up and enjoy every day.

I was raised to believe that Jesus had the answers that people need. At Floyd's retreat, I found out that in many cases, he did, but the answers were not the ones I was taught in church.

I found that "the later Jesus" who returned to Jerusalem was sharing the non-dual, Advaita teachings - teachings I had heard on occasion when I was younger but that no one in the church could or would explain to me when I asked about those statements.

I went to Floyd's that first time with a considerable fear of death (rooted, I would learn, in body and mind and personality identification). He suggested that if I was so afraid of death that the best thing I could do would be to "go ahead and die now."

Of course that was an anger-invoking, shocking comment to hear, but before I left, I understood that I could not die because I was not born - that what he was saying is that my ego(s) and my egotism must "die."

I understood after that retreat that I cannot truly live until this ego - this illusion - dies. To that point, I was entering Floyd's house one morning through the door he leaves open while he is preparing breakfast for participants.

As I entered, I shouted, "Knock knock ... anybody home?" He yelled back, "No." I got it ... I knew exactly what he meant, and that understanding has remained and I have since enjoyed the freedom every day of knowing I am no body ... nobody.

I came to understood that everything merely cycles and that timelines are a fraud, and Floyd also taught me the meaning of every part of his vision, and I learned by way of the eagle the difference in Subject-Object Witnessing and Pure Witnessing.

Why am I making this anthology available for all seekers to use now and to be available long after "floyd" and "andy" have taken mahasamadhi and are "gone"? First, because the books in this anthology offer the step-by-step process by which Realization can happen and, secondly, because the books helped me in that undertaking.

I want to preserve Floyd's vision and his writings for all who are seeking. I decided to support the printing of this anthology to make his teachings and methods available - to all that might be interested - because of what happened with me after sitting with Floyd and receiving the message that came by way of his step-by-step method which I realized was exactly what I had been seeking all of my life.

I am taking the action to help make these books available to interested seekers because I now know beyond a shadow of a doubt that if the understanding offered in these books - and Floyd's other books - could come to me, then the understanding can come to almost anyone.

May you allow the pure consciousness to see and receive the content of the works in this anthology and then also receive as a result the blissful freedom that came to me via the content of these and the other writings by Floyd Henderson.

Andrew Gugar, Jr.

Tyler, TX

FROM THE AUTHOR

This anthology contains four books that many seekers have used along their "path" as they moved to Full Realization.

The four-book series offers the following:

1. An opportunity for seekers to be guided through the seven-step "journey" from identification with the false "I" (via the content of the book FROM THE I TO THE ABSOLUTE) and to move beyond "The Seven Degrees of Separation from Reality";

2. An opportunity to understand the nature of Reality Beyond Self-Realization (with the content of the book CONSCIOUSNESS / AWARENESS);

3. An opportunity to understand that which was prior to the Absolute, namely, The Void, the Nothingness; and then

4. An opportunity to reach the Ultimate and Final Understanding.

To master all four of those levels of understanding is to enable the seeker to grasp Sri Nisargadatta Maharaj's pointer that "wisdom is knowing that I am nothing."

For most seekers, the "journey" ends when they reach the third of seven steps as they move along the first-stage "path," specifically, the point at which they adopt a new persona ("The Religious One" or "The Spiritual Giant") and then never move any further.

There, Maharaj said, they engage in what he called "kindergarten-level spirituality" and they "mistake the dawn for the noonday sun."

Only a few will truly understand the distinction between the consciousness and the awareness, and fewer still will be willing to abandon the notion that now they are Really Something and to consider the ultimate freedom of The Nothingness.

A synopsis of the four books follows:

BOOK ONE

FROM THE I TO THE ABSOLUTE

(A SEVEN-STEP JOURNEY TO REALITY)

Most of the so-called "Spiritual Masters" addressed at one time or another all of the steps that must be taken to shift from identifying with the false "I" to abiding as the Absolute, yet they did not present or explain the steps in the exact order in which they must be taken if Realization is to happen.

While all of the steps (or "stages" to use Sri Nisargadatta Maharaj's term) have been discussed for centuries, this is the first time that the steps have been offered and explained in simple language in the exact order in which the seven steps must be taken in order to move from "the lie of the I" to Full Realization.

Most of the content of this book contains the complete set of transcripts from audio tapings of a series of satsang sessions that guided the participants from step one to Realization. Some have said that by reading the questions from seekers and the immediate responses by floyd (all offered in their original, easy, conversational format), they have felt as if they were present in the room, actively engaged in the satsang along with fellow seekers.

For those who have studied any of the various types of yoga and who have studied either Traditional Advaita Vedanta, Neo-Advaita, Neo-Vedanta, or Pseudo Advaita: the author of this book is a disciple of Sri Nisargadatta Maharaj so he uses the Direct Path Method of teaching along with the Nisarga (Natural) Yoga.

Regards on your "journey" to Full Realization.

BOOK TWO

CONSCIOUSNESS/AWARENESS

THE NATURE OF REALITY BEYOND SELF-REALIZATION (PEACE EVERY DAY WHEN ABIDING AS THE ABSOLUTE)

One of the "final frontiers" of the Advaita Teachings is transitioned when the Nature of Reality is understood and when the Advaita Teachings are "applied" on a daily basis even in the absence of any "Applier."

The Final Understanding happens post-Self-Realization, but the nature of Reality cannot be understood until the nature of Consciousness / Awareness is understood. Understanding the Nature of Consciousness allows for abidance in the I AM, but what of THAT Which Is beyond, and that which is beyond the beyond?

Only abidance as the Absolute (and later, the Nothingness) allows for the remainder of the manifestation of Consciousness to happen in Perfect Peace.

BOOK THREE

FROM THE ABSOLUTE TO THE NOTHINGNESS

An understanding of the pointers offered in this book can allow the advanced seeker to shift even beyond SELF-Realization, even beyond an understanding of Consciousness and Awareness, and to an understanding of that which preceded the Absolute.

The content of this book can, in fact, allow the advanced seeker to truly comprehend the Reality of "no concept," of "no duality," of "no something," and even of "no nothing."

The Advaita Teachings offer an invitation to be free of all concepts, all beliefs, and all ideas in order to be totally free. Yet how many reach that "state," and how many who reach that "state" are able to fixate in that understanding and truly be free and thereby at peace?

This book will offer details of the way that can happen.

Consideration

Regarding one character in a Michael Connelly novel: "He was long past believing in God - the horrors he had seen documented had, little by little, sapped his stores of faith. In those seemingly final days, as his own heart withered and tapped out its final cadences, he did not grasp desperately for his lost faith as a shield or a means of easing the fear of the unknown. Instead, he was accepting of the end, of his own nothingness. He was ready. It was easy to do."

BOOK FOUR

The book THE FINAL UNDERSTANDING is

(a) for the few that are willing to consider that there is far more to grasp after having reached the third, spiritual step (which will only move seekers as far as "the dim light of dawn");

(b) for the few that have even the slightest awareness that the brighter light of the full noonday sun awaits; and

(c) for the few that have some sense that the freedom and peace which come with abandonment of the notion that they are Really Something will allow for the full shift into the no-concept, no-identity, non-dual Reality.

In THE FINAL UNDERSTANDING, the author discusses:

A. The myths of a "Prior Me" and a "Post-Manifestation Me";

B. The myths of "You-ness," "Me-ness," and "Them-ness";

C. Krishna's pointers about that which is beyond the beingness and the non-beingness;

D. Abandonment of "the personal" and "The Personal" and an understanding of Presence instead;

E. The truth of the composite unity (elements, breath, conscious-energy) as opposed to the falsehood of the triad of body-mind-personality;

F. The sixteen shifts in awareness which must happen in a step-wise fashion for misunderstandings to be abandoned and for the final understanding to manifest;

G. The pointers about religion and spirituality that were offered by Maharaj which allow seekers (who are trapped at the third step while playing their "new and improved persona or personas") to move along the entire "path" and then reach the final understanding;

H. A distinction between supernatural, unnatural, and nisarga (natural) living; and much more.

FROM THE I TO THE ABSOLUTE (A SEVEN-STEP JOURNEY TO REALITY)

A NOTE TO THE READERS

REALIZATION only came when one particular path was followed in one particular order. A vision came during a meditative session when the theta state of consciousness was reached. It laid out an exact, direct path from the false "I" to Realization; however, the vision made no sense to me at the time. Then, I began reading the transcripts of Advaita talks and they made clear the message of my vision. Talks on varied topics in varied orders eventually provided the understanding of each of the stages seen in the vision. The only thing remaining for an "Aha" moment to happen was to take his assortment of sharings and use them to understand the exact order to follow along the path. This book will offer to you the seven-step path to take and the order in which it has to be traveled.

After realization, a shift occurred in the way communication happened. In fact, instances of communication became fewer and farther between, and when the silence came, many noticed a shift. Some inquired as to the source and some came to hear more and some brought friends with them. A variety of questions were raised and the understanding was offered. Finally, it became clear that the Teaching should be presented in a more organized fashion, so a schedule of sessions was set up in which the seven steps would be offered in order. When one participant asked if her friend could tape the first session since she would have to miss that one, it was done. After that, all the exchanges were taped because a sense came that the 2001-2002 session might be the last. (A few of the exchanges that are included took place via e-mails or telephone conferences as well.)

Shortly after the last session, a retreat began that continues to this day. Days now pass mostly in the silence on the lake. Occasionally the Teachings are shared when contacted by e-mail or telephone, and on a website as well, but mainly the silence prevails. After realization, there was no path, no journey, no concepts … only the freedom of the Void and AS IF living afterwards. May you travel the path to freedom as well.

Finally, please note that a "Glossary of Terms" appears in the back of this book. The explanations and definitions are not those that will be found in Advaita lists that include the Far Eastern terms used by many gurus and teachers; instead, the terms are explained in ways that are relevant to this work in particular which tries to use everyday language when possible to provide as simple an explanation as possible while discussing what can be complicated subject matter.

Defining Advaita Vedanta

In its simplest form, "Advaita" is merely a system or an approach that can lead to Realization. Realization is what occurs when one becomes aware of all that he is not and eventually "Realizes" What He Really Is. The goal of the process is to allow people to eliminate all illusions and delusional thinking that result in dependence, in co-dependencies, in beliefs in superstitions, and in the mental and emotional dependence that results when we accept all the lies programmed into us through the culture's conditioning.

Mental and emotional restrictions occur when we adopt the ideas and beliefs of others without ever having truly investigated those attitudes. The Advaita approach allows us to become truly free. Being "truly free" refers to being free of the ideas, free of the emotional intoxication, and free of the beliefs that have been used to control us, to create fears in us, and to drive us to be influenced by illusions and lies. In its broadest use, "Vedanta" is simply that message that is beyond any written texts that are said to be "holy" or that claim to contain "truth." My own experience has shown that the truth is already within each individual and can be Realized when one experiences the Advaitic approach with a "guide" who has undergone that process, seen the false, and then comes to understand That— That Which Is Real.

The Seven Degrees of Separation from Reality

Some Westerners will likely think that certain of the entries on this site have a "too philosophical" bent. No apology for that shall be offered since one must either find a working philosophy or be doomed to adopt their ideology instead, and my experience shows that nothing is more destructive than buying into their ideology. For the most part, however, the version of the Advaita Vedanta (Non-Duality) message that I offer has been characterized by one protégé as being "Applied Advaita."

I will present the concepts of Non-Duality, yes, but eventually they are to be applied in everyday situations and used to bring peace and acceptance around the issues of the day. Ultimately, the concepts can be tossed, your everyday situations will be discarded, you will have no mind capable of being disturbed, and you will have no issues-du-jour. My teacher Sri Nisardagatta Maharaj was as direct and straight-forward as he could be while working in an Indian culture that tended to focus on its glossary of phrases and terms and words associated with Eastern philosophy. (That study, too, was a part of my "journey.")

Yet we must remember that the ultimate goal is for you to come to know You. You are invited to study the dilemma expressed in that "I don't even know who I am" complaint (which contains an ironic duality in itself, yes?) and come to Know the answer to the age-old question implied in that statement. Ultimately, your culture has created a seven-fold barrier that is separating you from Knowing THAT Which You Are. We'll discuss all seven eventually. The first of the Seven Degrees of Separation from the Knowledge of THAT Which You Are appears in the form of a manifested body. Offered as a meditation for today, therefore, I invite you to consider how the belief that you are a BODY might prevent your seeing the greater truth of Who or What You Truly Are. Are You your body?

PLEASE NOTE: The terms "wet charcoal" "dry charcoal," and "gunpowder" will be mentioned. You will read pointers that are offered at times in the discussions that will seemingly contradict what you might read in other books or on the Advaita website referenced earlier on the copyright page. Beginners (the wet group) will be given one piece of advice, those farther along the path (the dry group) will be given other pointers, and those who need only a few additional points for the truth to explode into consciousness (the gunpowder group) will be offered something different.

THE FIRST DEGREE OF SEPARATION FROM REALITY: BODY IDENTIFICATION

THE FIRST DEGREE OF SEPARATION FROM REALITY: BODY IDENTIFICATION, PART ONE

"THE Arms-Legs-Organs" Consideration can help people become free of the limiting, false belief that they are the body. Of the various self-concepts that block most humans from Realizing Who We Truly Are, body identification is the most basic and least sophisticated identity. Belief that one is the body preempts engagement in Self-Inquiry and—unless transcended—will prevent one from ever coming to know THAT Which We Absolutely Are. I offer the consideration now to you: If you were to lose your right arm, would You still be You?

You would still be You, right, even without that arm? If you were to lose your left arm, would You still be You? You would still be You, even without that arm… correct? If you were to lose your left leg, would You still be You? You would still be You, right, even without that leg? If you lose your other leg, wouldn't You still be You? You would still be You, right, even without that leg? Would You still be You if you have a heart transplant? You would still be You, yes? If you have a lung transplant, are You still You? You would still be You, right, even without your original lung or your original heart?

And if you looked into your own eyes in a mirror, wouldn't You still know that You are You, even though your physical body is only a shadow of what it once was? Then...Who Are You? Who or What You Truly Are must be something beyond the physical body.

If more than half of what most consider to be "you" were to be lost, Who Is That You that remains? Moreover, Who is that You that is sensing that You would still be You, and would still be complete, even after the loss of four body appendages and the replacement of two original organs? Please enter the silence of contemplation.

THE FIRST DEGREE
OF SEPARATION FROM REALITY:
Body Identification,
Part Two

With those first beginning a journey of Self-Inquiry, my teacher always addressed the illusion of body identification, so I too begin with that beginning. What's the problem with thinking you are your body? That misconception leads to chaotic behavior, insane conduct, and problems in relationship...especially with yourself. Regarding problems with others, occasional chances for a respite occur, but the problems with yourself are 24/7; worse, they not only create occasional misery and grief but often result in self-destructive behaviors as well.

Body identification can be chaotic and even fatal. Here's how. I once had a dog that, when it saw its reflection in a mirror, would go ballistic. He fought with that false self, biting at the mirror and trying to destroy himself/his own reflection. (In humans identified with their bodies, the deep-seated need to destroy the ego and false roles and to be true to Self is a subconscious, driving force that leads to self-destructive behavior or even suicidal assaults against the physical body. If I am my body and I am having overwhelming problems, then the way to be rid of those is to be rid of the body, so the unconscious, fallacious reasoning goes.

In fact, one need not be free of the body to be content, merely free of body identification and other false identifications as well. The goal of Advaita Vedanta is to use preemptive strikes to eliminate the notion that the illusion is real, for illusions incite all insane, destructive behavior.) Of course when my dog looked at an image and became fear-based and angry, he was never seeing anything but a reflection; however, once he took the reflection to be real and separate and threat-ening—thinking the reflection to be an "other"—he fought the foolish fight. (Humans do the same. They fight the foolish fight when they see reflections or illusions that they take to be the real.) Despite my greatest efforts to help the dog realize that what he thought he was seeing was not the real, he reacted as do most humans: If I can see something right before my very eyes, you are the one who must be insane to suggest it's not real.

How does believing in an illusion complicate one's life? The dog illustrates the point perfectly. When he took the image to be real, the dog tried to make himself appear even tougher. He adopted a phony persona and behaved more violently. He tried to appear to be even more intimidating than the image that he thought real; thus, he became even more aggressive. The more the illusion seemed to be attacking him, the greater his counterattack. The greater his coun-terattack, the more real and threatening the illusion appeared to be. He was trapped in a vicious cycle of war, all based in image.

Persons are at war with themselves—with their false selves and false identi-ties. Persons are at war with others, and those wars are based in illusion as well. By trying to appear to be tougher and to be something he was not, the dog reinforced the imaginary self in the mirror and became even more frightened, more confused, and more miserable. And the more frightened and confused and miserable he became, the more chaotic his life became and the more those around him were impacted by his chaos.

(Consider the result if persons in leadership positions were enlightened... not frightened by their faulty perceptions, not thinking that their illusions are real, and not utterly confused but completely logical instead. Imagine the effect if the Don Quixotes of the world Realized that the windmills are just windmills and that they are not threatening opponents. The leaders could then stop their jousting and those around them would no longer be impacted by the war and the chaos that the unenlightened create. That is what "Applied Advaita" would look like.)

But what about you? You now see the irony with my dog, correct? There never was any duality. All his madness was based in misconception and illusion. There was the "real thing" and a perceived image. Such is the case with persons. To believe that one is the body is to believe that "others" are separate and threat-ening and that the illusions and images reflected before one's eyes are real. As with the dog, just because a person can see a body does not mean that it is real, and just because a person can see the body does not mean that it defines Who or What He or She Really Is.

Is it seen that all duality is false, based as duality is in supposing that one or more real parts can co-exist with one or more other parts that are illusions? No "parts" exist and no illusion can "exist." It really is just illusion. Only the One Is Real, and by removing the Seven Degrees of Separation that prevent most from ever finding what The One Is, you will ultimately find the Real You...your True Self. Your body is not It. Are you seeing the lie of duality and the truth of Non-Duality more clearly? Please enter the silence of contemplation.

THE FIRST DEGREE OF SEPARATION FROM REALITY: BODY IDENTIFICATION, PART THREE

[The discussion of the illusion of body identification will continue via transcriptions of exchanges during workshops conducted during 2001-2002]:

Questioner: The "Arms–Legs-Arms Consideration" has shown me something, but I'm not sure what."

F: "Ha. OK. Hopefully, the consideration first reveals that you are not the body and then, secondly, inspires you to ask, 'Well, if I'm not my body, Who or What am I?' The body is momentary. That which is fleeting cannot be the Real. Consider the similarity with a melted ice cube that seems to have 'gone' or 'disappeared' when placed in a glass of hot water. In fact, that which 'the cube' truly Is did not 'go' or 'disappear': all of the pairs of hydrogen atoms that had grouped with various oxygen atoms still remain. Only the appearance of the form that those atoms had manifested in for a time led to the misconception that the cube was destroyed. As with the cube, when the body 'dies' and 'dissolves' away, the appearance of the form alters but all the elements from which the body was composed still remain. What 'disappeared' was an image wrongly perceived. In the 'Arms-Legs-Organs exercise,' the arms, legs, and some original organs of your manifested form seem to disappear, but just as the hydrogen and oxygen atoms of the cube remain, so remains That Which You Truly Are. You sensed that truth during the exercise. You did sense that You would still be You, right?"

Q: "Yes."

F: "Then what is That which you sense is remaining—even after arms, legs, and organs are gone?"

Q: "I sense that I still exist."

F: "Yes. You sense that You still Are. Specifically, You sense the 'I Am' or Your 'I Amness,' which we'll discuss later. Another way of understanding the results of the exercise would be to say that 'You experienced Your presence.' You experienced the truth of the fact that 'something' would be present even after most of the physical parts of 'you'—of your body—disappear. During the experiment, you are not sensing your complete body—for much of it is gone—but you are sensing a complete presence. That is what you are aware of when, even without those appendages and organs, you know that You Are still You."

Q: "OK."

F: "If you understood that pointer totally, no more would need to be heard, but too much remains to block that full understanding. So, we continue. Next, since we have seen that there is no duality, that there is no subject-object duality, Who (or What) can you now conclude knows that consciousness?"

Q: (Questioning look)

F: "Let me put it to you another way. What remains after the body parts are gone that is sensing that presence? What is conscious of that presence?"

Q: "I don't know."

F: "That's close! Ha. That which knows the presence or the consciousness of Self, since there is no duality, has to be…CONSCIOUSNESS! It's simple! It is that unprogrammed, unconditioned, prior consciousness that senses Itself in the manifest form which you call your physical body. Wordsworth wrote his 'Ode on Intimations of Immortality' after he had sensed his 'infinite Self.' The arms-legs-organs exercise affords you that same opportunity: to become intimate with Your Immortal or Infinite Self. (Later, we'll even amend that concept.) That Is What I Truly Am, and always have Been, and always will Be—hang the body. In the process of Self-Inquiry, we see the false, we see the mirages, we see the images, we see the "not real," and we thereby come to know what we are not. The exercise in intended to help you see first what you are not and then sense that You Are something beyond the body. You actually sensed Your own presence remaining, even after much of the body was discarded during the exercise. If you got even that much from the exercise, then you have received the basic benefit: you have been prepared to ask the next logical question. And what would that be?"

Q: "Well, as you said earlier: if I'm not the body, then What Am I?"

F: "Exactly." Please enter the silence of contemplation.

THE FIRST DEGREE
OF SEPARATION FROM REALITY:
Body Identification, Part Four

F: "Having been 'to the end' and having transcended the Seven Degrees that had separated me from knowing The Absolute, I was able to 'look back' from the place of Reality and see all the false. I can tell you that once I came to know That—the True Self—I no longer ponder any false ego-state, persona, or identity when I hear the 'Who or What Am I?' query. But you have not yet been to the end. You are at the beginning of Self-inquiry, so you must see each and every thing that you are not, and if you would know the answer to the question, you must transcend—in order—each of the stages which I'll make you aware of in our sessions.

Compare our journey to that up Maslow's Hierarchy of Human Needs. If you do not master level one, you cannot ascend to two. If you have not mastered levels one and two, you cannot transition to three. As with the climb up Maslow's pyramid to Self-Actualization, the journey to Reality cannot skip any of the stages I'll define, all of which must be transitioned. With each advancement along the path, you move farther away from the personal and closer to the Impersonal Reality. You must clearly see the illusion of each of the Seven Degrees that I define for you, and you cannot skip from one to three or from two to five.

You must consider each of the stages, see the lies around each, and only then move to the next. You have been led to believe that you are many things. All that you have ever been told to this point is a lie; on the other hand, all which is already within you that you have not yet experienced will serve as your vehicle to truth, and then all that is within you which you already know—but do not yet know that you know—will be revealed. Inquiry ends and You will Know The Real."

Q: "Would you say that again?"

F: "I'll repeat the part you should focus on for now. You must see each and every 'thing' that you are not. For now, seek not the truth. Only seek to realize all that is false. That is your beginning. When you eventually come to know The Great Reality—The Absolute—you will Realize that all perceived via the five senses is false and is nothing more than learned ignorance. It is learned ignorance that spoiled your pure consciousness and resulted in a 'mind.' The journey via the Non-Duality approach will detox your consciousness and restore it to its original, pure condition. Once you're 'out of your mind,' then You will know That which You know."

Q: "So consciousness is not destroyed at death? What about, 'He's lost consciousness'?"

F: "Ha. In that case, why not also ask, 'What about, "The earth is flat"?' Let's go back to the ice cube to discuss the false concept of 'loss.' If an ice cube melts in a glass of hot water, you might have seemingly 'lost' your ice cube, but have you really lost the clusterings of two atoms of hydrogen and one atom of oxygen?"

Q: "Of course not."

F: "So it is with consciousness. The ice cube resulted when clusters of three atoms combined in an exact pattern at a specific temperature. Even after the 'disappearance' from your view, that which it was…remains. It is. I am sorry to shatter another popular illusion, this one relating to what a special gift you were from some entity, but now is an appropriate time to report to you that your body resulted nine months after two plant-food-eaters entered into an exercise of friction. That's it. (Laughter) You are consciousness manifest, and when the body 'disappears,' conscious energy cannot be destroyed. It is not lost. Now, you should be moving to a clearer understanding that you are not the body."

Q: "But the cube was at one point and now it isn't."

F: "If you believe that, then you'll continue to cling to your body identification. Your journey ends here. You will never get past this first degree, much less be able to negotiate the next six. If you look at a steel girder from a distance, and then look at the same girder through an electron microscope, what you report seeing in those two instances will appear to be very different. When you see the girder at an atomic level, it looks nothing like what you thought you were perceiving with the naked eye. Did you lose the girder once you looked into the microscope? No. The only thing you lost was a wrong perception regarding what that girder really is."

Q: "Clarify, please. It seems the girder is both what I see with the naked eye and what I see through the microscope."

F: "So you choose to abandon non-duality and adopt duality? In that case, you're excused. You may leave. (Laughter) No, please be seated. I was joking, though I can assure you that my teacher would have run you out of his loft the second you made that comment." Please enter the silence of contemplation.

THE FIRST DEGREE
OF SEPARATION FROM REALITY:
BODY IDENTIFICATION, PART FIVE

Second Questioner: "Speaking of running people away from his loft, I've read his talks and you don't really sound like him."

F: "Ha. Well, thank you. I thank you and, were that manifestation before us, it would thank you. Study the enneagram system and you'll see that there are nine very different personality types. Some will relate to my experience with non-duality and some will not. Too, some are ready to hear and some are not. And some who do not 'get it' from me might get it later from another. My teacher was not the first teacher who tried to give me the Understanding; he was merely the last. He became the last because he was the first to show me that the greatest teacher is within. Those who knew my teacher's guru said that my teacher did not sound like his guru, and they were correct. If you hear what I say, OK. If you do not, maybe you will hear it from another…or not."

2nd Q: "Fair enough."

F: "And you, too, are lucky I'm not my teacher. I would have to run you out as well. Ha." (Laughter. Then to first questioner) Back to your comment about the girder. In non-duality, there's no place for your comments about 'It looks like this and also that' or for your thoughts that something 'was' but now 'is not.' That too is just more duality. If you drop an ice cube into a glass of hot water, and the cube dissolves, and you know that cube was a cluster of hydrogen and oxygen atoms in combination, can you rightly say, 'That which once was, now no longer is'?

Q: (Hesitates) "No."

F: "Can you say, 'Now it is not'? Can you rightly draw that conclusion, knowing what you know about atoms?"

Q: "No."

F: "On the other hand, can you rightly claim that 'the cube' still is?"

Q: "No."

F: "The atoms that had manifested in the shape of a cube no longer have a 'cube-shaped appearance,' but they remain exactly what they always were and have always been. So all that you need say is, 'That which I originally thought to be a cube with a particular shape, a perception rooted in my faulty programming, was not that at all. What I thought it was that I thought I was seeing has disappeared from my view, and now I know that what it really is, was, and always shall be…still IS. Now, say the same about your body: 'That which I originally thought my body to be, based on my faulty perceiving and programming, is not what it seemed to be at all. What I thought it was that I thought I was seeing has disappeared from my view (during the arms-legs-organs exercise) but what it really is, was, and always shall be…still IS."

Q: "OK! I see that!"

F: "In the case of ice cubes dropped in hot water and in the case of bodies losing parts and eventually 'disappearing,' we are seeing evidence of cycling, that's all. Some groups fabricate a concept called 'time' and speak of 'an eternity' and geographic places where they believe their bodies and minds and personalities shall exist 'forever.' Claiming to be 'spiritual,' they are actually focused on nothing but body and mind. Ignoring cycles, they speak of a timeline with a beginning, a middle, an end, a judgment, and then eternity in one place or another. In fact, if eternity runs infinitely along their line in that direction (pointing right) then logically eternity must run forever in that direction (pointing left) as well. Infinite is infinite. 'Infinite' knows no direction. If infinity is to follow their 'death,' then infinity must have preceded their 'birth' as well. If all is energy and if energy cannot be created nor destroyed but just IS, then what is this talk of a 'creation'? And if there is talk of a creation, then talk of "a creator" usually follows since the ancient pagan myths have been handed down and thrive in the newer religions. In Reality, infinite is infinite. Let your thinking mind dissolve and sense the cycles. Truly know infinity rather than imaginary timelines. Here's what I'm writing for The Board of Directors of Wars: Begin in the silence. Experience the reality of the cycles. Know that the timeline of birth, life, death, judgment, eternal damnation or eternal salvation represents nothing more than an Anglo concept. In the place of such limited, linear thinking, try to actually experience—at the innermost core of your being—the cycles. Then you won't attach to that "I love spring, but I hate winter" mentality. You'll stop over-celebrating what you label as 'good,' and you'll stop over-mourning what you label as 'bad' because you'll know the temporary nature of all conditions in this existence. All will cycle into something else. Once you fix that truth at a core level, and once it resonates through each and every fiber of the fabric of your transitory existence, then why would you sweat the penetrating heat or the bitter cold if you know it's not the real, not the permanent?' Give no regard to anything that is temporary, for it is illusion. Detach from all illusion. Now, back to consciousness. Consider its energy aspect. (Picks up a card and reads) Szent-Gyorgyi correctly observed, 'What drives life is thus a little electric current, set up by the sunshine.' Can you create energy—that 'electric current'?"

Q: "No."

F: "Can you destroy energy?"

Q: "No."

F: "Can energy cycle?"

Q: "Yes."

F: "Then realize that energy-consciousness is eternal and that it can manifest in that which has no eternal form. When the form ends, the manifestation of that consciousness ends, but the consciousness itself does not end. Sense the cycles. The Real is eternal; the temporary is not That. Apply that understanding to your body and stop believing that the Real You is a body." Please enter the silence of contemplation.

THE FIRST DEGREE
OF SEPARATION FROM REALITY:
Body Identification, Part Six

F: "Now it is seen that consciousness cannot be 'lost.' I do not have consciousness. I Am the consciousness—the consciousness currently manifested in what you perceive as a body. When you recall that the physical elements of the entire body can be reduced to the size of a small urn, then you understand that the body is mainly space. The space/elements in which that consciousness is manifested is temporary, but the consciousness is eternal. I am not the body. I Am the consciousness that is aware of its presence; thus, I Am eternal, though the body in which I Am presently manifested is temporary. The form of the body (like the form of the ice cube) is not forever, but that which is Real (like the atoms of the cube) are forever. What is Real is forever; thus, the body cannot be the Real. The charges jumping across the synapses between the neurons of your brains right now are all part of the movement of electrical energy-consciousness. Consider, for example, the EEG. It measures electrical impulses as it charts consciousness. Consciousness is 'electrical' or a form of 'energy' in its nature, so I cannot be destroyed. Neither was I created. I Am, infinitely. Now, having done the 'Arms-Legs-Organs exercise' and having sensed that You would still be You even if you 'lost' more than half of your original physical body parts, the consciousness should be seen as perceiving Its presence. At some point, the consciousness will be released through the process you call 'death' as the combined elements return to dust—to the earth. Just as the elements might recycle to form 'new' bodies (or not), the energy can recycle...or not; however, those same elements will never re-form to make the same body with the same mind with the same consciousness. But more importantly, when the body ends, you cannot destroy the 'freed' ashes or the dust of the body and you cannot destroy the 'freed' consciousness. For now, grasp this: your body is only a manifestation of plant food. It is sustained by plant food (or, for many Westerners, by animals that eat plants and gain the energy-consciousness that can be passed to you when you eat them). As long as the body takes in the plant food, it shall experience consciousness if the breath is also cycled. At the 'death of the body,' the body components shall eventually return to the pool of universal elements, the breath shall join the reservoir of universal air, and the consciousness shall enter into the vast 'field of consciousness.' During the process whereby a body was formed, whereby consciousness became manifest, and whereby a 'birth' of a body happened, eventually breathing also began. In that entire process, from the frictional activity to the slapping of a rear to inspire breathing, no earth elements were created. No air was created. No consciousness was created. So what is this talk that associates 'birth' with 'creation' but ignores natural and simple cycling? The elements, the air and the consciousness merely cycled. And of those three, the consciousness is that which can know Itself/Reality when it is manifested, and Itself/Reality are not two. That is what Advaita Vedanta is offering to you: the understanding of not two."

Q: "Then why does consciousness not Know Who or What It Is in the case of every human?"

F: "Because of the faulty programming and conditioning by your cultures—the processes that contaminate the Pure Consciousness and bastardize it with lies and roles and personas and false identities and beliefs and emotions and attitudes and fears. What we have seen is that body identification is the first illusion that serves as an obstacle to separate you from knowing What You Truly Are. It is

The First Degree of Separation from Reality. The "I Amness" is first separated from knowing Itself by body identity. Pure consciousness knows it is not a body, and knowing that much allows us to consider the next of the Seven Degrees of Separation. If you complete the 'journey,' all that you are not shall be known so that What You Truly Are will be known. Of course, there is no actual journey to make since there is no one to take that journey. There are no real degrees of separation. All aids only point to that knowingness which already is. Seek 'within,' not without. Eventually, no aids will be needed. All concepts will have been discarded, including these offered in the sessions that will guide you along this seven-step 'path.' The shift from not knowing Who You Are to the Knowing of What You Are is a transitioning by degrees from a dark, contaminated state of consciousness (resulting from all the conditioning and programming and assumption of lies) to an elimination of that darkness with the light of Full Awareness of THAT Which You Are. In the next session, we'll discuss the second of the obstacles—the 'mind'—that stands in the way of clearly perceiving Who or What You Are. Please enter the silence of contemplation.

THE SECOND DEGREE OF SEPARATION FROM REALITY: MIND IDENTIFICATION

THE SECOND DEGREE OF SEPARATION FROM REALITY: MIND IDENTIFICATION, PART ONE

F: "During this session, we begin discussion of what I call 'The Second Degree of Separation from Reality'; however, please recall a comment I offered during the last session: There is no actual journey to make since there is no one to take that journey. There are no real degrees of separation. All aids only point to that knowingness which already is. Seek 'within,' not without. That said, let's continue. Here's an overview of what I am calling a 'journey' (in a symbolic sense for the sake of discussion only) in order to help some of you visualize the 'return' to pure consciousness as you become free of the negative effects of consciousness corrupted by adopting their beliefs and ideas as your own. At the beginning is the false "I"; at the end is THE ABSOLUTE. On our fictional journey, in between the false "I" and THE ABSOLUTE—which are not two and which are not separate at all—are seven stages that must be transitioned in order for the I AMNESS to know all that it is not and then Realize THE ABSOLUTE. We saw that the first of the seven 'obstacles' standing in the way of Full Realization is body identification. The second obstacle is mind identification. The content of your 'mind'—which includes all the lies and programming added to your originally pure consciousness—blocks your realization of Reality and thus prevents the bliss of being-without-desire."

Q: "Why? It seems the mind should be a tool for helping me find that bliss."

F: "The thinking mind will completely prevent your ever 'finding' bliss. When the thinking mind goes, the natural intuitions and instincts engage. Humans suffer from the rattlings of the thinking mind; the deer relaxes by living naturally under the guidance of what some teachers call the 'working mind'—the natural, internal guidance system. I hesitate to give the term 'mind' any credibility. Humans are self-destructive because of their thinking minds; deer are self-constructive because of their natural mode of living. The words I offer are pointers to guide you away from the unnatural thinking mind and toward the bliss of natural living."

Q: (Nods)

F: "How could bliss possibly manifest alongside the frustrations of a mind's imaginings of unmet needs and unfulfilled desires? All needs and desires are figments of the corrupted mind. Joy begins where desire ends. The mind may be referred to as 'the variable mind,' 'the superficial mind,' 'the imperfect mind,' 'the thinking mind,' 'the private mind,' 'the programmed mind,' 'the personal mind,' or 'the conditioned mind.' Ultimately, though, your mind is—at this stage of the game—a repository of all the falsehoods not yet known to be false. For the not-yet-realized, all of the ideas or beliefs or emotions or attitudes or pieces of dogma accepted as 'fact' and 'truth' now form the various bars of the prison called 'your mind.' To reach Full Realization, the thinking mind must dissolve. To reach Full Realization, the source of mental illusions must be known and transcended at this stage. Once the thinking mind dies, learned ignorance—and its resulting insanity—die as well."

Q: "But Floyd, the way I feel is not illusion. I am miserable. I am not happy."

F: "If the goal is to experience the freedom of Non-Duality, why begin by calling Me 'floyd'? And why place 'miserable' and 'happy' after 'I am'? Mark well your words. A thought-life of endless dualities leaves one mentally unstable. How can one know 'the great Reality' if out of touch with reality?"

Q: "Good question."

F: "Thank you. [Laughter] One comes to know Reality by following the pointers that point away from lies and toward the truth. The lies must first be seen to be lies before one can ever hope to know Truth. The false selves must be seen to be false before one can ever begin to glimpse the True Self. Why reinforce the illusion of duality by speaking to the consciousness as a body with a name? Why promote an illusion of 'miserable-happy' duality? I don't believe in 'floyd.'

I only believe in Me. Come to know What You Are, then the instability of dual-mindedness ends when the light of Reality strikes. Follow the pointers and your false beliefs will dissolve as Truth explodes into awareness."

Q: "But I'm sure I've seen you happy at times and miserable or angry at times."

F: "All of that which you feel sure of at this point is precisely what will prevent Realization of the True Self. Your ideas and beliefs prevent your seeing Reality. On some occasion, anger might have been witnessed as it rose and fell. On another occasion, joy might have been witnessed when it rose and fell. Whatever was thought to have been seen by you was in fact merely happening and merely being witnessed."

Q: "No…I have seen both the anger and the happiness, specifically."

F: "So have I. I was like the eagle, soaring above it all and merely watching." Please enter the silence of contemplation.

THE SECOND DEGREE OF SEPARATION FROM REALITY: MIND IDENTIFICATION, PART TWO

[Received by e-mail as the sessions were being conducted]

Q: "Do thoughts create our reality? I've played with this for years and watched how 'my' thoughts created my so-called reality. Can you explain? Thanks, Andrea."

F: "Wise of you to write 'my' thoughts and 'so-called' Reality, indicating that you already suspect the fallacy of that notion. 'I create my own reality' is a popular statement nowadays, and once again we see that what is popular is often in error. I would ask those believing in that concept, 'How can there be a "your reality" and a "my reality"?' Reality duality? They just 'created' a seventh system of yoga! Reality is Reality, period. Some might want to bring the 'self-fulfilling prophecy' concept into the discussion with you, but even if something results from that, it does not create Reality. What is Real we do not create. The Real has always been, always is, and always shall be. Suppose a male and female engage in an act of friction and then earth elements cycle during a nine-month period and consciousness manifests. At the moment of what is called 'birth,' a child 'appears,' air is introduced, and breathing cycles begin. The question is, 'Was anything really created?' The answer is, 'No.' Everything that regrouped into that 'new' space existed already: the air existed already; the conscious-energy existed already; the earth elements all existed. Nothing was created—things merely cycled. Consider again the ice cube metaphor that we've been using. If I fill an ice tray with clusterings of two-hydrogen-and-one-oxygen-atom groupings and place the tray in the freezer, can I rightly proclaim that I have created ice? Did I create the basic elements? Did I create hydrogen and oxygen? No. Though the clusterings took the shape or appearance of something 'new,' no appearance is ever the real. Since matter/energy cannot be created or destroyed, nothing about the cube was created. The form of the cube cannot be real since it is changeable. The Real is permanent, was not created, and cannot be destroyed. So it is with our imaginings that appear to be 'our reality.' Raise a child while telling him that white is black and black is white and then send him off to school after six years of that programming. When his belief system around black and white is challenged in the classroom, he'll be certain that those who know the truth are fools. How much of what we were told as a child is fiction? How motivated are most to seek the fictional non-truths and challenge those belief systems? Not very motivated at all, in most cases. People love to take credit for 'creating' when, in fact, cycling is merely happening. To understand that no creating has ever occurred, please consider this: Have you have ever been invited to realize 'infinity after you die'? Is so, why have those extending that invitation not also invited you to realize 'infinity before your birth?' Infinite is infinite, and the Real has been the Real infinitely. Recall: 'In order to be sane, you must be out of your mind.' What the thinking mind comes up with is fiction. What the brain understands can be fact. So, you cannot create Reality, but your ability to know Reality is within you already; however, it will never be known with the thinking mind. One can discard the false 'realities' once assumed to be true, sanity can be restored, and then one can know Reality. Again, your reservations about what you have been told about 'creating reality' are valid and are an excellent sign of your capacity for realizing the truth and the True Self. Best regards, Floyd. Please enter the silence of contemplation.

THE SECOND DEGREE
OF SEPARATION FROM REALITY:
Mind Identification, Part Three

F: But my question is, 'What do you think is the source of your misery'?"

Q: "My wife leaving me. She said, 'I don't even know who I am,' and she took the children and left. I'm miserable over losing everything...wife, family, property. I lost it all."

F: "First, if she said that she doesn't know who she is, we can believe that is the case. Obviously, you don't know who you are, either."

Q: [Frowns]

F: "Secondly, if it is truly understood that one does not have a body and therefore cannot 'lose' the body, how can one lose the bodies on your list? The world of misery you speak of is imagined. You do not live in the world. More importantly, your freedom will come in knowing that nothing on the list is the source of misery."

Q: "I don't think you appreciate the hurt involved."

F: "If you truly understood the illusion of the body, you could not have an illusory mind that would speak of a 'lost wife' and this lost person called 'husband.' To be free is to be in a state of total independence. The person lives in total dependence. Each illusion of personality requires two codependent bodies as well as two codependent minds. It is that illusion of dualities which prevents a person from being free and which blocks a person from continuing on the path to realization."

Q: "Two bodies and two minds?"

F: "Two bodies and two minds are required for any role to be taken as an identity. You cannot play the role of 'husband' alone. She cannot play the role of 'wife' alone. You each must have a body in order to play out those roles, you each must have another body willing to play the counter role, and you each must have a mind that has been programmed to believe that the roles you play actually identify who you are. Two bodies, two minds. Duality squared. If you are 'husband' and she leaves, you are not 'husband' any longer in your variable mind. According to that belief system, What You Truly Are can vary, depending on who is in your physical presence! But the reality is that What You Truly Are can never vary. All personalities (or 'personas' or 'false identities' or 'roles' or

'states-of-being this' or 'states of being that') are dualities. The Real is permanent whereas dualities, being illusions, always appear to come and go. In that
instability, one lives in the depression around perceived loss or in the manic state
of joy around perceived gain. Neither state lasts, so one is constantly in a state
of flux and desire, clinging to current dependencies while trying to accumulate new dependencies. 'The employee' cannot exist without 'the employer'; the
'lover' cannot exist without a separate 'lover'; the 'father' cannot exist without 'a
child.' If 'wife' leaves, 'husband' thinks he's dying. How tenuous your existence
becomes—how absent of freedom life must be—believing in the illusion that
your existence is totally dependent on all those 'others.' How vulnerable and
fear-based that life must be…feeling so dependent and needy and incomplete.
Do you see that if each assumed personality requires the physical presence of
another person, then two codependent bodies are required to sustain the illusion
of each false personality? Trying to live in that duality, with no freedom at all, is it
any wonder that you speak of misery?" Please enter the silence of contemplation.

THE SECOND DEGREE
OF SEPARATION FROM REALITY:
MIND IDENTIFICATION, PART FOUR

Q: "I need some help to really process all that."

F.: "Then let's try this: we're on a seven-step 'journey' to Reality, if you will.
Let's go to the 'end' and work 'backwards' for a moment, since all merely cycles.
Let's consider when the consciousness was manifesting in the space in a womb
with the non-beingness about to cross the borderline to the beingness. The days
of the bliss of the womb were numbered."

Q: "If I had known then what I know now, I wouldn't have come out."
(Laughter)

F: "I'm in charge of humor here. Don't intrude. Ha. (Laughter) Regarding
your leaving or not leaving the womb, as well as all that has happened since then,
there has never been any choice on your part. A natural process forced the space
to exit a birth canal. An initial act of friction between your parents resulted in
this space in which consciousness manifested. Actions began to happen, but they
were driven by instinct. No one taught you to protest if hungry; no one taught
you to seek a breast to suckle."

Q: "Right."

F: "In a manner of speaking, that's as 'close' to the True Self as you've been since that slap on the rear triggered your breathing cycles."

Q: "Why?"

F: "Because you were mainly being. They had not yet taught you. A fictional mind had not yet resulted from hearing the lies about who or what you are and had not yet assumed any false role or identity or personality. You wore no masks. All merely happened via natural instinct and body chemistry rather than programming and conditioning. You mainly focused on nothing and were just being. You were manifest but still mainly in a void, though becoming increasingly conscious of pain and discomfort. If fed and clothed comfortably, you were fairly free of strife or worry...whether sleeping, dreaming, waking, or fully conscious. Not until they taught you would you be forced into the bondage of concepts and the mental and emotional pain of duality. Eventually, you would always be in a sleep state—whether in bed, driving, at work, talking, whatever."

Q: [Nods head in agreement]

F: "Next, at some point you began to witness. You saw a mobile spinning in the crib above you. You saw huge faces being shoved into yours. You heard sounds coming from their mouths. You began to witness. Unless they made loud, alarming noises, you witnessed objectively and had no perceived fears. You had no opinions. You had no beliefs or concepts. You had no array of attitudes and judgments about what you were witnessing. Since contradictory beliefs had not been introduced, you had no quandaries to weigh, no disparities to consider, no ideas about 'good' vs. 'bad' or about anything else. You were merely witnessing. Do you understand what was happening when I spoke earlier of being like the eagle, soaring above it all and merely watching?"

Q: [Head moves in the affirmative]

F: "Soon, having sensed a body presence, you would believe yourself the subject and assume that you were witnessing other objects. Do you see why, at its very root, this life becomes a lie...setting you up to assume that dualities are the real and feeling apart from?"

Q: "Yes. I never considered that aspect."

F: "Add to that 'setup' all of the concepts that they would soon begin to teach you and you should understand the source of your future bondage: the assumption of duality. Their teachings, combined with that initial assumption of subject-object, would soon result in a programmed, variable mind. The mind would begin moving constantly. No rest or peace will it ever know again, unless you follow the path from duality 'back' to the unicity." Please enter the silence of contemplation.

THE SECOND DEGREE
OF SEPARATION FROM REALITY:
Mind Identification, Part Five

F: "Later, they began labeling you as 'our child,' 'our son,' 'our boy,' 'our teen,' 'our young man,' and later…'an adult.' But Your True Identity cannot change; any variable labeling can only name what you are not. As their 'child,' they began teaching you concepts, giving you ideas and a personality, 'whipping you into shape,' so they claimed. Then, they introduced one of the earliest and most limiting of all dualities—the source of so many nightmares in this culture. They presented their concept of 'good' vs. 'bad.' That illusion began to dominate your mind and affect your behavior. With the 'good-bad' concepts feeding your illusory 'mind,' you were becoming more and more ignorant, even as they claimed to be making you more and more knowledgable. All the concepts and ideas and beliefs and dogma they offered became your learned ignorance. They then began assigning roles for you to play and to assume as identities. You probably received their earliest 'spiritual' role or persona: 'a gift from God.' That fostered egomania and set another destructive ball rolling! [Laughter] Self-will became a liability because, the more false 'selves' you assumed as identities, the more the agenda of each false self—the desire to be—began to drive you. You were constantly in a fight to preserve those false personalities. The chaos of self-will ends when the self dies—when the false ego-states or false identities dissolve. Until then, you will have much to fight for, as your current body-mind-personality experience shows."

Q: [Nodding]

F: "Back to the 'downward' journey through the stages that has now left you out-of-touch with reality. Next, they took you to church and religious roles and identities were assigned there. You took their learned ignorance and began seeing even more "others" and using religious concepts to judge others and to label them and their behaviors as 'good' or 'bad.' The next stop was school where teachers programmed you, teaching you their version of what is 'good' and 'bad,' encouraging you to read the words of 'experts' and learn from their knowledge. They told you to listen to newscasts so that you would always be informed. 'The more you know, the better,' they claimed. They filled your brain with what they called 'facts' and 'knowledge' and contributed to your variable mind. That mind became dominated by its 'good-bad' duality perceptions as that mind tried constantly to process all the contradictions in your false world. Your mind is the chattering of a thousand monkeys, trying to process all their 'stuff.' As you became older, you could drive down the road alone and be in group therapy, right?" [Laughter]

Q: "That's still the case!" [Laughter]

F: "Of course it is. Every picture ever taken of you is a group photo because you believe yourself to be all those false identities that they assigned to you." [Laughter]

Q: [Smiling]

F: "All in positions of influence over you were rewarding you in order to reinforce behaviors they considered 'good' or were punishing you for what they thought to be 'bad.' You would become confused, though, since what half in the culture labeled 'good,' the other half considered 'bad.' You did something once and got a kiss. You did it again and got slapped. Contradictory opinions never convey the truth, so you were receiving more and more lies and becoming more and more confused."

Q: "So how do I know your words are the truth?"

F: "I make no such claim. My words can't convey the truth, either, yet they might allow you to see the lies in order to make way for the truth within to become known…that is all. But truth has not created your nightmare. For now, forget trying to find truth. For now, look to the actual source of the misery you speak of—the lies you believe and the false identities you have assumed. You believe all of those lies which form your corrupted mind and which you think define who you are. You have scores of personalities—dozens of false identities— and each has a love-to-be. It is that love-to-be of each ego-state that inspires you to cherish your false personas. It is your corrupted mind that is inspiring you to fight to maintain each false identity or to be miserable when you see that the role has ended. That mind and its identifications will convince you that it is you— not a role—that is dying." Please enter the silence of contemplation.

THE SECOND DEGREE
OF SEPARATION FROM REALITY:
Mind Identification, Part Six

Q: "So do you have a pure mind?"

F: "To understand 'where I am,' go back to the beginning of this tale of your 'downward spiral' into the state of misery you speak of. Recall the being and non-being?"

Q: "Yes."

F: "I am beyond even that, so why speak of a mind? Look to yourself, your false selves, which are just images in your mind. Those leave you miserable and feeling as if you're dying. All of your problems and all of this talk of misery arise because you are driven by that early training-programming-conditioning, combined now with the fact that you define yourself by the use of labels that limit you. Limitation restricts freedom. Restriction of freedom prevents peace. You are limited; I Am limitless. And you wonder why I sit here in peace while you sit in misery?"

Q: "Hummm."

F: "You've been a mental prisoner of war, locked up and tortured, but not by her. You've physically escaped the prison through no effort of your own, but mentally you are bemoaning that fact and begging to be allowed to return to your prisoner state. You want that 'husband' to experience a continuity of being. You are willing to continue suffering for the sake of that continuity. You prefer the guaranteed pain of the familiar over the potential bliss of the unknown."

Q: [Grimacing]

F: "Once they introduced that duality of 'good' and 'bad,' you began a life-long quest to earn the 'good' label and avoid the 'bad' label. The woman you married thought you were 'the best' at the time; at a later time, she thought you were 'the worst'."

Q: "You had a camera in our house!" [Laughter]

F.: "Ha. No, I just already know the ending to every movie, having observed so much of the flickerings across so many screens. The way you felt varied constantly, dependent upon the label being applied to you at any given moment. Talk about vulnerable. How fear-based that existence must have been."

Q: [Look of sadness]

F: "Your consciousness-in-motion, and hers, became the seat of all the pain-pleasure duality, so both of you felt happy one moment and miserable the next. In the end, when she felt miserable, you were blamed. Well here's a consideration: Suppose you had nothing to do with how she felt? What if that was determined by her chemistry, her personality, her programming, her conditioning and her delusions?"

Q: "That would be freeing, to get past that blame."

F.: "Not really. Her blaming you is not the cause of your perceived misery. What will free you is to understand that, if you had nothing to do with her feeling miserable then, she has nothing to do with your feeling miserable now. She is not involved at all with this misery you claim. She is a figment of your imagination."

Q: [Nods] Please enter the silence of contemplation.

THE SECOND DEGREE OF SEPARATION FROM REALITY:
Mind Identification, Part Seven

F: "You each created dependencies, expecting another person to make you happy; now, you each blame another person for making you sad. If that belief were true, your case would be hopeless and I would not waste another breath. I would say, "Well, I hope she returns because then you'll be happy; if she doesn't, your situation is hopeless and you're going to be miserable forever. I hope she fulfills all your desires, but ultimately…everything in your life depends on her. Good luck and goodbye." Instead, I tell you that your suffering is rooted in a false sense of threat combined with attachment and resistance. Taking yourself to be a person results in the imagined sense of threat; your attachment comes from believing that you are your body and mind and the role you played; and the resistance is to the refusal to question all of your beliefs so you can move on. Freedom from all of that is only a few steps away…specifically, the five steps remaining on this path. But you have not yet mastered even the first step."

Q: "Meaning?"

F: "You told me that you understood that you are not the body, but if your body has disappeared, how can any person remain? And if no person remains, how can a mind remain? You take the body-mind-personality to be who you are. You allow the impure mind to convince you that you are the persona called 'husband.' Your suffering is likely exacerbated by idealizing certain memories and by trying to cling to a prior lifestyle. The memories are about the mind and the lifestyle is about the body. If your consciousness were purified, you would not tell me that your misery comes from the absence of false roles and assumed personas that you once played but can no longer play. Think about that! You aren't hearing the full implication. Basically, you're admitting, "My misery is caused by a false role which is a complete illusion"! Finally, you've said something that I can agree with! [Laughter] I might as well tell you that I'm suffering miserably from the pain of an auto accident that occurred yesterday when I saw a mirage ahead in the road but drove my car into it anyway." [Laughter]

Q: [Nodding, smiling.]

F: "I may as well report that my back hurts because someone stepped on my shadow just prior to this session. I will never find the actual source of that back pain and will never receive effective treatment until I stop assigning the blame for it to some illusion that I hold to be true. If you realized the freedom of the unbounded expanse that You Are, then you would not desire any of your former, limiting identities. You would know that no false personality can define Who You Are. You would imagine no body, no mind, and no personality...yours or hers. Your dream-nightmare would end. Only full enlightenment can clear away the darkness of your conditioned mind." Please enter the silence of contemplation.

THE SECOND DEGREE OF SEPARATION FROM REALITY:
MIND IDENTIFICATION, PART EIGHT

F: "Once enlightened, the illusions dissolve and you live freely, but they made you believe that you are a body. Then, they programmed your mind to assume one role after another and to use your body to play out each role. You've been an actor on a stage, but your insane misery is rooted in the fact that you have acted a part for so long that you now think the part is real and that the play is real. They set you on a track to create dependencies of the most debilitating order. We saw earlier that each role you play must have another person willing to play the complementary part that gives your role its false impression that it defines who you are. Your conditioned mind works with dualities like the 'good-bad' pairing, a combination always accompanied by the 'reward-punishment' duality. The 'husband' is dependent on the wife's thinking him 'good' in order to allow him to continue to exist. Talk about dependent! Talk about vulnerable! Believing that you are 'husband,' your 'life' is in her hands. [Turns] Any of you females who are assuming the identity of 'wife' or 'girlfriend' or 'good daughter' or any of the other roles you play, the same applies to you. Your 'life' is in the hands of another person. How fragile and chaotic an existence, one person always in fear of loss, the other person always desiring more! [Back to Q.] The deficiency you now imagine to be caused by her leaving is actually based in your mourning the dissolution of a false identity that has struggled for years for permanence. You have been so wrongly programmed by them that you think that you can only be happy if the temporary is permanent! What an impossible state!"

Q: [Sadly] "You're right. That's insane."

F: "Yes, and your sanity returns only when you are in touch with Reality. Here's what you've been up against: your driving force in life was to work to do all you could to convince a person that you were 'good' enough in order to earn the reward of her staying and in order to avoid the punishment of her leaving. What a job!"

Q: "But she left right when I started on this path and was improving."

F: "Who is improving? Your false identity wants affirmation that it is improving and 'good' so she'll come back and so this personality called 'husband' can experience continuity. You're trying to perpetuate a myth. You believe that you can only be happy if you can make reality out of a myth. You may as well believe that my back will feel better if someone gives my shadow a massage. [Smiles] You wanted her to see that you were changing, but that which changes cannot be the real, so you were living a lie. Misery had to result. Further, some spouses stay and some spouses regularly leave when a partner begins to follow a different path. Some feel driven to go when they can no longer sleep comfortably with one who is always awake." [Laughter, applause]

Q: "You got that one right! But it sounds to me like you're contradicting my counselor who is suggesting I process the trauma rather than repress or deny what I'm feeling."

F: "Even Realized you can feel. If your counselor wants you to process and you want to process, then process. But if you complete this journey, then we'll talk one day and you will not speak of either processing or repressing. You will not attach to any roles, you'll witness feelings rise and fall, and you'll not have any ego-states that react and react and react ad infinitum and create further harm. Nor will you be trapped in the state of emotional intoxication currently being experienced via your body-mind-personality triad. I suggest you each focus on the 'I Am' only. You are not your body and you are not your mind. You are not who they told you that you are. Stay with the 'I Am' alone. If you see yourself inserting any word after that, stop and return to the 'I Am' only." Please enter the silence of contemplation.

THE SECOND DEGREE OF SEPARATION FROM REALITY: MIND IDENTIFICATION, PART NINE

F: "To conclude the discussion of The Second Degree of Separation from Reality, Mind Identification, I'll read an excerpt from the interview at the end of a non-duality novel I'm working on."

Editor: How can the readers' realization, and thus their freedom, come?

F: "By realizing that there is no duality. The labels we accept, the roles we play, are the very constraints that imprison us mentally. Consider this, please: if you work during the week and are off on the weekends, and you have a job that is very challenging, even draining, then you might experience something like the following. On Monday, your alarm goes off. You unthinkingly shut it off. Just gaining consciousness, you know 'I am.' The knowledge of existing in this body begins to come to you. As you awaken more, you remember you are 'The Employee,' and you have to get up and leave the comfort of your bed, your room, your house or apartment, and go off to play that role and to try to meet all the expectations and demands that come with having accepted that role and believing it is you. Quickly, the ego will promote you to 'Super Employee,' and eventually you'll be convinced you're not getting the money or the respect you deserve. Frustration will build as a result of accepting that role. You take things personally, for you are playing a persona, a role, accepting a false identity. If you get fired, you might feel as if you're dying. To exist, 'The Employee' must have a job. Your very identity seems challenged, so your very existence seems at stake. Consider that same 'employee' on a Saturday. No alarm goes off. The awakening comes slowly. As one gains consciousness, one knows 'I am.' Then, the fact that it's Saturday settles in. One does not have to go to work. One does not go into the mode of 'The Employee' but rolls over in bed and enjoys just being there. To stay in the 'I Am-ness' prevents accepting false roles and identities. To stay in the knowledge that 'I Am, period' allows one to relax. Free of that false identity for the day, one remains in the 'I Am,' in the 'Is-ness' only, and thus at ease. That same mindset, seven days a week, will allow the perpetual peace and the constant ease to manifest. That person is not playing the role that day, is not trying to meet expectations and demands, and is free and feels free. What he is really free of is accepting the label. How many who consider themselves to be men or women are really nothing more than a bundle of concepts and labels and identities assigned by this culture? Is it any wonder that most, before making it to the grave, will wonder 'Who am I?' or will state flat out, 'I don't even know who I am'? To be free is to be free of the false identities that jerk us around and jerk around the people in our vicinity who allow our role-playing and role-demands to impact them. Once we come to know Who We Really Are and stay in the 'I Am' state, we accept no false roles as identifiers of Who We Are, no false labels as identifiers of Who We Are, no dependencies as a result of believing we are what we do." [from the non-duality novel entitled The Twice-Stolen Necklace Murders, available at www.floydhenderson.com]

F.: "In any discussion of the mind, the key pointer is that…in truth there is no mind. A series of false ideas and wrong concepts are thought to be truth. Abandon the body. Abandon the mind. Abandon all false identities."

Q: "But I really am an employee. How can I not be driven by that role?"

F: "No, You are not an employee. Since you do not yet know What You Truly Are, you don't see all that you are not. Peace came with my understanding of What I Am and with the subsequent shift to pure consciousness. When I was 'The Teacher,' promoted instantly to 'Super Teacher' since egoism accompanies all roles, I was frustrated when lessons were interrupted and 'Super Teacher' could not do what he had planned to do. Peace came with the realization that all merely happens. That allowed me to flow along with the realization that 'Today, teaching will happen…or not.' If it happened the way I planned, okay. If it didn't happen at all because of circumstances far beyond my control, so it was. Either way, I merely witnessed teaching happen, or I merely witnessed teaching not happen. I could just be, unaffected by what did or did not happen, unaffected by any employment-role delusions. Know that you are not what you do. Peace."

Q: [Nods]

F: "Stay in the 'I Am.' That means shifting from the corrupted mindset that allows any word to follow the phrase 'I am.' If a word follows that phrase, reject it: not 'I am an Employee/Super-Employee.' Just, 'I Am'." Please enter the silence of contemplation.

THE THIRD DEGREE OF SEPARATION FROM REALITY: RELIGIOUS AND/OR SPIRITUAL IDENTIFICATIONS

THE THIRD DEGREE OF SEPARATION FROM REALITY: RELIGIOUS AND/OR SPIRITUAL IDENTIFICATIONS, PART ONE

F: "I'll mention before we begin that you might want to buckle your seat-belts. If this session is typical, we may be in for some turbulence. Ha. [Light laughter] Our 'journey' has reached the third stage. It is here that the broad highway narrows to a tapered path."

Q: "And why is that?"

F: "Because a narrow, tapered path will handle the low volume of traffic from this point forward. Most will not move beyond the obstacles discussed in this session. The majority who quit abandon this seven-step journey at level three. Early on, my teacher guessed that one in ten thousand might make it to the 'end'; later, he predicted one in a million. He was only guessing, but he might have been close."

Q: "Not very good odds."

F: "Indeed."

Q: "Maybe we need better teachers." [Laughter]

F: "Indeed."

Q: "No fight? Ha."

F: "None. The variable is not the teacher. The readiness is all. Are you ready?"

Q: "Yes."

F: "We'll see." [Laughs] Let's move to the Third Degree of Separation from Reality: assuming Religious Roles or Spiritual Roles as actual identities. Note, please, that I speak of religious or spiritual roles as obstacles. Why are they obstacles? Two reasons: first, they are personas. They are just new personalities adopted to replace other roles or to 'co-exist' in a conditioned mind with other states-of-being this or being that. Secondly, religion and spirituality—by their very nature and by virtue of the manner in which they are practiced by most—foster duality. They are steeped in duality."

Q: "I disagree completely. The ultimate message of both religion and spirituality deals with atonement and oneness and that can't do anything but help all mankind. How can a message of oneness be 'steeped in duality'?"

F: "You speak in suppositions; I speak of actualities. You dream of a bountiful yield; I see the fruit already in store." Please enter the silence of contemplation.

THE THIRD DEGREE OF SEPARATION FROM REALITY:
RELIGIOUS AND/OR SPIRITUAL IDENTIFICATIONS, PART TWO

Q: "None of that supports your claim that religion and spirituality foster duality."

F: "In the earlier sessions, did you not see how the phenomenal existence of everyone in this room has been made miserable as a result of being trapped in your debilitating preoccupation with trying to earn the 'good' label and avoid the 'bad' label and earn a reward and avoid a punishment?"

Q: "Yes. That was clear. I got it."

F: "I disagree. If you truly 'got it,' why would you defend roles that supports the 'good-bad' duality now? Why would you assume personalities that are preoccupied with the 'good-bad' duality's companions—'reward and punishment'—and strive for some earthly 'reward' now and some 'ultimate reward' that you want to experience eternally? Only because of your faulty conditioning and wrong programming. How has living in that duality worked for you so far? And 'who' would experience the benefits now and the reward forever? Your body-mind-personality. The sources of so much mental anguish in this temporary existence—that body-mind-personality triad and that 'good-bad-reward-punishment' quartet—you have been invited to discard in order to see truth and to be at peace, now. Instead, you want to assume and defend two false identities that will perpetuate the effects of those dualities in this existence and then seek to extend them for eternity. And that's only a fraction of the duality that dominates these two false personalities."

Q: [Pause. Begins to speak. Doesn't.]

F: "Would being occupied with the material while claiming an occupation with the spiritual constitute dualism?"

Q: [Pause] "Go ahead."

F: "Then look to the practice rather than the words. If we are speaking of 'abandoning the material to deal with that beyond the material,' are you going to suggest that the pious have abandoned the material? Or do they require a constant influx of the material to operate? Can creeds be practiced without material churches, temples, mosques, material accouterments, money, etc.? All of those material elements are required to sustain dogma and spread doctrine. That is material-spiritual duality, but only the beginning of the duality we'll see."

Q: "I don't do all that any more. I focus only on the words of Christ."

F: "As you will. Then look to his history and see that it reinforces my point. He began in the temples, talking about the content of holy texts; later, he left organized religion and its temples, spoke on hillsides and in homes, and offered talks that were beyond the texts. He had been exposed to the Advaita Vedanta Teachings during his 'lost years' and tried to shift his audience away from traditional religion with its dualistic nature by offering the message of non-duality that I'm speaking of now."

Q: "Christ had a non-dual message?"

F: "He said, 'Before Abraham was, I AM' and 'When you speak of me, speak of me as I AM' and 'Heaven and earth shall fade away' and 'No one shall ever see heaven—it is within' and 'A dual-minded person is unstable in all ways." That manifestation called 'Christ' tried to offer the Advaita Vedanta Teachings. But how many who assume the persona of his followers have a clue of the Advaita content?"

Q: [Pause] "Hummm. No one ever pointed it out to me. [Another pause]

Alright, granted that organized faiths have to mix the material with the spiritual, but spiritualists have no churches or budgets. Why group the two together? You're spiritual, aren't you?"

F: "I am neither spiritual nor material."

Q: "Are you a sage?"

F: "Ha! Do I sound like any of the authentic sages you've heard or read?"

Q: "Not really."

F. : "So, there you have it; however, my teacher was a sage. I'm but a voyager who listened to the words of a sage who knew of what he spoke. He spoke of That Which He Truly Is, and I read his words and first came to know all that I am not. That facilitated my coming to know exactly That Which I Am. Like the early explorers of the earth, I embarked on a journey following a sage's directions, I have seen that which is at 'the end,' and I have returned to tell you of its wonders. Now I can guide you 'there' as well, should you be ready to follow the same path. There is no difference in you and me. The appearance of any difference is merely a result of the fact that What I Am...I know. What You Are, your questions and comments show me you do not know. So let's continue with the journey. You used the word 'spiritual.' What do you take 'spiritual' to mean?"

Q: "Spiritual to me simply means abandoning the material to deal with that beyond the material."

F: "Good enough. We'll use your definition for our discussion, but let me ask first, 'What might be the detriment of shifting one's focus to the spiritual and abandoning the material before having thoroughly examined all of the 'material'?"

Q: "I don't think there can be any detriment." Please enter the silence of contemplation.

THE THIRD DEGREE
OF SEPARATION FROM REALITY:
RELIGIOUS AND/OR SPIRITUAL
IDENTIFICATIONS, PART THREE

F: "On my 'journey,' when I turned too soon from the material and began focusing only on what I called 'the spiritual,' I merely developed a new persona:

the role of a 'Spiritual Giant.' I did not move farther along 'the path' until my teacher's words returned my focus to the material long enough to see every falsehood. Many want to see the truth before they have seen all of the false. It cannot happen. So far on this 'journey,' we've focused on nothing but the material—the false material body, the false mind concerned with the material, and the personality concerned with the material. As for the 'spiritualists' you mention, they are as dual-minded as the pious if occupied with material trappings and posturing. My teacher gave short shrift to those playing spiritual roles, showing up in his loft with saffron robes, wooden crosses, beads, gold crosses, special beards, restricted dietary plans to please gods supposedly concerned with gastronomic issues, drums, bells, crystals, rituals, whatever. They were often 'asked out,' so to speak."

Q: "I don't see what any of that hurts."

F: "It's diversionary, misdirecting the focus from the I Am and The Absolute, accumulating more material 'stuff' on what is supposed to be a journey toward de-accumulation, and thus halting the journey. It supports the false beliefs that 'I have arrived' and 'the path ends here' and 'this material stuff helps me be more spiritual' when, in fact, the journey is not yet even half complete. Some want to flaunt material evidence of their assumed spirituality. So be it. My words are for those who know they have not reached the destination. My teacher knew that nothing external could abet the process of knowing that which is within. Even the guru is within, he said."

Q: "Maybe those elements bring a touch of the material to the spiritual, but that doesn't make the spiritual dualistic."

F: "Of course it does, along with many other aspects. All roles are dualistic as soon as a person assumes an identity and then assigns attributes to that false personality. By assuming a role-with-attributes as a new and improved identity, one takes that which claims to have transcended the material but then assigns material attributes—an act which immediately gives the role a phenomenal character. Duality is an inherent component of any role, but it especially marks these two limiting personalities that are the repository of all 'good-bad' concepts and all 'reward-deserver' and 'punishment-avoider' personas. While body identifications and mind identifications prevent taking the first two steps of this journey to Realization, these two dual-natured roles will bring any journey already begun to a halt if not transcended. Before anyone here who is assuming a religious or spiritual personality wants to rush to the defense of a false persona, let me make this point: an interesting shift can occur at this juncture. The remaining obstacles I'll discuss can still separate travelers from reality, but they also have the potential to facilitate the journey to realization. The key lies in transcendence."

Q: "Transcendence meaning what, exactly?"

F: "Meaning, if one transcends level three and the levels that follow, the stages can become stepping stones used to continue along the path. The challenge is that along the way two hindrances usually appear. First, some encounter what they take to be a cool oasis of religion or spirituality, tempting places to stop, to abandon the journey, and to spend the remainder of one's life; in fact, anything prior to reality is a mirage and ultimately offers no stability. Second, along other parts of the path, many obstacles appear and some become frustrated and abandon the journey. To continue, all roles must dissolve, including the limiting religious and spiritual personalities."

Q: "I see the problem with some of the roles you discussed earlier, like the way the 'husband' role or 'employee' role or 'wife' role traps people. But it just seems that the positive role of 'spiritualist' would have some benefit. It seems different from the others."

F: "So let's say that you're a patient in a study group among those dying of cancer. Your group is receiving the placebo and the other group is getting the real thing. You're telling me that you'd be willing to stay in the placebo group of cancer patients and not get the real thing if the researchers will just give you another placebo that is 'different from the other' placebos that you've been taking...but a placebo nevertheless? [Q. frowns] All personas are false. Nothing false can help differentiate the true from the false." Please enter the silence of contemplation.

THE THIRD DEGREE
OF SEPARATION FROM REALITY:
RELIGIOUS AND/OR SPIRITUAL
IDENTIFICATIONS, PART FOUR

Q: "You have a knack for turning around my statements in a way I don't mean them."

F: "I'm not trying to turn statements around or even offer a different perspective. All perceptions are illusions, so I suggest their dissolution. The personas you're trying to defend are just more states of being this or being that. Some want you to adopt all of their beliefs. I invite you to abandon all of your beliefs."

Q: "So you're claiming that these two states have never helped anyone?"

F: "What is 'help'? [Pause] Let's try this: can a canoe help one cross a river?"

Q: "Of course."

F: "Then imagine that seven rivers separate you from a destination. Imagine also that at each crossing point is a canoe. I ask you, if you use a canoe to cross a river, do you need to drag that canoe along to the next river if a guide assures you that another canoe will be ready to help cross the next obstacle? Is there any reason you should carry along the first and second and third canoes as you approach the fourth river? Why drag with those three canoes the fourth, fifth, and sixth canoes when the seventh canoe awaits? Why burden yourself by dragging along all those canoes that can only inhibit free movement along the path? Now, did the canoes help? They were there and you used them. So be it. But to say, 'Well, I had to do everything I did on my journey' is a lie. The truth is that you could have crossed the rivers in other ways, and some of those other ways might have been much easier. Not far from the canoes were footbridges. In some places, the rivers narrowed to shallow streams that you could have walked across. Large traffic bridges crossed the rivers elsewhere. Did the canoes help...or hinder? The more relevant question now, since you've gone the canoe route, is 'Don't the canoes now need to be abandoned so you can move on effectively?' The answer to that is, 'Yes'."

Q: [Raises eyebrows]

F: "I'll take that look as an affirmation that you get the point. When I speak of transcending, I refer to the fact that you must transcend all body identity, all mind identity, and now ... all religious or spiritual personalities as well. You might feel they have helped you along, but they are not the end and they need not be taken along after having served whatever purpose you think they served. All identities must dissolve between now and the end of the fourth degree of separation or you cannot go on and know the child ignorance and the witness, nor the True Self, nor the beingness, nor the non-beingness...much less be fully in touch with Reality and know the Absolute. It will be impossible. We have reached the point along the path where religious and spiritual roles must be transcended. Any benefit that you believe they might have provided up to this point, so be it. But in order to continue, these roles too must dissolve."

Q: "If all roles are dreamed up in the mind and played out by the body, why are these two in a separate category from the other mind identifications you discussed?"

F: "Excellent question. The answer is, first, because in the vision in which these seven degrees came to me, these two roles were the third degree."

Q: "What vision?"

F: "The vision I'll share later at a more appropriate time. That said, these personalities also deserve a category that allows for their thorough investigation since they have far greater impact in the relative existence than any other body or mind identifications. Look to yourself and see how they are 'fighting for their lives.' Typically, these personalities are the earliest to be planted in the conditioned mind. Being the oldest ego-states, these personas are the longest held. Like an obnoxious guest at a party, they are often the first to come and the last to go. Even if the roles are assumed during the adult years, their power to dominate the behavior of those with a conditioned mind is demonstrated daily."

Q: "So why do they have a greater impact than other roles?"

F: "For several reasons. First, playing a religious role will either prevent the journey from beginning or will end a journey that has begun. This Teaching requires that we question everything. Faith in dogma requires that you question nothing. The journey only begins when questioning begins. The journey only continues if questioning continues. Second, having been told he has all the answers and having been trained to ask no questions, how could anyone so programmed continue the journey? Next, the programming and conditioning administered in such venues create minds with unwavering belief in dogma or theory, resulting in a rigidity that prohibits the consideration of opposing views. That I know from my years of being mired in both roles. Further, no other ego-states trigger more emotional intoxication. Also, most persons have had their entire phenomenal existence frustrated by the dualities of 'good and bad,' 'reward and punishment,' 'heaven and hell' and the struggle for their souls by 'dual gods': the god of good and the god of bad. These two personalities are the seat of those concepts of dualism that are so debilitating, but to suggest that the concepts are harmful and should be questioned will usually earn you a new label, maybe something like, 'New Age Agent of Satan.' [Loud laughter] Don't laugh. That's one I've actually heard. Ha. Next, imagine how difficult it is to shake off decades of such conditioning and programming. Finally, all roles are ego-states and thus foster egotism. Once the stance that 'Our way is right and your way is wrong' is taken, no room remains for facts or truth or opposing views. Fix bayonets ... cock and load." Please enter the silence of contemplation.

THE THIRD DEGREE
OF SEPARATION FROM REALITY:
RELIGIOUS AND/OR SPIRITUAL
IDENTIFICATIONS, PART FIVE

Q: "Your talk about moving beyond these roles is scary because I've always been taught this is my only hope."

F. : ...... "How's that hope working for you? Can losing false identities harm your True Self, or would the loss of all false identities finally reveal your True Self? What you find 'scary' is not this talk. What you fear is the loss of continuity of the body and mind and personality. You want immortality for something that is temporary! Set the personas aside and your fear will be replaced with peace. See the immensity of the Totality, not the limited life of a body-mind-personality. Get free of your unachievable desire to make the transient into the permanent. Seeking the unachievable will assure you a lifetime of feeling separate and angry. You'll exhaust yourself with needless effort."

Questioner 2.: "You really bother me, saying religion and spirituality aren't the final answer. I'm only alive today because I found a spiritual solution to my problem."

F: "The best question I could ask in reply would be, 'Who is bothered?' but I'll go with second-best and ask, 'Who said to let religion or spirituality dissolve?' I see no likelihood that either will fade from the screen. Each of you, on the other hand, has an opportunity to be free of two additional, limiting personalities. I identified the next two obstacles that must dissolve in order for the journey to continue: religious and spiritual persons. Personas are false. How can anything false progress? The journey halts when personalities believe they have arrived. Don't consider the inseparable I Am/Absolute as 'separates' by believing that these 'Seven Degrees of Separation from Reality' are real. They are the illusions."

Q. 2: ..... "I think that I'm a spiritual creature having a human experience."

F: "I read that book too, so you now think what another person thought.

Aside from what any human or religious or spiritual person thinks, what do you know…within?"

Q. 2.: …."I know I have the power of faith, which it doesn't sound like you have."

F: "Ha. Oh, I have faith … faith that the Totality will function. Functioning will happen. My teacher said that there's a current of energy that flows within the space when manifested. He suggested that I know that energy and its functioning. I do, so I have faith that happenings will happen, infinitely."

Q. 2.: …"I think your problem is that you must have been given a negative concept of God along the way. I came up with a God of my own conception. If you can't like that God you were raised with, I suggest you come up with a God of your own understanding that you can be comfortable with."

F: "Yes, I've also read that book, but after making that suggestion to choose your own idea of God, it tells you to 'cast aside all ideas.' So which is it?"

Q. 2: "I don't care what you say. The bottom line is, I have a Power that you don't have."

F: "Actually, you've proved that your Power doesn't exist."

Q. 2.: "Hardly."

F: "You told us that you have chosen your own conception of god, that you 'came up with a god.' You created god. That itself is a very interesting twist in the dogma. But more to the point, you admit that your god is a concept—an idea fabricated by a conditioned mind. You're admitting that you dreamed up a concept and now believe in the dream. If one dreams that he's sleeping with his favorite starlet, he's no less alone. If he awakes from that dream and still believes that she's there, a delusion exists. We're supposed to be moving away from the dream state and to the awakened state. All concepts are just notions or inventions or conceits. We're on the path to no concepts, not more concepts."

Q. 2.: [Raising voice] "I know for a fact that my Higher Power is real. He's given me the power and peace I never had." [Note: "Q2" was in a Twelve-Step program. Few persons in any such program seem to be aware of what their founders had to say about the "Higher Power" and "God," but what they said is relevant to all readers at this point…whether "Twelve-Steppers" or Advaitins. In the appendix of their book, an appendix entitled "Spiritual Experience," they make clear that though earlier in the text the writer used gender-specific pronouns such as "He" or "Him" to refer to a male god with personal attributes, that is not what most of the founders took the Higher Power to be. Q2 had the same gender-specific concept of the power. The appendix in their book reveals that those founders who had a "spiritual experience" no longer saw the Higher Power as a male entity but saw it as an "inner resource," to use their words. (That resource is, of course, pure consciousness.) The appendix goes on to say that it is only their religious members who speak of "God-consciousness." So according to their own literature, most of their founders had a spiritual experience and were conscious of the consciousness within—of the "inner resource" as they called it. Only the religious members continued to speak of a male "God." The point made in their appendix is exactly in line with the Advaita understanding, as is their point that, after having had a spiritual awakening, they tapped into their "sixth sense" and "intuition" and lived in a fashion that was "automatic"—not unlike the "spontaneous living" of the Advaita teaching. Now the dialogue will continue.]

F: "You seem to read a wide range of books. You find in your books what you don't know and then you believe you know it. The content of all those books you're quoting amounts to learned ignorance. I hear you quoting what you've read, but I hear no evidence that you have found what you already know… within. You and I both know what's in the books you're quoting, but do you know what is beyond those texts? If not, whatever peace you claim to have received is tenuous, vulnerable to being shattered with a few words, as your voice seems to be confirming. Fix bayonets…cock and load."

Q. 2: [Frowns, shouts] "I wasn't angry until you started talking blasphemy!"

F: "Make no connections where connections don't exist. That's just more duality. A common reasoning fallacy claims, 'I am unhappy; I am in your presence; you are making me unhappy.' See the truth: one, you are unhappy; two, it just so happens that you're also in my presence."

Q. 2: "You're a real piece of work."

F: "Let's stay with your conception. You've created a concept in your 'mind,' and now you depend on that concept. My teacher cautioned against anything that makes one dependent. You also probably concentrate on that concept, you likely pray to that concept, you perhaps even try to model yourself after that concept, but you admit it's just your conception—an invention of your 'mind.' Other ideas you've believed about that god were ancient concepts fabricated in the minds of other men. In the last session, you obviously didn't grasp that the personal mind produces powerlessness, not power. The variable mind doesn't provide peace. It robs you of peace. If you want lasting peace, abandon your

mind, your concepts, and your ego-states. Then, seek within to know the Real."
Please enter the silence of contemplation.

THE THIRD DEGREE
OF SEPARATION FROM REALITY:
Religious and/or Spiritual
Identifications, Part Six

Q.2.: "I wasn't in the last session, but my own experience shows that my
Higher Power has given me the power to accept the things I cannot change ...
things like you, for example. So I'll keep doing my spiritual work, and He'll keep
giving me power and peace."

F: "Actually, since you weren't in the last session, and since we're taking the
steps of a journey in a specific order, you won't be able to make this journey with
us at this time, but I'll finish our discussion. You speak of having to work to get
peace. My life is without toil since all work involves working to ignore mirages or
working to accept mirages. No more mirages ... no more work."

Q. 2.: "You know what? It's obvious that you've got nothing to give, so you
can't really be of any service to anyone."

F: "I agree. I am not of service and I have nothing to give; in fact, I'll take
everything away from those who can hear."

Q. 2: "Say whatever you want. The fact is that I serve God and help others
while all you're doing is harming others. And someday when we both stand in
judgment before Him, I'd a helluva lot rather be me than you."

F: "You have merely been re-programmed while what is called for is to be
de-programmed. When your mind dissolves, so will every concept that you've
ever dreamed up, including the god of your own conception. As far as helping
others, who can know what any 'others' need, long term? Since there is no separation, my teacher advised that each should focus on helping the only one he or she
can help—herself or himself. Then, the relative improves for all."

Q. 2: "I can't help myself, but I can help others."

F: "So a man who cannot swim can rescue others who are drowning?
Hummm. And how do you claim to help these 'others'?"

Q. 2.: "I share my experience, strength, and hope with them."

F: "All experience is about the five-sense, phenomenal existence, which is a mirage. Strength is about power, and power is about control, and control is about ego, and ego is a mirage. Ultimately, ego is about fear…generated as a result of one knowing at some level that he has no power. Hope is merely about desires for the future, but the future is a mirage; therefore, your experience and strength and hope are all mirages, outgrowths of phenomenal desires and phenomenal fears. What help is derived from sharing ideas about mirages that are based in desires and fears? Worse, fear and desire are the sources of anger, and anger is the source of all hostility. Hostility becomes the source of all harm. [Look of hatred from questioner] Right now, it seems that anger is what you're experiencing, so the point I offered earlier—that your peace is fragile and can be destroyed by words alone—is confirmed."

Q. 2: [Expletive]

F: "I'll offer a final consideration, and then suggest you go find a quiet place and follow my grandmother's three-moon rule. She advised that each take any consideration into three days of quiet contemplation before accepting or rejecting the point. So here's the final consideration for you: before dedicating your life to serving others, why not first serve yourself by investigating whether or not there might be a reality beyond your current spiritual identity that could lead you into a stable and never-ending position of neutrality around the words or actions of others? If it's peace you want, realization can result in an unshakable peace."

Q. 2.: "I think instead that I'll follow my sponsor's advice and go home and pray for you. I can't hate anyone I pray for."

F: "So be it."

Q. 2.: [Harshly] "Yeah, so be it!" [Exits noisily]

F: [Pause] "Turbulence." [Laughter] Please enter the silence of contemplation.

THE THIRD DEGREE
OF SEPARATION FROM REALITY:
Religious and/or Spiritual
Identifications, Part Seven

F: "Well … it seems the pointers that I intended to offer verbally, you have now received experientially. Ha. [Laughter] In that exchange, you didn't see these two personas at their worst—they can be far worse—but you did see the emotional intoxication that these roles can generate."

Q: "So, is his attitude about you right…you don't believe in God?"

F: "I don't believe in the mind, so I certainly don't believe in what someone says is a concept dreamed up in the mind. Some use the term Brahman to point to the Absolute Reality and some speak of the 'matrix' or of Prakriti. In the West, some claim that those terms refer to their 'God' (which has personal traits) but the Absolute Reality is not some omnipotent person. The Absolute is impersonal. Better for you, go to the end of this path and see for yourself. For me, the issue is moot. There's no reality in any concept, so this is the stage where the serious move on and the players stay behind. It's time to start purging the mind and being rid of all concepts."

Q: "But I've always had a sense that some kind of external power must exist."

F: "Of course external power exists. The sun is an external power source, but someone thousands of years ago projected himself onto an imagined source, gave it personal traits, and ever since, humans have repeated the tale to impressionable children. More to the point, you never had any innate sense that some personal external power exists any more than you had an innate sense that Santa Claus exists. You believe what you were told. You believed for years that there was a super-human male at the North Pole who was omnipotent and omniscient because you were told he exists. You believed that he knew if 'you'd been good or bad' and you also believed he was old, white-bearded, kind, giving, loving, residing in a remote location, unseen, etc. You didn't come up with all that, but you believed it when it was told to you as fact by people you trusted. An entire culture joined in, and if you asked any of them about this far-out tale, they supported the lie. But inside, as you became older, you had a notion that the story was rubbish. Even then, though, it's possible that when an older mate on the schoolyard first suggested 'Santa isn't real,' you were probably ready to fight, not unlike the man who just stormed out of here."

Q: "Ha. Guilty!"

F: "Why? You wanted to believe…in order to receive forever the gifts from that super-powerful being. And when did you finally learn that there was no Santa? Did they come to you voluntarily to tell you the truth? No. They didn't say, 'Hey, we need to come clean. We need to be honest with you. We lied. Somebody just made up all that rubbish and we just repeated it. All of that wonderful story and all of those wonderful traits rolled into one super-powerful being…it was all a lie. Sorry to set you up with such great hope and then disappoint you.' No, you found the truth when someone offered an opposing view and suggested that you question what they told you. You had to confront your belief systems. You had to say, "This Santa tale actually sounds like a bunch of rubbish. Is this real, or not?" That's my invitation to you. Go into the silence and question it all. Ask the tough questions."

Q: "Easier said than done."

F: "Why would you delay, having already seen exactly how the minds of the people who programmed you actually worked at that time? Their minds told them, 'We think it would be a great idea to lie to this child and tell him that he's being watched every second—asleep or awake—by an unseen male who lives at a faraway location and who knows if he's been good or bad. We'll also tell him that the male is keeping a list and will either give a reward or withhold a reward depending on the good-bad label earned.' The same people who thought it would be good to lie you—and then later admitted that they were liars—those very people then gave you the same story over again but used a new name for the male. But you didn't question that story the second time around? Why not? You questioned the first lie they told you, even knowing you'd end the illusion and not receive any rewards eternally. Why do you not have the courage right now to question their revised version as well? Seek the answer, knowing that this time, you need ask no one. The answer is within. Ask, 'Is it possible that personal power sources were dreamed up and tales of them are now passed on as a result of human desires and human fears and human resistance to the fact that man can do nothing, and need do nothing, to become free of the bondage of misery-causing fear and frustration-causing desires that result from accepting the body-mind-personality as self?' You'll see that all misery comes when fear and desire meet at the same point."

Q: "Meet at the same point?"

F: "Take as an example the display of misery you witnessed earlier. The dream of having power now and being guaranteed eternal life for the body-mind-personality creates a desire that is accompanied by fear. The body-mind-personality desires power and eternal life, but at the same time it fears eternal punishment. The desire and fear met at the same point—at the point of the concept of eternal continuity. You witnessed the result. If you challenge the method that someone is following to pursue a desire or to avoid a fear, then expect emotional intoxication to ensue. In the same fashion, when 'husband' thought he was dying, the misery resulted when desire and fear met at the concept of 'wife.' The role of 'husband' desired her and feared he would lose her." His desire and fear met at the same point…at the concept of 'wife'."

Q: "You're right!"

F: [Staring at Q., without comment. Eventually smiling. Light laughter from the group.] "Let's return to the original pointer. The journey we are on aims to put us fully in touch with reality. To be out of touch with reality is to be insane. This journey is about getting in touch with reality in order to be free of the bondage of the illusions and falsehoods of a mind exposed to years of enculturation." Please enter the silence of contemplation.

THE THIRD DEGREE
OF SEPARATION FROM REALITY:
Religious and/or Spiritual
Identifications, Part Eight

F: "If freed of the bondage of the illusions of a mind exposed to years of enculturation, you'll be sane—no longer believing lies to be true. That restoration to sanity activates natural behavior—rather than the subconscious mind or the thinking mind—to conduct one through the relative existence. We just saw a demonstration of why these two roles form their own category of major obstacles on the path. Nothing impedes the shift to the sanity of touching reality like emotional intoxication and the resulting madness that is generated by these two states-of-being…of being 'religious' or being 'spiritual.' [Pause] Now, my original intent for this session was to start with a pointer from Maharaj. Actually, his words will probably be even more relevant now than before. Maharaj said, 'There are so many who take the dawn for noon, [who take] a momentary experience for full realization and destroy even the little they gain by excess of pride.' Why pride? Who, claiming to be a religious person or a spiritual person, will not also claim that he or she is better as a result? Typical is the claim, 'I'm a better person for being religious,' or 'I live a better life since becoming a spiritual person.' The truth is, both are assumed personas, mistaken for the real but nonetheless limiting."

Questioner 3: "But don't you think the world does need to be better?"

F: "My world is perfect. 'Perfect' comes from the Greek teleios, meaning 'complete.' Christ was not perfect as a result of being without sin. The text said he was teleios ... complete. He understood his 'completeness' after receiving the Advaita understanding and then demanding, 'When you speak of me, speak of me as I AM.' For me, I need nothing. That's perfect...complete...whole. I'm not fractured into dozens of false identities. I'm not even two. As we discussed earlier, if you assume a role, you are incomplete. Why?"

Q3: "You said every role requires another person to play the counterpart. This gentleman [pointing] thinking he had to have a woman willing to play 'wife' for him to exist as 'husband,' felt incomplete without her."

F: "Excellent! I am no role that requires a co-dependent partner to complete a false identity. No roles...no dependencies. No dependencies ... no incompletion. I'm whole. I'm 'perfect.' What's with this imagined need to be better if you're already 'perfect'?"

Q3: "Finally!" [Pause, then laughter from others] "Well...I got it!"

F: "[Pauses, allowing for full absorption of the awareness. Then ...] For most of you, your questions and comments show that your case is different. Instead of being in the world, the world is actually in you, meaning…in your mind. The world you see is you, projected by you, so it's not whole. It's incomplete and imperfect and fractured. That leaves you with a sense of being unfulfilled—you have unfulfilled desires and imagined fears about the state of the world. You haven't yet lost your mind."

Q. 3.: "I've spent my entire life up to now thinking the ultimate goal was to be spiritual and to work forever at being better." [Exhales, slowly. Looks down, then to side. Looks up. Shakes head, seeming to reveal a new understanding.]

F: [Continues to wait, then ...] "The religious and spiritual levels are only the beginner's stage. Those who stop there on the journey haven't even reached a halfway point. If you complete this journey, you're going to see exactly, step-by-step, how you got from the Absolute state to the false belief that you're a body. And you're going to see how to get from believing that you're a body to realization of the Absolute. And seeing that complete cycle, then you're going to understand all the cycles, how the happenings happen over and over and over again."

Questioner 4: "I'm processing what you said about completion, but I'm still thinking about what he said earlier, [pointing at Q. 3] about making the world better. Don't you think, over all the years, that religion has helped millions?"

F: "You love your religious and spiritual identities, don't you? [Pause] Aren't you seeing the relief that's coming to him as he's dropping this burden of working all his life to be better? And imagine the relief that'll come to others around him who won't be dealing with him trying to force them to be better. [Laughter. Q. 3 smiles. Then to Q. 4] You may have reached the end of your road. I suspect you're going to be stuck right here. For me, I deal in facts. I know that millions and millions have died from fighting over religious beliefs, but that's not the pointer. The point is that, when I was assuming religious and spiritual roles— which I played with just as much enthusiasm and anger as that person who walked out of here—I was seeking eternal existence for a body-mind-personality triad. Required was the transitioning beyond the dogma and doctrine and beliefs as well as the continuation of the questioning that ultimately revealed the lies which in turn allowed the truth to be seen in order to be free of fears and desires. Until then, I remained trapped in anticipation and regret, focusing on the 'ever-lasting fate' of a personal body. I was seeking the 'good' label to earn my reward and working to avoid the 'bad' label in order to dodge eternal damnation and punishment. Don't you see that the religious seeker is still being driven to have his desires fulfilled and to have his fears abated?"

Q 4.: .... "Aren't there at least some who are motivated simply by a desire to help?"

F: "Again with this 'helping.' Again with 'desire.' An entirely new ego-state is given birth to if one goes out to reform the world and make it a better place. The closest you are to 'complete' right now is being completely trapped in your ego. Your words tell me that you really do want to change the world, and that's the height of ego if you think you can. But you're not willing to let dissolve that which is within you that you're projecting as 'the world'."

Q. 4: [Frowns]

F: "The irony is that anyone seeing a horrible world is simply projecting himself onto what he calls 'the world.' And how would the world be a better place via a reformer's religious or spiritual service, according to his beliefs? All would eventually think and feel and behave as dictated by his doctrine. They would live in the image of the reformer. They would think, feel and behave as he does. The egotistical belief is that the world would be better if all would just become clones of the reformer. Foster that belief system, and those with contradictory religious views—all trying to compel others to model them—will meet as they travel to the 'four corners of the earth' and they will clash at every turn. As those persons go forth, the rest of the people of the world will have their every thought, feeling, and behavior labeled as 'bad' or 'good' and the misery and destruction of dual-mindedness spreads. If you think that the power of a parent's definitions of 'good' and 'bad' can drive one all his life, imagine the power of believing in a god of duality as he defines what is 'good' and what is 'bad' and describes in vivid terms exactly what eternal reward or never-ending punishment will look like. The no-single-cause understanding will be missed and another concept of a divine plan will be assumed to be the cause. The cause of all is all that has ever happened before, but if you seek a prime cause—or a singular 'causer'—then a person playing a religious or spiritual role will be glad to fabricate some concept of causation for you or will encourage you to dream up your own." Please enter the silence of contemplation.

THE THIRD DEGREE OF SEPARATION FROM REALITY:
Religious and/or Spiritual Identifications, Part Nine

Q. 4.:. "So you don't believe there's a Prime Cause—or 'causer' as you say?"

F: "You still want to bring up concepts that were dreamed up in some mind and then repeated by programmed people for millennia. Forget trying to find out about ancient concepts and find out about the True Self now."

Q. 4.:............ "So, I guess there's no chance of you believing in the Trinity?"

F: "The Trinity? The Trinity?! [Light laughter] I speak of non-duality. I Am the unicity. Why would you mention a duality, a trinity, a quadrility, or anything other than the unicity? We're discussing the Advaita Teaching. If you want to examine trinities, study the ancient words of the gurus. Know the three gunas; study the inner, the outer, and the supreme; find the sat, the chit, and the ananda if you like; focus on the material, the spiritual and the essence; talk of the 'I Am,' the 'I,' and even the 'I-I.' The ancient form of The Teaching abounds with trinities that you can study. But you continue to want to bring up concepts after we've discussed in Level Two all of the misery associated with such mind clutter. I've addressed all of that. I spoke earlier of groups dreaming up concepts like 'time' and 'eternity' and 'far-off places' for dust-to-dust bodies to re-form and gather with other re-formed dust-to-dust bodies for some eternal reward or never-ending punishment. That's all about the desire for continuity of a body-mind-personality triad. To even ask that question, you show that you're still ignoring the cyclings. Energy can't be created or destroyed, so how can there have been a 'creation'? And if there's no creation, what need for your creator concept or Prime Cause? You've modeled our dearly-departed guest and are dreaming up your own conception and then wanting to talk to me about the content of a dream. Understand the facts and then answer the question for yourself. [Pause] For now, just listen."

Q. 5:"So how did you get past this point in your journey?"

F: "After all of my study and searching and 'spiritual work,' I spent an evening applying my teacher's words to the vision I'd had. Realization came on an April 21st, a little after 9:30 one evening when I was doing nothing…nothing but resting in the silent contemplation after reading the words of my teacher and focusing on all the lies I'd ever been told…open-mindedly and objectively questioning it all. When I finally saw it was all a lie—including every belief and idea that had contributed to all my assumed personas—the illusion of a 'personal I' dissolved and the understanding of the functioning of the Totality was realized."

Q. 5:"You make it sound so easy."

F: "It wasn't for me, but it can be for you. It took me half a century. It need take you but seven steps. Take advantage of the offering."

Q. 5:"Here's the part I don't get. Remember how you said a shift in consciousness came and you didn't have to quit your job teaching to be at peace…you just let teaching happen … without attachment?"

F: "Go ahead."

Q. 5:"Why can't religious or spiritual practices 'just happen' too?"

F: "They can, but not for any of you at the present. [Pause] Consider this: I once loaded a car in Lucerne, Switzerland one morning and began a trip to Venice, Italy. Seven and a half hours later, I pulled into Piazza Roma and parked. I unloaded the baggage. I arranged for a gondola, and forty-five minutes later he delivered us to a canal-side entrance to our hotel. We checked in. We negotiated narrow steps with our luggage and finally arrived in the room. After more than nine hours, I fell backwards onto the bed and relaxed. The journey was long and tiresome that day, but for the next several days, we spent hour upon hour in the main square, just enjoying the orchestras and watching what was happening. We did nothing. All just happened and we just witnessed it. Now, you're in Lucerne, wanting to relax in the Venetian square, without having completed any of the journey in between … without unloading any baggage…without giving up every false identity. You can feign detachment and tell me you're just amusing yourself, but I know you're as attached as ever to the personalities and the body-mind that sustains them. You must give up these two roles and all others, take this entire journey, see all that you must see, and know the functioning of the Totality. Only then can you practice AS IF living and truly be free. Your ego is telling you that you've arrived and can pull that off. You cannot. Playing the roles at this point will attach you to the role identifications. In truth, your questions show that you haven't abandoned the roles at all. The only thing 'happening' for you is an on-going struggle to preserve your illusions."

Q. 5:. "The trouble is, I was raised the same way he was, [pointing at Q. 3] being taught that reaching the spiritual state is the end of the road."

F: "None of you were likely raised in a more unyielding, religious environment than I. I'm proof that such cannot prevent seeing truth and abandoning rigidity. But are you ready for your road to end? I'd much prefer to reach the true end of the journey and then live a life in the relative with the peace afforded by understanding the functioning of the Totality. But for those who choose to stop here, so be it. Many certainly do, but they miss out on the filtering stage of child ignorance, on the clarifying stage of the witness, on the sense of Oneness gained via knowing the True Self, on the bliss of the beingness, and the Full Understanding of the non-beingness and the Absolute. If you don't know all of that, and if you don't know THAT, then you will never know the 'teaching-just-happens-or-not' existence. If none of that seems worth the continuation of the journey, camp out here and the rest of us will wave to you on our way 'back' to a lifetime of wonderful AS IF living! Ha." [Laughter] Please enter the silence of contemplation.

THE THIRD DEGREE
OF SEPARATION FROM REALITY:
RELIGIOUS AND/OR SPIRITUAL
IDENTIFICATIONS, PART TEN

Q: "So if being in touch with reality restores us to sanity, and you practiced strict religious and spiritual disciplines along the way, were you insane?" [Laughter]

F: "Totally. I was out of touch with reality, limited by accepting these two ego-states as the ultimate. That arrested my journey at this third level for years. In a book I'm writing, one passage will describe those years when I was trapped in the dogma and attached to spiritual exercises: [Picks up a folder of papers, begins reading] In his energy-consuming search for salvation, he'd been dipped, dunked, sprayed, spayed, sprinkled, and neutered; in the quest for truth, he'd been blessed, cursed, cussed, lectured, scolded, and praised; in his pursuit of Life's Meaning, he'd been communion'd, Om'd, grape-juiced, wined, ahsram'd, accepted, rejected, Mu'd, and yoga'd; in his chase for service-work-opportunities, he'd been pulverized, martinized, and frappéd; and in the endeavor to attain Life Eternal, he'd been baptized, Buddha'd, New Aged, powwow'd, Far Eastern Indianized, incense'd, sage'd, Tao'd, Peru'd, Tibet'd, washed in the blood, dunked in the waters, and purportedly purified. (from The Twice-Stolen Necklace Murders) [Huge laughter] I had as active an addiction to spiritual workaholism as ever existed. If it had led to Realization and a life marked by consistent peace, I'd be recommending it all to you right now. But ultimately, none of that allowed me to escape the duality, and I have never seen any person living in duality who is free. Krishna said, 'Those alone who understand that I, the Absolute, am beyond the states of being and non-being realize my true nature, and all others are fools.' Can you be consistently free if you're consistently 'being fooled'? Only by seeing all the lies and then the truth within can one not be fooled."

Q: "I'm just having such a hard time even considering the possibility that the spiritual state in not the supreme state. The goal for me has always been to work to be more godly."

F: "Then you need to study the early Advaita Teachings to learn what the supreme state truly is. Or, you may complete this journey and know. The seven-step journey merely offers abstract concepts in concrete terms to facilitate Realization. At Realization, all concepts and all 'abstracts' and 'concretes' dissolve. As for your working 'to be more godly,' what I have witnessed is that persons who believe in a judging and punishing god—when they become godly—are judging and punishing in their relative interactions. And persons who believe in a god that gives rewards for good behavior—when they become godly—give rewards with strings attached in their relative interactions. Find the True Self that has no attachments and no rewarding-punishing dualism."

Q: "You don't believe in a creation event, but I was raised to believe in the creation story in the Bible."

F: "Those very same people also raised you to believe in Santa Claus. Do you still believe in that concept?" [Laughter]

Q: [Defensively] "I believe in the creation story as told in Genesis."

F: "Which one?"

Q: "I said the one in Genesis."

F: "Which one in Genesis? There are two totally different and contradictory versions of creation in that one book."

Q: [Long pause, confused, thinking] "I've never heard that."

F: "You've never heard anything I will say, and you never will unless you investigate all your beliefs and see them for what they are: ancient myths and superstitions handed down for so long by so many that they are unquestioningly taken to be truth. I invite you to question it all. You speak highly of your sacred text and accept its content as fact without even having read thoroughly the first chapter of the first book. [Tightens lips] Not unusual. I've witnessed that to be the case with almost all who quote their holy texts. I invite you to forget what they told you that they thought they knew and find out what You know, within. You take offense when you are told that you must transition these two personas and all others, but identified with these two ego-states, you take my words PERSONAlly. [Smiles] All personalities are limiting. These two will limit your ability to see all else that must be seen for realization."

Please enter the silence of contemplation.

THE THIRD DEGREE
OF SEPARATION FROM REALITY:
Religious and/or Spiritual
Identifications, Part Eleven

Q: [Sarcastically] "So what do you know about creation?"

F: "Ha. I know that what you call 'this universe' is a result of a single hydrogen atom manifesting in a vacuum, a process now being duplicated in the scientific laboratory. I know that hydrogen atom split and paired and eventually smashed into a subsequent helium atom. I know that all is a result of that original movement of energy and that's why this universe is composed of hydrogen more than any other element. I know that the process of photosynthesis allows plants to use the energy from the sun to produce sugar and then ATP via cellular respiration. I know that results in a form of energy that can be used by all living things, including the two plant eaters who would be called 'my parents.' I understand that the conversion of unusable sunlight energy into usable chemical energy allowed those two plant eaters to consume plants that would automatically form sperm cells in one and form eggs in another. I know that this space called 'floyd' is a result of an act of friction between those two plant eaters that set into motion a chain of happenings that would result in this manifestation of consciousness. That's what I know about creation, but none of that knowledge was required for realization! What was necessary for the full understanding was already within me. I needed to but clear away the debris field of lies and myths and superstitions that had been blocking awareness of the truth. Once the debris was fully removed from an incorrectly programmed and wrongly conditioned mind, the full understanding of the functioning of the Totality happened. Steps four and five are where that purging can happen for you. Krishna said they have fooled you, and that has happened so thoroughly that you don't even know Who You Are. What can you possibly claim to know as truth when you don't even know that? Either you question the myths and find the truth or you live forever in the darkness of their tales and superstitions and all of the resulting ego-states of being this or that which now trap you in the misery of your desires and fears. If you can release the attachment to these two roles, you'll move to the Fourth Degree and a significant shift occurs. The first three degrees of body and mind and personality identification have all separated you from Reality. In the discussion of the third degree, you've been invited to transcend the two most entrenched personas. If you can release the hold of these two personalities, then you'll have a chance to complete the purification process in the fourth and fifth steps. If that happens, awareness of Your True Self will occur. And the interesting shift is that, while the first three degrees blocked you from reality, the next levels can all facilitate the coming of the full understanding. If you can successfully transition beyond these two false identities, then you'll enter The Fourth Degree of Movement toward Reality. What is called for now is for you to take into focused meditation all that we've discussed and allow all you've heard to be understood." Please enter the silence of contemplation.

THE FOURTH DEGREE OF MOVEMENT TOWARD REALITY: CHILD IGNORANCE

THE FOURTH DEGREE OF MOVEMENT TOWARD REALITY: CHILD IGNORANCE, PART ONE

F: "We have reached the fourth level ... the level where a shift occurs. We discussed the first Three Degrees of Separation from Reality. Now, at this fourth step, we'll begin talking about 'The Fourth Degree of Movement toward Reality.' Again, in truth there are no steps and there is no journey, no separation, no movement. These are all concepts used to help you shift from being asleep to being aware. These are just thorns being used to remove thorns, after which all the thorns will be tossed."

Q: "That's appropriate. The last step was very painful." [Laughter]

F: "And what pain do you imagine you experienced?" [Light laughs]

Q: "I did what you said and really focused on my subject matter during my meditation. I didn't try to reach some no-thought state but really paid attention to the assignment. I also double-checked some things you said." [Laughs]

F: "Double-checking non-duality. Interesting." [Laughs]

Q: "The first day, I read part of Genesis and I saw the two conflicting versions of creation you mentioned, and then I sat with that. I also saw where he plagiarized the I AM THAT I AM and used it as his own, and I meditated on that."

F: "And?"

Q: "And at the end, for the first time ever, I had to ask, 'Can this text really be considered 'infallible'?" [Pause. Quiet. Finally ...] I'd like to apologize for getting angry with you."

F: "Who would have been offended? Better yet, find who got angry."

Q: "I know who got angry. I saw by mid-week that my roles really were fighting for their 'lives' with you. By the end of the week, I saw that all of the fighting I've ever done in my life was being fought by one ego-state or another."

F: "Have any others come to a similar understanding?" [Several raise their hands]

Q. 2: "I talked with someone who did these sessions with you before and she said you had her write a list of every role she's ever assumed as an identity. I did that and was blown away by the length of the list." [Laughs]

F: "Would that it were always so easy to blow away the personalities. [Laughter] So what did you find?"

Q. 2: "In about twenty minutes, I listed over seventy roles I've played in my life!" [Laughter]

F: "You obviously needed to spend more time considering and writing if that's all you came up with!" [Laughs]

Q. 2: "I have no doubt I could probably double the list." [Laughs]

F: "There's that double again. [Laughs] How many can tell me unequivocally that you have realized, or that you're realizing, how the body-mind-personality triad has blocked you from any possibility of knowing Who You Truly Are?" [Everyone raises a hand] Excellent. Now, without raising your hands but just considering this for a moment, how many are aware of a dropoff in the level of tension you've brought into the room and how many are aware of their more relaxed condition right now? [Pause. silence. Looks of awareness begin crossing most faces. One hand goes up.] Please, no comments or questions for now. Just consider for a moment. [Pause. Quiet. Then...] Nothing need be said. You're seeing the results of taking even this much of the journey. Shifts are occurring. [Pause.] Let's move on. Where I said the first three levels separate you from Reality, steps Four through Seven can move you toward Reality. The Fourth Degree is the level of Child Ignorance. We've been told by the sages that all knowledge is 'learned ignorance.' Before there was learned ignorance, there was Child Ignorance. To move beyond this point on your 'journey,' you must reject the learned ignorance and seek to shift into the 'state' of Child Ignorance. Let me describe the arrival into this state and as I do so, know what your life can be like if you return to this 'state.' Please hold your questions until I finish the description

and see where this next step is inviting you to 'go.' [Pause] After the space manifests, there's a period of witnessing … without judgment or even knowing. The
child then becomes more aware of its presence. Consciousness becomes aware of
consciousness. At that point, the child is aware that it IS, but it has no learned
ignorance that it's a 'girl' or 'boy' or 'baby' or 'human' or 'gift from god.' The
labels and false identities will come later. Remember that we're taking these steps
in the cyclings in reverse order. The original journey was from the Absolute to the
misinformed state of body identification. If the first stages of the original cycle
were from non-beingness to beingness to Self to witnessing to Child Ignorance
to being programming with learned ignorance, then on our 'reverse journey' we
forfeit the labels and identities to enter again into this more peaceful state. At
this point 'on the way in,' so to speak, the child had no thoughts, no beliefs, no
ideas, no programming, and no conditioning. All that was happening within
the space was happening automatically. The heart was beating without the child
having to think, 'I need my heart to beat.' The lungs worked automatically. As
long as the child was fed, digestion happened automatically. If the mind is the
storehouse of ideas, thoughts, beliefs and attitudes, then the child was living in a
no-mind state. This is the state where a brain was functioning and consciousness
was present and the child was aware of its presence. How do we know that awareness of presence was there? Pop your palms together loudly in a child's face and
the child will react automatically—intuitively—to a sensed danger or threat, but
the consciousness that allows for that self-awareness had not yet been contaminated with what adults would later model and teach. So the child had a sense
at that point of its presence. It sensed the "I Am-ness" without even knowing
any words or concepts. And in the awareness of "I-Am," without any personality or concepts, peace prevailed. Then, as the child became older, they began
teaching the child concepts. The level of peace that a child enjoys in that state
of 'ignorance,' prior to programming and conditioning and being assigned false
identities, is never realized again in its lifetime, in most cases. The exceptions are
those such as you, the ones who take these steps and return to that 'state' of peace
that exists when we are once again free of learned ignorance and the influence
of the illusions of the body-mind-personality triad." Please enter the silence of
contemplation.

THE FOURTH DEGREE
OF MOVEMENT TOWARD REALITY:
CHILD IGNORANCE, PART TWO

Q: "Whoa!"

F: [Pauses] "Yes?"

Q: "I just got a glimpse ... like, the big picture."

F: "Meaning?"

Q: "I mean the cyclings. I've lived by that timeline you mentioned—beginning, middle, end, judgment, etc. But you dropped a few hints that registered... the 'movement,' if you will, from the Absolute to body identity."

F: "Actually, I've dropped those hints all along. You evidently just weren't ready to hear. Ha." [Laughter]

Q: "Well, I'm seeing it—the 'order,' so to speak—from awareness to the sleepwalking we talked about."

F: "You've seen only a portion at most, but for now that's sufficient. Remember M.'s warning, though—don't mistake the dawn for noon. As for this method, it works for some and not at all for others. I can offer only what led to Realization: a vision, reading the words of a sage, sitting in focused meditation on his words, understanding the vision and the seven levels that had separated me from knowing the source, and finally knowing I Am That source. For others of you, you might pass a few hours in here and in meditation and find you need to go to the next teacher. So it is. There's no competition I know of, and no single way. I told you that I tried many, many Advaita teachers and was exposed to a variety of approaches in offering one single truth—but I didn't 'get it,' as you say. [Laughter] Then, my vision and the words of Maharaj came together."

Q: "Whatever. All I can say for now is that things I never understood before are becoming clearer."

F: "We'll see. [To the group] If you walk into a forest and become lost, backtrack. Follow your steps back to the point of entry. The most direct way out of a mess is to follow in reverse the steps you took getting into the mess. Otherwise, you'll wander in the forest forever. You cycled step-by-step from the Absolute to body identification. We're backtracking. We're following the steps back to Who We Really Are, leaving behind body identity, mind identity, personalities, the ignorant programming and conditioning ... all of it."

Q: "I'm seeing it."

F: "Then let's continue. You've touched the truth of the journey. We're 'going back,' so to speak. We're cycling 'home.' Here's the next step: if all that you've learned is the problem at this stage, then the solution at this stage is to unlearn all."

Q.2:......."It's difficult—I've always been taught that knowledge is the key."

F: "Ha. I hope you're finding that your knowledge, far from being a 'key,' is actually the very thing that locked the door of your mind and shuttered all the windows that need opening for you to see."

Q: [Nods in acknowledgment]

F: "It's useless to try to use your mind and its knowledge to seek outside yourself for the truth of Your Self, which is within. It is that very mind—the conditioned mind—that has prevented the knowing."

Q. 2: ... "Here's the piece I don't get about the no-mind of child ignorance: if there's no mind, how am I supposed to ever have peace of mind?" Please enter the silence of contemplation.

THE FOURTH DEGREE OF MOVEMENT TOWARD REALITY:
Child Ignorance, Part Three

F: "Let me see if you understand what you're really asking for. You want a mind that is always at perfect peace, but consciousness is energy and thus is not immobile if manifested. So you are saying that you want your consciousness to be unmanifested—that is, you want to die. Ha." [Laughter]

Q. 2: .... "Okay. Real funny, but you described a superconscious state when you talked about the vision that came to you."

F: "True. The samadhi state was reached, but M. said that it's the nature of consciousness to be 'busy.' More to the point, however, do you see that you're speaking of another desire? We've already seen the ramifications of desire. Who wants this perpetual peace? Take all the steps, find how this consciousness manifested, and then you'll be free of the misery caused by a mind conditioned with learned ignorance. That's the focus of this step. Complete all the steps and natural living will happens."

Q. 2: "Then the relative existence will be peaceful?"

F: "Ha. Again, a desire. I hear both a fear of something and a desire for something. Once realized, what is, is. Then, all happens, and all happens without attachment. Movement...no movement...whatever. [Pause] Consider the deer that lives naturally rather than with a thinking mind. Generally, the deer is what you would probably call 'at peace.' Yet during the days when I went into the woods regularly, I often startled a deer as it was feeding. It would 'freeze,' raise it's head and stare, and then its heart would race as the adrenals kicked into over-drive. Next, seeing my movement, it would bolt away. I would not say that deer was 'at peace' even though it had no thinking mind and no false identities. But I noted that the deer would often move to an adjacent clearing and, seeing that I was moving on, its fear would dissipate. It would then ignore me completely. It would return to grazing. Something happened, consciousness witnessed what was happening, no persona was assumed so no attachment followed, and the tasks involved with sustaining the consciousness continued. With the deer, happen-ings were happening, then a happening was witnessed, then fear rose and fell, and then other happenings happened. Voila. But consider this: how peaceful is the deer's existence as long as it has a body to tend to, as long as it must search for food during seasons when less is available to eat, when it must fight on occasion to preserve its territory or to protect its partner from other deer trying to move in during mating season? I don't know how much 'peace' as opposed to how much 'not-peace' that deer had in the relative, but it was certainly freer than persons whose thinking minds accept false identities that experience fear and desire all day long, every day."

Q. 2: "Right."

F: "The deer did not take offense, having no persona that felt it had owner-ship of that field where it was eating. It was not driven to attack me as a result of a 'how dare you come into my space' mentality that always accompanies ego. Its consciousness knew its presence—it knew the 'I-Amness' since it ran away from a perceived threat in order to continue its presence—but the actions taken to protect that beingness were intuitive. That left it free of attachments and emotional intoxication. Without a thinking mind and without a personality, it did not feel driven to work at trying to avoid or gain, as you're doing. Forget trying to find ways to avoid what a body-mind-personality experiences as a result of its learned ignorance. If you take that triad to be 'you,' fears and desires will always be experienced. No rest will come because your personalities will always be engaged in a never-ending quest, and the quest is an impossible dream since in effect you're trying to avoid illusions. You're crossing an imaginary road in terror, dodging cars that you're only imagining are coming toward you. How futile, that constant jousting with windmills! You're trying to address the symptom rather than the cause. The cause is the assumed triad and the learned ignorance. Get to the root and understand this step. Devalue your knowledge and learned ignorance. Let dissolve any remaining personas. See all that you have learned to this point as being useless and let it all fade. Then no body-mind-personality illusion will be occupied with desires for peace of mind or with fears of losing peace of mind." Please enter the silence of contemplation.

THE FOURTH DEGREE
OF MOVEMENT TOWARD REALITY:
Child Ignorance, Part Four

Q.2 :"Is 'marriage' a concept?"

F: "Of course. Anything you can name is a concept."

Q. 2: ."So, if all has to dissolve and one has to give up every concept, must marriage be abandoned in order to continue this journey?"

F: "I invited you to allow all personas to dissolve. Just because the role of 'husband' dissolves does not mean that a series of happenings must stop. Sex, reproduction, work, house-sharing, child-rearing…all that can continue to happen. The difference is that after realization, all those happenings will continue to happen, but no person will be involved with the happenings; also, the absence of ego-states will herald an absence of emotional intoxication. No images believed before to be real will be taken as the real after understanding the functioning of the Totality, but the full array of all those happenings can still occur. With no persona to experience anything, the experiencing of the fears and desires that accompany the assumption of false identities will end. Persons experience; consciousness experiences nothing. Impure consciousness believes experiences to be real; pure consciousness simply witnesses. The fourth level we're discussing is about purifying, about filtering. It's about returning to that state when the child was conscious of its presence but not conscious of any beliefs or ideas. The consciousness was pure, devoid of lies and fabrications and prior to programming and conditioning. This is the point at which the effects of your learned ignorance, your conditioning, and your programming should be seen and cast aside, once and for all. You are within two steps of seeing your True Self. Obviously, the True Self can only be seen when Truth is seen, and Truth can only be seen when all the false has been noted and discarded. The True Self springs into view when the last state-of-being dissolves. The Child Ignorance step begins to purge the corrupted, variable mind of all false identities so that you can know the True Self. We are looking at all that you take to be 'within' that is false before we move to the witnessing level and see that all that you take to be 'outside' is false. In truth, none of it is anything more than movements in contaminated consciousness. There is no triad of perceiver, perceived, perceiving. The first two are illusions and even the perceiving will dissolve when consciousness is no longer manifested."

Q. 2: "So, how to be rid of all my ideas and beliefs once and for all?"

F: "See that there are no 'my' ideas or 'my' beliefs. They are theirs, and theirs are dreamed up…not real. They are false. Accept that and then let all ideas and beliefs dissolve, including mine after realization. Now, enough talk about forfeiting the learned ignorance. We've reached a juncture where meditation is called for. I suggest you spend time now in the quiet. Focus consideration on where we have been so far on the journey: review our discussions regarding the misery of accepting the limiting view that you are your body, of taking a corrupted mind's beliefs as real, of the various personalities you've assumed. Review the power of two personas in particular that—if assumed to be who you are—will prevent any further movement along the path. All knowledge has availed you nothing, so you're being invited to let it all go. If you reach that no-body, no-false identities, no-false beliefs stage, then you're ready for the witnessing stage. Go now and meditate on these words. See the body lies, the mind lies, the personality lies … see all the lies." Please enter the silence of contemplation.

THE FOURTH DEGREE
OF MOVEMENT TOWARD REALITY:
CHILD IGNORANCE, PART FIVE

F: "Before we move to the Fifth Degree, it's time to share with you the content of a vision that came years ago. The vision will clarify the understanding of the four levels we've transitioned. It will also allow you to know the next level (The Witnessing), and will guide you through the remainder of the journey …

to the True Self ... to the beingness ... to the non-beingness ... and to a full knowing of the Absolute which will be accompanied by an understanding of the functioning of the Totality. I'll be offering the vision in parts, and I suggest that—after reading each part—you enter the silence of contemplation. The goal will not be to reach a no-mind or superconscious state at this point. The goal will be to become so awake, so aware and so conscious of what is being revealed through the vision that you know the truth of the pointers offered regarding each level we have discussed. Eventually—via your meditating upon the content of the vision—you will complete the journey on your own through the remaining levels. In today's part of the vision, see the first of the shifts as You leave behind on the journey all that is not You in order to know All That Is You. After reading today's segment of the vision, close your eyes, feel your presence in the vision as you walk through it again on your own, and contemplate the content until you know the truth of what it reveals."

A Spirit Journey to Your TRUE SELF

Envision yourself standing at one end of an open field in a very remote area. At the far end of the field is the edge of a forest. See yourself moving across the field and toward the woods. As you walk closer to the edge of the forest, see a gap in the trees that allows clear access to a trail. Follow that path through the woods, noticing the sounds along the way. Walk until you reach the side of a small creek bed. Turn to the right and see yourself walking along the bank of a "branch," one of those small, usually V-shaped mini-gorges, cut into the ground ten to twelve feet at its deepest, not as much by rainwater as by constantly flowing springs that surface from below. Observe an emerald-green moss that covers the walls and the bed; it seems to shine with a luminescence in spite of the fact that the thickness of the overhead foliage prevents much sunlight from striking the creek bed or the sides of the chasm. The earthen walls look rough-edged, for stones jut out all along the way, their tips exposed by years of erosion. Colors typical of the region come into view along the way: earth-tones, rust-colors, and sometimes blackness, but always brightened by the ever-present grayish and fluorescent-green moss.

As you parallel the edge of the creek on the beginning of this journey, see yourself reaching a place where the land slopes sharply, and the watery swath cut into the earth follows the oblique contour of the land. Next to the slanting branch rests a series of natural, sandstone steps descending to a granite arch twice the height of a human. From the arch shines a pure white light. An illumination this bright should easily blind you, but instead it soothes you. It seems to spotlight the steps, and as you move down the stones, first your feet and then your legs and then your torso become bathed in the glow. Eventually, by the time you reach the dead-flat area at the bottom of the natural walkway, you stand before the arch, and the luxuriance of the light bathes you fully in its warmth. The clear spring waters from the branch flow through the archway, and you follow.

Stepping inside, you look over your shoulder to see that your physical body has remained outside the arch. You sense some degree of separation from the material.

F: "Keeping your eyes closed, I now invite you to consider: are you fully convinced that You are not a body?" Please enter the silence of contemplation.

THE FOURTH DEGREE
OF MOVEMENT TOWARD REALITY:
CHILD IGNORANCE, PART SIX

F: "After you read the second part of the vision, close your eyes and picture yourself in the setting. Relate the content to the level of separation that we discussed earlier."

When you turn to see where the arch has led, you notice that the spring waters have suddenly multiplied into a slow-moving stream. The stream runs the length of a plateau and then cascades over the edge at the far end. You will soon see that the waters drop from the highland and then flow, in waterfall fashion, down the cliff side and into a pool some twenty feet below.

Trees line either side of the stream, and you begin walking through them toward the sounds of the water crashing below. Astonished, you noticed that you are literally walking through the trees. As you progress, fauna of several species join you: a black bear rubs against your leg in the manner of a docile housecat; a cougar does the same on the opposite side, and each playfully swats at the other as if to proclaim dominion over both of your legs; a lamb skips along ahead as a heron brings up the rear. He walks as if on stilts, taking more time than needed, looking rather judgmentally, it seems, at the wasting of energy by his peers.

As you near the edge of the cliff, you walk across the top of the water, not becoming wet at all; your new companions either lead or follow. As you approach the left side of the plateau, the animals nudge you toward a winding walkway of sorts, cut from the stone side of the cliff naturally, definitely not made by man. After swinging down and around and back to your right, you find yourself on a level piece of ground jutting out from the side of the cliff. You see that a pond is overflowing, part of its waters cascading down the cliff side and pooling in another flat below.

That same pattern repeats itself until the waters reach a level valley. You watch the falling waters eventually form a river that winds its way across the desert basin. Along the river has sprung up a variety of shade trees. All else appears brown and dry. Then in the far distance, hills grow into mountains. In the forefront arise huge columns of stone, cathedral-like, forming spires of varying shapes and heights. The colors vibrate with life, offering images of the blues and oranges and browns and beiges like those of Venetian palazzos when reflected in the waters of the Grand Canal.

In the far distance to the left stand even grander mountain ranges. Puffy clouds float slowly across the sky. You focus attention on a fire burning next to the pool, and you feel yourself being nudged there by the bear, nudged in a very persuasive way. Then, from behind, the cougar lifts its front paws onto your shoulders and forces you into a cross-legged, seated position before the camp-fire. Finally, all four animals form a semi-circle around you, from your left side, behind you, and to your right.

Looking at the animals quizzically, you notice that each is focusing on an object in the distance. Allowing your eyes to follow the path of theirs, see a bird of some kind flying directly at you, drawing nearer by the second. Its speed accelerates as it moves dart-like across the skies, aimed at your chest like an avian arrow. Yet you feel very calm. As the bird approaches closer and closer, you extend your arms and, with the sides of your hands touching and your palms up, you form a landing area for the fowl. A raven, the bird of death that comes from the spiritual realm, now slows as it approaches even nearer. Why had you not made that association between spirit and death and this bird? It swoops upward to curb its flight and, with only a slight, backwards fluttering of wings, settles gently into your outstretched hands. The other fauna watch but do not react.

The bird stares at you, and you at the bird. You sense the bird drawing forth something from within you that is flowing out via your eyes and moving directly into the eyes of the bird. You watch as the bird leaves, but you feel as if you have left and that your mind has stayed behind. A second degree of separation you seem to detect.

F: "Keeping your eyes closed, I now invite you to consider: how convinced are you that You are not your mind?" Please enter the silence of contemplation.

THE FOURTH DEGREE
OF MOVEMENT TOWARD REALITY:
CHILD IGNORANCE, PART SEVEN

F: "Is it your belief that your relative existence should play out in the limited confines of a narrow dungeon where you feel imprisoned and struggling each day? Should you feel as if you are at the mercy of the whims of a plethora of guards, including the guard of accumulation, the guard of politics, the guard of religion, the guard of austere disciplines, the guard of personalities, the guard of fear, the guard of 'others,' or the guard of desire? How free do you want to be? Are you willing to leave the prison behind? I come to tell you again, the bars of the prison of your body-mind-personality triad are made from the ideas that you hold to be true and the beliefs that you hold to be sacred. The instant you leave the physical and mental prison of personas behind, in that very instant you are well on your way to freedom. Today, you're invited to leave behind the other personas that have such a limiting hold. Please close your eyes and listen to the next section of the vision." [Please read the vision first, then close your eyes, place yourself in the setting, and move through the vision again.]

The raven soars over the valley, flying high, then flying low, and then flying high again. Its spirit is high. Soon, it makes a direct course for the mountains, for it is driven to try to reach the mountaintop. You no longer watch from the cliff but see everything below through the eyes of the raven. After missing the mountaintop, the raven passes beyond and begins a fast descent toward an ocean which has come into view just after topping the peak. The raven begins to dive lower, and lower, and lower yet. Suddenly, the spiritual exuberance of the high-flying raven seems to be unraveling into an imminent and deadly crash against the ocean's surface. Following a huge impact—one that you take to be the end of you—the waters first splash upwards from the collision and then fall back into the ocean. Ultimately, the waves settle, and the sea surface smoothes out to a mirror finish.

F: "Keeping your eyes closed, I now invite you to consider: how convinced are you that You are not the religious or spiritual roles that you've played?" Enter into the silence of contemplation.

STEP FIVE

THE FIFTH DEGREE OF MOVEMENT TOWARD REALITY: WITNESSING

THE FIFTH DEGREE OF MOVEMENT TOWARD REALITY: WITNESSING, PART ONE

[Note: Visit the advaita blog link at the front of this book for in-depth discussions of the two levels of witnessing]

F: "To be disillusioned is to be disenchanted or disappointed. For any person who has ever felt disillusioned, the remedy is to become 'de-illusioned.' Only for the sake of discussion will we talk of 'illusions within' and 'illusions without.' In truth, there is not an 'inside' vs. an 'outside.' All illusions are illusions, and all illusions are within the corrupted mind. They are the corrupted mind. For purposes of discussion, though, since many students of the Teaching have seen the difference in stages, let's review the illusions taken to be of an 'inner' nature. The 'inner' illusions involve taking the body to be an actual identity, taking the mental (ideas, beliefs, attitudes) to be real, taking emotional intoxication to be justifiable or normal, and taking false personas to be real. Through the first four levels, the goal has been to allow all of those identities and beliefs and personas that are held 'within' (within the conditioned mind) to dissolve. That having been accomplished, one enters the Child Ignorance stage and then transcends that to the 'Witnessing Level." Again, merely because some have seen the false in stages, we'll say that the witness is objectively seeing the illusory nature of all that is 'without.' What we're really seeing are all the lies ever believed about self and about who one is as well as all the lies believed about others and about who they are and about all else seen that is supposedly outside myself."

Q: "Such as?"

F: "Such as 'seeing a spouse.' You were struggling early on with the perceived 'loss' of a 'wife'."

Q. : "I'm amazed at how I've shifted away from all that."

F. : "The shift is not amazing at all. It's so simple when a person sees that all he believed was a result of faulty programming and wrong conditioning. But to the point: you have an image of yourself. You also had an image you showed her when you were dating. She had an image of you. That's three images of you. The same three images were in place with her. The 'honeymoon was over' when you were together long enough for both to begin seeing that the images weren't real. If a person can look at a coiled rope and believe that it's a snake, then a person can look at a snake and believe it's just a coiled rope." [Laughter] The point is, when you die, she dies; when she dies, you die. Why? Because that personality you call 'wife' is just the image in your mind of who she is, but she is not that at all. Your detailed description of her would differ completely from a detailed description of her provided by your children, from a description provided by a stranger, from a description provided by her mother and father, from a description provided by friends or by former lovers that she ended relations with, etc. If you ask one thousand people who know her what she's like, you'll find that there are one thousand images of her. When those thousands eventually die, each of their singular, unique images of her will dissolve. There are as many images of 'her' as there are people who think they know her. That's an example of a so-called 'outer' image that is an illusion; of course, as I said, there is no 'inner vs. outer' duality since the images of that 'external wife' are not external at all. They are really internal images in the conditioned minds of those who think they are seeing her for who she is…but are not. Thus I say there are not inner or outer images—all images are internal, held in the conditioned mind, perceived via corrupted consciousness. There are the images of self that are held within the corrupted mind and there are the images of others or other things held within the corrupted mind. As the eagle in the vision—the witness—sees the noneness of it all, the True Self will see the oneness of it all. Now, let's return to the vision as we see the eagle enter into the setting and begin to witness. In preparation, envision an eagle, soaring above the arch-desert-mountain-ocean location of the vision. The eagle could see a mouse scampering among the trees that border the stream that runs through the arch. If it were hungry, it could swoop down, capture the mouse, and eat. Furthermore, it might see a stick that is casting a shadow that might look like a mouse—that might appear to be a mouse. The eagle, however, is so observant and so knowing that it does not mistake the shadow for a mouse and attack it. In the case of the shadow, the eagle is not really witnessing any 'thing' but is recognizing an illusion as an illusion. It does not react, attack, or even waste another moment with the image, once it notes that it's just an image. Such is the possibility when you enter the witnessing stage. That having been said, let's move to today's segment of the vision. Close your eyes and enter the realm of the vision."

For a time, the eagle soars, glides, and mainly just witnesses. You feel the remnants of the gull; you sense the remains of a raven; you look at "you" seated at a fire and see only a mental image; you look through the arch and see the figment of a body imagined. Another degree of separation.

But now You the Eagle have no time to contemplate, for you feel yourself being pulled deeper into the universe through a clear-walled tunnel in the remotest part of the heavens.

F.: "Keeping your eyes closed, I ask: are you sensing the detachment of the eagle as it merely witnesses? Is it possible that everything that appears in the material realm is nothing more than an 'outer' image registered 'within' your consciousness and misinterpreted as a result of all your programming and conditioning and beliefs? If you have given up all your beliefs and ideas and attitudes that were mistakenly taken to be the real by your conditioned mind, is it also possible to take everything you see with your eyes and admit that it is not at all what you thought it was? Is it possible that when the last belief is allowed to dissolve, and when the last illusion of 'things seen' is allowed to dissolve, that then—and only then—can you turn and see that which is Real?" Please enter the silence of contemplation.

THE FIFTH DEGREE
OF MOVEMENT TOWARD REALITY:
Witnessing, Part Two

Q: "Okay, I understand there's no 'inner' or 'outer,' that all images are within the mind—or make up the 'mind'—but the notion of witnessing something and then believing that 'I'm not seeing what I'm seeing' seems impossible."

F: "Why?"

Q: [Pause] "Because I can be skeptical about what I hear, but people take what they see to be what they see."

F: "After Realization, the supposed seeing ends and what is known will be known and what was once supposedly 'seen' will be 'seen' no more. But why should the current pointer seem 'impossible'? You once took the concepts of your parents and priests and teachers and friends and culture at face value, but now you've rejected those. You questioned those most basic ideas and beliefs and discarded them. Why can't you accept that what you think you see—and the way you perceive—can be in error?"

Q: "I just said...because even the most skeptical typically accept what they can see."

F: "So you cling to the notion that the coiled rope is truly a snake? [Pause] Return to the steel girder. If you look at that beam from ten feet away, you're going to have one perception of what that beam is; however, if you look at that beam through an electron microscope, then you're going to see a reality that is completely different from your original perception, aren't you?"

Q: "Right."

F: "What's the difference?"

Q. : [Pause] "The closer view."

F: "Okay, the closer view or...the view gained by seeing more clearly with an aid. The satsanga is your aid, your microscope, your new pair of glasses. Eventually, You will see clearly on Your own and can discard the glasses. For now, you need assistance. Your perception has been fogged by decades of distorted enculturation. [F. points to his own body...] What do you see here?"

Q: "I see Floyd."

F: "Oh my gosh ... I'm sending you back to the Level One sessions! [Laughter from group. Points to a woman next to the man.] What do you see?"

Q. 2: "I see chemicals, elements, energy, consciousness, and mainly … just space." [F. smiles broadly, then looks with a mock sneer at Q. as the group laughs.]

Q: [To Q. 2] "Teacher's pet."

F: "If you must label her, call her 'an electron microscope.' Credit her with having 'a third eye.' She sees far more clearly." [Laughter] If the witness sees clearly, then a large world becomes available for this manifested space. You no longer believe in the limited, confined, restricted, restrictive, small world of a body-mind-personality. What she knows [pointing at Q. 2] is that 'A' is not looking at 'B,' 'B' being a mirage; what she knows is that 'A' is witnessing that there is no 'B'—no 'Floyd'—to see. Thus, she's able to understand what actually is. Fixed in the childlike state and just witnessing, the eagle can look at the entire field below—can 'see' all that is in its field of consciousness—but it will experience no emotion and will form no opinions and will draw no conclusions about what it witnesses in the field. It will understand that the shadow of the mouse is a shadow and will ignore it [snaps fingers] that fast. It now witnesses with 'filtered consciousness,' made purer by having discarded all of the false; it 'sees' with the clarity of an electron microscope. Since all is illusion that the eagle-witness witnesses, nothing is really witnessed; therefore, no opinions, attitudes, offenses, or reactions are registered and attached to. Later, even this will change as the True Self will 'see' accurately—will understand—all that it witnesses."

Q: "I don't see any application for the relative existence."

F: [Pause] "You and your application. Who is always seeking to gain more when I invite you to know the bliss of less? [Pause] When a person screamed that I was a 'New Age Agent of Satan' for believing in 'that Advaita stuff,' only a faint buzz was detected for an instant…as if coming from a ghost, from something transparent … artificial … illusory. No longer are voices coming into my head. No longer are voices that once originated from my mind taken to be the Real. No mind exists that can either register or generate such nonsense, so to be called some name has no more effect than someone throwing a rock at the moon. The voices are all gone since the mind that once registered them is gone. Apply that. [Pause. Q. still confused.] When driving along those long stretches of road in the deserts of the Southwest, I don't swerve my car to avoid mirages in the road. By the time I'm closer to where the mirages had supposedly 'appeared,' that closer view shows that the mirage had just been a momentary flickering across the screen of consciousness. In pure consciousness, images cannot register as being something 'real.' [Pause] Take the closer view. Always take the closest view possible until you see the Absolute, then You will have the grandest, broadest view of All. You will understand the functioning of the Totality. Stay on the path until you see every illusion and all of the Truth." Please enter the silence of contemplation.

THE FIFTH DEGREE
OF MOVEMENT TOWARD REALITY:
WITNESSING, PART THREE

Q: "So I could just stop here and live as the witness for the remainder of this relative existence."

F: "I just advised you to stay on the path until you see all the Truth, and then you say that?"

Q: [Grinning sheepishly. Laughter.]

F: "Since nothing is really being witnessed, the witness is not the real, either. After the subject-object dissolves, you still want the subject to remain?"

Q: "So what's next?"

F: "You're going to see in the vision that the eagle is drawn into a tunnel which allows the movement from awareness reflected in consciousness via the witness to Pure Awareness. Once the witness turns on itself after realizing that all in the phenomenal realm is illusion, the witness also dissolves. A sleeper can have a dream that seems so real that he can wake up screaming and sweating, but when full consciousness comes, he realizes that none of it was real—that it was all a dream."

Q: "I still don't get how everything that I see is false and how it's not all about just witnessing."

F: "You teach science, right?"

Q: "Yes."

F: "Consider this parallel: in the earliest micro-second during the formation of this universe, the 'original awareness' happened when a hydrogen atom became aware of the presence of a helium atom. The two interacted and, voila...we have this [waving arms in a full circle to indicate 'the universe']. There was no seeing or witnessing during that original happening in awareness. Nothing happened phenomenally. There was no five-sense perception. It happened nomenally.

Awareness happened without any element of 'seeing' or 'hearing,' etc. What you think you see has nothing to do with what is known via awareness."

Q: [Finally nods in understanding]

F: "For the rest of you, forget the science and know the truth, which is within you already. The witness is not the end of the journey. 'I am the witness' is not the Truth. The I Am is witnessed since the only 'identity' of the manifestation is a sense of presence, consciousness knowing consciousness; therefore, the advanced stage of witnessing is mainly involved with becoming aware of consciousness and its movements. The 'Eureka' sensation that happens when the understanding of the functioning of the Totality becomes known will be the ultimate liberation from all the misunderstanding that has plagued your phenomenal existence."

Q: "So again, what's next?" [F. stares at him, noting Q's impatience. The group laughs.]

F: "To witness the body-mind-personality triad as illusion is to allow that which is witnessed to dissolve. Persons take 'observing' to involve observing 'self' or 'others.' When the eagle reviews the Medicine Place—the scene of the vision— and realizes that the body was an illusion, that the mental state was an illusion, and that the spiritual and religious identities were illusions, then the eagle knows there is no 'one'—there is nothing real—to observe in that realm. The eagle is not witnessing others. It is coming to know, for what they are, all those move- ments in consciousness—all those illusions—that preceded this eagle/witnessing 'state.' That's why I said that the advanced stage of witnessing is about becoming aware of consciousness and its movements. Eventually, the witness, once freed of any mistaken belief in a subject-object duality, will also dissolve. Closing the door on all the illusions opens the door for True Self awareness. [Pause] So what's next, you ask? The witness will eventually give way to the True Self. The witness sees the false without judgment—without reacting—but nothing Real is seen until the True Self knows ItSelf and sees the Oneness. That True Self, which we can point to as the 'Universal Witness,' will eventually dissolve too...into the non-witnessing state of the Absolute. How, knowing we haven't reached the Absolute, can you have had an earlier notion that the journey is complete at the witness level?"

Q. 2: [To Q.] "There are seven degrees, you know!" [Laughter]

Q: "You're pushing your luck!" [Laughs]

F: "You're both pushing your luck. [Laughter] The shift via witnessing occurs when the personalities—when all the ego-states—dissolve. As long as a person is trapped in playing the roles of false personas, that person's ego will demand that the person stay focused on the false self and will demand that all 'others' stay focused on that false self. No witnessing of the false can happen in that 'sleep state,' so persons walk about in their sleep, dreaming dreams while believing they're awake and that their dreams are real. The movements that are typical of a sleeper in the delta or theta states of consciousness are mistaken by persons in the beta state of consciousness to be the real. A person is always the focal point in his dreams, rendering him self-absorbed, selfish, and self-centered...and all of those are about the false self. When the last ego-state fades, witnessing begins in earnest. The focus is not on the false 'me' but is on all that remains that must be seen as illusion. When all of the false is seen and fully accepted as being false, then the Truth—and the True Self—can be known." Please enter the silence of contemplation.

THE FIFTH DEGREE
OF MOVEMENT TOWARD REALITY:
Witnessing, Part Four

Q: "So what's the difference in the True Self and the witness?"

F: "If the eagle/witness sees itself as separate from what is 'seen,' then it can't know the Oneness. The eagle imagines that it is alone, not all-one. It's the True Self as the Universal Witness that knows the known and the knower, and even the knowing, as One. The witness witnesses the illusions...the nothingness that in the past had garnered so much hoopla and triggered all that 'much ado about nothing.' While the witness comes to know the nothingness, the True Self can come to know the 'everything'...the Oneness of it all...the Truth. The actual unicity beyond the imagined multiplicity is understood. On my journey, once the True Self became known, the phrase 'I am nothing and I am everything' became understood. After understanding the functioning of the Totality, I understood Krishna when he said that he was even beyond the beingness and the non-beingness. You must complete the entire journey to be able to know all. At this point, you can know the false, but you cannot yet know the Truth. Let the witness come to know all that is false and believed to be separate; let the Universal Witness come to know all that is true and known for a fact to be One.

In 'universe,' the prefix makes clear what the Universal Witness 'sees': it sees the unicity."

Q: "I was taught that the witness is the vehicle for seeing it all."

F: "First, 'all' is not to be seen. All is to be known. You're not listening. You're confusing the witness and the Universal Witness, the witness and the Real Self. The True Self knows ItSelf and from that point can know the beingness, the non-beingness, the Absolute and the unicity. The eagle/witness is only a point of awareness that allows for the further movement along the path to finally knowing the Absolute as What You Are. We'll see that from this vantage point, the light of the Absolute begins to reach the witness and enables this point of awareness to happen. We are 'close,' but only the Real Self can see the Real. Only the True Self—the 'Truth' Self—can know the Truth."

Q: "Another teacher spoke of elimination, purification, renunciation, and liberation. It seems a lot is being missed here."

F: "Evidently, you missed it all there; otherwise, why would else you be here? One who has reached the final destination does not continue traveling. But I, too, have covered all those elements of the Teaching."

Q: "I don't recall any mention of any of those."

F: "What do you think the first three levels were about if not about elimination? What do you think the fourth level was about if not about purification and renunciation? What do you think the fifth level is about if not liberation? Shedding the remnants of any remaining personas or concepts is purifying and liberating. Only pure consciousness can know the True Self, can know ItSelf. All on this journey has been in preparation for that knowing, but that's not the end. 'Full Realization' is realizing fully the Absolute, realizing You Are That, and realizing the functioning of the Totality."

Q: "So we're very close to seeing the Absolute?"

F.: "Not at all. You'll not see it; you'll know You Are it. Then Mr. Give-Me-a-Benefit and Mr. I-Want-Application can know the deep sleep peace while being fully awake in the relative." [Laughter] Please enter the silence of contemplation.

THE FIFTH DEGREE
OF MOVEMENT TOWARD REALITY:
Witnessing, Part Five

Q: "This is the point where I've always become totally confused. The Self is the Absolute, right?"

F. "Right."

Q: "But you've talked about the false self. Then I hear talk of a self that seems to be embodied and a Self that's Real and a Self that's 'Beyond....'

F. "Granted the various uses of the term can generate confusion, especially in English translation and with Western audiences. Ramana Maharshi spoke of 'levels of reality' in his teachings, but of course there is only one Reality. I'll take a few moments to discuss 'levels of Self' with you, but of course there are not two...there is only One. The term can refer to the Absolute when discussing What One Is, really. For the sake of discussion with the yet-to-be-enlightened I sometimes refer to a True Self and a Supreme Self. The jnanis speak of 'the person' (vyakti), 'the Self' (vyakta), and 'the Supreme Self' (avyakta) and Maharaj spoke of a real self as swarupa. Let's go over those for a moment, but I want to lay out a working definition that we'll use for purposes of discussing the sixth level of our seven-step journey. The person, the 'outer self' is illusory. You've heard me refer-ring to that person as the 'false self,' an 'ego-state,' a 'persona,' the 'personality,' the 'assuming-you-are-this-role-or-that-role,' a 'state-of-being this' or a 'state of being that,' etc. For the sake of these discussions, we'll assume that the 'True Self' is manifested and we'll add the word 'true' to distinguish it from 'the false self.' When Maharaj spoke of the real self as swarupa, he was pointing more toward one's own real nature. In contrast, the false self believes the lie that it is the real and is always 'concerned' since the false self is a mistaken identification with the body and the mind and the varied personalities and all of 'their' problems and concerns and desires and fears. The True Self knows better. Shakespeare said, This above all: To thine own SELF be TRUE and it must follow, as the night the day, thy canst not then be false to any man. That's the sixth level Self we'll be discussing: the Self that knows the Truth and can no longer be false. The vyakta/Self is the evolved, manifested 'matter' as opposed to 'the person'—which is not evolved—and as opposed to the unmanifested Supreme Self. You have evolved beyond body identification, mind identification, and religious-role or spiritual-role identities. You have evolved through the 'state' of Child Ignorance. You have evolved to the point that you've witnessed the false beliefs and false ideas that unaware, unevolved persons believe. Therefore, at the sixth level, consider yourself to be the Supreme Self appearing as the Witnessing Self (which I will call 'the True Self'…the Self that witnesses and knows Truth). Now, you are not looking for the false that needs to be discarded. That's done. You have evolved to the point where you can now know the Truth. That Self with the ability to know Truth serves as an 'intermediary' of sorts and allows for the understanding that 'I am not a person and I know unequivocally that anything associated with a person is false.' So, for purposes of our discussion, I'm calling the vyakta/Self the 'True Self' only because it is the manifested Self that has evolved and can know that which is 'True.' 'Self' and 'Real Self' and 'True Self' can as easily refer to the Supreme Self or the Absolute since there's no duality. I'm only making a temporary distinction for the sake of moving you through the next step along a path, as Ramana Maharshi did when he discussed 'levels.' At the end of the journey, you'll transcend the Self anyway, so what does any of it matter? If a mule dies the moment it delivers you to your destination, bury the mule. Do not drag a mule about for the remainder of your relative existence. In the end, you'll finally realize that there is no journey since there is no one to make a journey, and you'll know that there's nothing to gain since there's no one to benefit. More importantly, use the words I offer to assist in finding the answers within to the questions 'Who Am I?' and 'How does the Totality function?' Then, You'll know what That is and You'll understand the cyclings by way of understanding the functioning of the Totality. All the rest is just semantics, in the final analysis…just thorns removing thorns. What's to be known is already known. You only need to realize what you know that you don't yet know that you know. For simplification, I'll speak of the 'True Self' in the next stage, but understand that, just as I can say both 'I Am' and 'I Am That' without contradiction, so I can say both 'Self' and 'Supreme Self' without contradiction. The atman and swarupa and parabrahman and paramatman will be totally understood when the truth of not two is totally understood. In due course, none of it will matter since the bottom line is…to know the Self is to be the Self and to know the Absolute is to be the Absolute." Please enter the silence of contemplation.

[PLEASE NOTE: With advanced seekers, two witnessing stages are discussed. There is Subject-Object Witnessing and there is Pure Witnessing which aligns with the witnessing that happens via the True Self. For more on the two levels, visit the Advaita website mentioned at the end of this volume and search for those two types of witnessing by name.]

STEP SIX

THE SIXTH DEGREE OF MOVEMENT TOWARD REALITY: THE TRUE SELF

THE SIXTH DEGREE OF MOVEMENT TOWARD REALITY: THE TRUE SELF, PART ONE

F: "Ramana Maharshi spoke of finding the Self in the "cave of the heart." Let's return to the vision. During the last installment, we left off with this: You the Eagle have no time to contemplate, for you feel yourself being pulled deeper into the universe through a clear-walled tunnel in the remotest part of the heavens. As I read today's part of the vision, feel yourself—as the eagle—transcending the material realm via the tunnel. Then feel yourself exiting the tunnel and entering into a cave. As the Witnessing Self, discover the unicity. Close your eyes now as I read the next portion of the vision." [Readers: Please read the vision, then close your eyes and move through the vision again.]

You feel yourself accelerating at the speed of light. In fact, at the end of the tunnel, you can see nothing other than light. Your speed now nearly doubles, and just as you reach that point of mach two, with the deafening sounds of the winds racing by your ears, you crash through a veil of sorts and find yourself in a mostly dark, crystal cave. You stop abruptly and then are swooped into an upright position, floating near the ceiling of the cave. You feel at this moment as if you are exactly between nowhere and . . . nowhere. Never have you known such peace. Sensing yourself in only the vestige of a human-like form, you drift toward a lake below that covers most of the bottom of this huge cavern. You experience a fifth degree of separation—as if estranged from all illusionary roles, as if removed from a phony world left behind, as if moving closer to a degree of connection with the Real.

Your slow descent allows time to study the cave. Across the way a dome glows brightly, the source of the vivid light you'd seen through the arch and more recently at the end of the tunnel. A huge pipe organ sounds from the highest peak of a cliff on the far left side of the gigantic grotto. To your left and to your right drift millions of forms, and on closer inspection, You see that they are . . . You! Each looks to be a clone—maybe a transparent clone but a clone neverthe-less—of You!

F: "Consider this: is it possible that the tunnel could represent the gap between awareness of the not-real and the awareness of your True Nature, your Real Nature, that you can come to know via the manifested Self? What the eagle witnessed in that material realm cannot be the Real and cannot be Your Self. Is it possible that the tunnel represents that which allows the movement, or the shift, from awareness reflected in consciousness to Pure Awareness? Is it possible that the True Self can turn its back to 'the world' and actually practice non-witnessing and just be? Is it possible that the True Self has evolved to the point that It can perceive the Reality of the Essence? Is it possible that the darkness of the illusions in that material realm, if left behind, will facilitate the knowing of Reality...the knowing of The Light? Is it possible that impure consciousness is transcended by degrees of purification and these steps we're taking are the purifiers? Is it possible that consciousness is being de-toxed and thereby eliminating the darkness via this movement to the light of awareness?" Please enter the silence of consideration.

THE SIXTH DEGREE
OF MOVEMENT TOWARD REALITY:
THE TRUE SELF, PART TWO

Q: "I still don't have a clear understanding of the way you're using the term 'True Self' since this level seems to be prior to the Absolute."

F: "The label merely points to that which is not 'the false self.' Substitute the more traditional terms if you like and use 'Impersonal Consciousness,' 'Beingness,' the I Amness, whatever. I use the term to distinguish this level of impersonal Consciousness from personal consciousness, that's all: 'True Self' as opposed to 'false self.' More important is the teaching in the vision: in today's portion see that 'the True Self' is not a 'do-er.' From this 'state,' all merely happens. The false self is the personal self. The True Self is not personal—it's without personas. As long as your food body continues to function with this manifested consciousness, the options are either to live in the misery of the desires and fears and delusions that are always generated by personal consciousness or to exist in this state of impersonal Consciousness. You've come to know that You Are certainly beyond the false self; ultimately, you'll come to know that You Are beyond this impersonal Consciousness—this True Self—as well."

Q: "So I can take the True Self to be Impersonal Consciousness. It's just pointing to the beingness?"

F: "Precisely. Now, set aside your focus on the terms and note via the vision what it's like to just be. All of these steps have been invitations to abandon everything you've ever been told and everything you've every read and everything you've ever thought and then just be. At this level, to 'just be' means that you simply remain fixed in the I Amness. Abiding in this impersonal Consciousness, you'll find within the understanding of what yet remains to be understood. [Pause] Remember that due to faulty programming and wrong conditioning, you came to believe that you're personal consciousness, adopting false identities that you assumed to be definitions of who you are. You took your personality—or personalities—to be real and to define who you are. All of that was all a misunderstanding...a belief in lies. This distinction is not difficult...I'm distinguishing between personal consciousness and impersonal Consciousness. You should understand that at this level You Are that universal Consciousness. Here, You reside in the Truth of I Am and not in the false beliefs of 'I am this role' or 'I am that role.' From this platform, you'll be able to see that You Are even beyond the impersonal Consciousness and that You're the Absolute. Then You'll know that You were never born and that You will never die. You're closer to realizing that What You Are is not even this I Amness and you'll be closer to understanding what Krishna meant when he said, 'Those alone who understand that I, the Absolute, am beyond the states of being and non-being realize my true nature, and all others are fools.' This level is 'the state of being,' but hear his words. Do not be fooled into believing that even this is What You Are. Even this impersonal Consciousness is temporary. It will leave the space one day. That which is temporary cannot be the Real. Clearer?"

Q: "Yes. Thank you."

F: "Then let's continue with the vision. As you close your eyes and I read this portion, find the unicity. Find the state of beingness referenced by Krishna. At this level of I Amness, look for the way that all just happens. Imagine a relative existence lived out in that fashion." [Readers: Please read the vision and then close your eyes and sense the content of the vision again.]

As You near the water, You automatically pivot so that Your back faces the opposite shore. Sinking shoulder-deep into the water, You feel Your feet rise. Your entire body stiffens momentarily, Your feet rise further, You float onto Your back and then You bob on the surface of the water. Now relaxed, You begin to be moved along, gently propelled toward the opposite side of the cave. Your movements just happen, no effort on Your part required. The music of the organ—ethereal and heavenly—sounds softly, beautifully; the waters are now calm and warm.

You float with millions of Your likenesses, or so it seems, flowing toward gigantic, granite steps cut amphitheater-like into the opposite wall of the cave. Yet the likenesses aren't likenesses at all. They Really Are You!

F: "Consider what it is like for those who know the True Self in the relative manifestation. Know what it's like to just be. Know the I Amness. What might your relative existence be like if you spent your remaining years of manifestation in the same fashion as the True Self in the vision?" Please enter the silence of contemplation.

THE SIXTH DEGREE OF MOVEMENT TOWARD REALITY:
THE TRUE SELF, PART THREE

F: "Know the cycles. You must know how this body 'came to be' in order to understand All. Expunging from the corrupted mind all of the superstitious and magical and doctrinal attitudes around that natural act of friction and 'birth' is the simple key to understanding All. How did the water, the air, the other elements, and the conscious-energy function in unison to facilitate this manifestation? On the 'way in' to manifestation, this True Self state is the state of unconditioned

Consciousness. On the 'way back out'—on the way to the unmanifested 'state'—the True Self level is the state of 'de-conditioned' Consciousness. It is one, the same. In the cave, You Are in position to know the manifested self, the True Self, and the Unmanifested Self; to know the temporary self, the unconditioned Self, and the Infinite Self; to know the I Am now and the I Am That eternally. It is in the cave—having discarded all of the myths, superstitions, half-truths and complete falsehoods of the material realm—that You will find the Truth of not two. Allow the Witnessing Self to witness the cycles. See the truth of 'the coming' and 'the going.' If you see how the ephemeral body came to be, they will never, ever again be able to fool you. You will never be fooled again. Want peace? Stop allowing them to fool you. If You turn, in order to see what You Truly Are, the appearance of desires and fears will dis-appear. Close your eyes and enter the cave." [Readers: Please read this portion of the vision, then close your eyes and move through the cave again.]

The steps ascend from underneath the waters, breaking the surface and then rising and narrowing upwards, converging on one point—at the door to the dome. As You near the steps, You feel Your body stiffen again. This time You rotate in the water so that You sail along face down. Just before Your head might have bumped into the steps, You are stopped. Your feet begin to be lowered, and You find yourself in an upright position, standing on steps in chest-high water. You begin to ascend the steps, leaving the water behind. You, and millions of Yous, walk in exactly the same fashion, moving toward the narrowing peak that leads to the door of the dome. You wonder, How could so many be entering the dome? It really isn't that large, now that I can see it more clearly. It seems that much that You perceived as more is really…less. But the nearer You All move toward the door, the more You witness a siphoning effect of sorts. As All near the door, All seem to dissolve into a form of light being drawn inside. As You approach, You feel the last remnants—remnants of whatever You had formerly thought yourself to be—gradually fading away. The dissolving seems to be occurring in slow motion, and you feel ecstatic. It's almost as if You are feeling blissful as your beingness seems to be dissolving into non-beingness.

F: "Where were you during the days and months before you were 'born?' Krishna said that only a fool does not understand, does not realize, that his true nature is beyond both the beingness and the non-beingness. Do you realize how they fooled you? Do you see how they fooled you with the words they used, with the ideas they gave you, with the beliefs they passed on, with the false words they claimed to be true by virtue of appearing in books said by others to be 'holy'? (holy means 'different from,' so the very word reinforces duality. See why this Teaching is 'beyond any texts.') Do you see totally how you have been fooled? Only ego refuses to admit to having been fooled. When the final ego-state dissolves, the struggle with admission ends. When the struggle with admission ends, all struggling ends. To be independent and free is to be totally independent and free. Degrees do not exist. Partiality would amount to duality. To know that the totality of all that they said and wrote was a total fraud is the only way to come to understand the Truth of the Totality of the functioning of All. Are You finally understanding the cycles? Are You glimpsing that which is beyond the two 'states' of being and non-being?" Please enter into the silence of contemplation.

THE SEVENTH DEGREE OF MOVEMENT TOWARD REALITY: THE NON-BEINGNESS

THE SEVENTH DEGREE OF MOVEMENT TOWARD REALITY: THE NON-BEINGNESS, PART ONE

Q:"You said earlier that the sanity of being in touch with Reality allows life to be lived out in a self-constructive way instead of a self-destructive way, but the talk about the beingness dissolving into the non-beingness as 'blissful' strikes me as being self-destructive. It almost sounds suicidal."

F: "I detect a fear of death. Who is this talking about this concern with the concept of death? Who is seeking continuity?"

Q: "Personas aside, it seems that if I am sane I should want to take the best care possible of what you've called this food body."

F: "If living occurs in a natural fashion, the body will be cared for via natural instincts. If living in the delusions of body-mind-personality, the body will be cared about. Persons are driven by a desire for continuity, and that creates attachment and fear and misery and preoccupation. Natural instincts protect while operating without attachment or fear or misery or preoccupation."

Q: "Explain 'for' and 'about'."

F: "Recall the deer that lives naturally. If you startle the deer, it will instinctively run from what it takes to be a source of danger. But after it has moved away from that supposed danger, it will not attach to that experience and thus it will not live the rest of its life—because of one incident—in fear or misery or preoccupation. [To another participant] How long did it take your wife to say that she was leaving? Give me an answer in seconds."

Q3: "Uhhhh … maybe two seconds."

F: "And how many seconds did it take her to leave?"

Q3: "About ten seconds to get to the car and drive off."

F: "But how many times did you 'relive' those twelve seconds in your mind?"

Q3: [Silence. Thinking. Shocked, then a look of sadness.]

F: "Exactly." [Pause]

Q3: [Pause. Seeing how long that happened.]

F: [Finally …] "Only the 'present moment' has the potential to be 'real' in the manifestation. The past is an image and the future is nothing more than what a person is imagining as well. But you've taken an image from the past and made it your 'present moment' for thousands and thousands of times. That action has been 'relived' over and over and over in twelve-second increments—in innumerable sets of seconds, expanding into minutes and days and weeks and months and years. The persona lived in the mental and emotional prison of that twelve-second image for years. [Pause] The persona lived in an attachment to the events of a twelve-second period imagined by that persona to be real, and the attachment to that image resulted in fear and misery and preoccupation. The personality was living in a 'false beingness' instead of in awareness of the being-ness, the non-beingness and beyond."

Q3: "Meaning?"

F: "Meaning that the person was living in a state-of-being husband and then for an even longer period in a state of not-being husband. You've now been shown how to live in a state of pure beingness while knowing the non-beingness and thus being free of attachment and the subsequent fear and misery and preoc-cupations of false roles. If you don't live in the beingness while knowing the non-beingness and beyond, then you cannot live in the present moment. You'll never know the power of now, and you'll live instead in the misery of a moment 'past' or in an imagined 'future' that the conditioned mind of a person will take to be the real in each and every current moment."

Q3: "Unbelievable."

F: "Yes. Now apply that adjective to all you've been told before, read before, thought before, or thought you saw before…and then you'll be free."

Q. 4:..................... "But your comment still sounds like an endorsement of self-destruction."

F: "Correct."

Q4: [Shrugs as if to ask, "What?"]

F: "I'm offering the point that self-destruction…little 's,' is to occur. You've left the cave and gone back to the material realm for a moment. So it is, but come back to the cave. The entire journey to this level has been about destruction of the 'self,' of the illusion of 'self'. [To Q.] You speak of 'death.' If I had ever been born, I'd tell you that I died years ago and that it was Absolutely delightful. Ha." [Laughter]

Q. 4:[Pause] "Okay … I got it."

F: "Welcome back. So, let's continue. In the vision we're crossing the borderline between beingness and non-beingness, leaving the last of the seven levels that separated us from knowing the Absolute. Even my teacher said that making clear the understanding of that borderline is difficult. The way I offer the understanding is to say that we are entering the 'territory' of no self—with a small 's.' This is the territory of selflessness—with a small 's.' Later, it will be understood that even beyond this is a territory of Selflessness, with a capital 'S'."

Q: "That can't be."

F: "Ha. It can't? Let's continue with today's segment of the vision, and if questions remain after a period of silent consideration, then we'll talk. Close your eyes, please, and enter the cave." [Readers: Please read this segment of the vision, then close your eyes and move through the vision again.]

Finally, You merge with the All, into the light, and it seems . . . it seems over. It seems as if everything is over, is finished, is very near complete. Then some degree of consciousness seems to linger after this additional degree of separation fades. Even without a physical body or an earthly mind or a spiritual body, a subtle body detects a series of chambers leading to other universes. All then fades into light. It is sensed that nothing represented in the vision is the Real. It is understood that only by peeling back all the layers of false identities—including the body, the mind, the spiritual identity, the child ignorance, the witness, even the True Self—could That Which One Really Is be known. It is understood that what You Really Are Is That, That which is often removed from awareness through many degrees of separation. In the fading moments, as beingness transitions into non-beingness, You come to know that You Are That common building block of All in this universe, in All universes.

F: "Please enter the silence of consideration."

THE SEVENTH DEGREE
OF MOVEMENT TOWARD REALITY:
The Non-Beingness, Part Two

Q: "That last part of the vision was amazing! I finally get it … I'm blown away!"

F: "Yes, we can watch the images and personas and roles being blown away, then we can see it All. [Pause] I said that the understanding of the functioning of the Totality can end attachments that result in fear and misery and preoccupation. If the cycles, the unicity, and the way the food body came to be are understood, how could an egotistical posture be assumed? How could it be believed that 'I am a great and successful executive' or 'I am so much better than you and deserve so much more' or 'I am the greatest of all' or 'This body is the key to my success'? [Pause. Looks of understanding from participants.] This space called 'floyd' is a phase in one cycle among the endless cyclings … cyclings unknown to most who believe in a birth-life-death-judgment and punishment or reward timeline. The body-mind-personality desires physical continuity, but in Truth, the only continuity is in the cyclings. The only constancy is in the interaction between matter and conscious-energy, in the manifestings or unmanifestings or restings that are repeated in infinite cycles. If a person looks at this food body and believes that he is seeing something other than elements, conscious-energy, and mainly space, then he's not in touch with Reality. The space is fleeting, just a temporary combination of elements and consciousness, and thus cannot be That Which Is Real. [Pause] Look at that picture by Martin Heade hanging there on the wall. [Points to Martin Johnson Heade's 'Cattleya Orchid and Three Brazilian Hummingbirds 1871.' All eyes turn.] I have that painting there for a reason, and I refer participants to its message at this point in the journey. Study it and then explain how it depicts the cyclings by telling me where the cycle in the painting 'begins' and 'ends'." [Waits]

Q: "I see eggs in the nest. The cycle starts there."

F: "You've evidently heard nothing."

Q: [Frowns, offended.]

Q2: "I see where it starts."

F: "Thanks, but give her a moment to reconsider."

Q: [Pause, studies painting] "Ah, I got it. It begins near the upper right corner…with the light, the sun."

F: "Bingo. [To Q.2] That's what you were going to say?"

Q2: "Yes."

F: "So we have that energy source of hydrogen, emitting its energy in wave form and particle form. Then?"

Q2: "Then, the elements and the manifestation of plants."

F: "Next?" [Pointing to another participant]

Q3: "Plants evolving, consciousness manifesting…the life forms in the painting."

F: "Go ahead…the next part of the cycle is…?"

Q3: "Birds … and the eggs that came about as a result of friction between two of the birds."

F: "Voila! And after the hummingbirds in the painting, which are merely conscious-energy manifested, what's next in the cycle being shown?"

Q3: "The oversized orchid in the foreground. I take it to represent an additional evolutionary stage of plants, more evolved than the ones in the background. Maybe it even represents us when we evolve into the fullness of awareness."

F: [To the group] "Agree?"

Q2: "I love this! I see why you have it here now. I've glanced at that painting and actually thought it was a bit feminine to be hanging in a single guy's house. [Laughter] Sorry."

F: "Quite alright ... but now I must ask you to leave." [Laughter] What's next? How about you?"

Q5: "Continuing in the clockwise direction, I'd say we go to the upper left corner and see the dead limbs. 'Death' follows after the flower has been around long enough to reach a fullness. But I take the flower to have more than one meaning."

F: "Okay. Continue."

Q5: "It struck me that the orchid could represent the ego or persona state. Look how it dominates the picture. It's larger than anything else in the cycling. It's like it represents the personality that thinks it should be the center of attention. Narcissism, if you will. [F. smiles] It's like it's the most beautiful thing, physically, and so it's more 'full of itself' than anything else in the picture. It's like the flower could be the 'I am this great and beautiful body.' On the other hand, I see how it could also just be the I Amness. It's almost like the lovely, physical form can take itself as the real, but then as the cycle advances, the real that's beneath the outer appearance is known. The flower is doing nothing but living the 'beautiful life,' so to speak."

F: "I think we need to change seats! The student has become the teacher!" Please enter the silence of contemplation.

THE SEVENTH DEGREE OF MOVEMENT TOWARD REALITY:
The Non-Beingness, Part Three

F: [Laughter] "Continue, please."

Q5: "If it really represents the I Amness, its like the flower is just being and just taking in what it needs—taking in the light—and enjoying the fullness and this height of completion. It doesn't have to think or do anything. It's all just happening. [Long pause, considering] That's why I came here. That's what I was looking for. [Another pause, then very quietly...] And I've found that, and more." [Pauses again. Finally, all look at F.]

F: "Okay, that does it. Come take this chair!" [Huge laughter]

Q5: "Remember how you talked about 'perfection' not having anything to do with being 'flawless' but having to do with being 'matured'? That flower looks fully matured ... 'complete' or 'perfect' or 'whole,' I think you said."

F: "Teleios."

Q5: "Yes. It's in the material realm but it's like I can sense that it has something else that transcends it's physical beauty. There's more to it than the eye can see. [Pause] I'm seeing that we can be like that, at this stage."

F: "Temporarily, yes. But then you rightly noted that the next level of the cycle, after this 'beautiful life' is...[points at top of painting] 'death,' the end of that manifested space. [Most nod in understanding]. Can you see that the 'flourishing' orchid and the 'dead' limbs are actually the same, the only variable being consciousness manifested versus consciousness unmanifested? [Longer pause as all study the picture.] Okay. Let's move on. Next, the clockwise direction takes the eye to...?"

Q: "To another group of dead limbs in the upper right, but then...back to the light."

F: "Exactly. [All are staring at the picture. A pause continues for a minute or more. No one says anything. Finally...] What I've described during these sessions, in words and in a vision, Martin Heade has depicted visually in a painting. But what he presented in the painting, he didn't see in this material realm. No flower is that large in proportion to its surrounding elements, setting aside artistic perspective and being totally literal for a moment. He never went to that spot in the Brazilian jungle. The birds did not pose for him. So where did he find the subject matter when he painted this scene?" [Pauses as participants reflect]

Q: "Within?"

F: "Is that a question or a statement that you now know to be fact?"

Q: "It's a fact."

F: "Yes. And that knowledge of infinite cycling has always been within each of you, but the programming that you were exposed to in your western culture taught you that a single cycle ends with a body-mind-personality experiencing physical continuity. Their programming was able to fool you—there's that word again—because their explanation had a remotely familiar element that resonated with what you knew instinctively. And that led you to say, 'But Floyd I just know, deep inside, that there's got to be a "this" or a "that" after I die.' They fooled you first, then you spent the rest of your life using their ideas and beliefs to fool yourself. During the worse days of your relative existence, which became so miserable that you were forced into the submission of finally questioning everything, you were at least conscious enough of that inner truth to say, 'I don't even know who I am.' [Pause] What makes your case different from that of persons who yet walk about in their sleep is that you asked the follow-up question: 'If this is not who I am, then who am I?' The asking of that question allowed you to begin a journey that enabled you to reach this level of understanding. [Pause] Now, as a means of review, let me ask you to consider this: is that orchid conscious-energy manifested?" Please enter into the silence of contemplation.

THE SEVENTH DEGREE OF MOVEMENT TOWARD REALITY:
The Non-Beingness, Part Four

Group: "Yes."

Q6: "Explain, please."

Q5: [As F. pauses] "May I say something that could help clarify?"

F: "Go ahead."

Q5: "I read that some scientists had injected into plants the same chemical that makes fireflies light up at night. They wanted to be able to film plants at night and see what was happening without using camera lights that would 'throw off' the plants' night-day rhythms. What they found was that plants actually 'sleep,' so to speak. The vital fluids and energy 'rest.' Then, as morning approached, the scientists were able to film in the remaining darkness the chemicals as they began to circulate, and they saw that the plants raised up—like raising up their heads after sleeping. Then, it was like they were using some kind of radar to adjust the alignment of their leaves. The scientists had to measure the plant's movement into a new position in fine increments, but they observed that every day, the plants re-aligned themselves in order to be aimed directly at the position where the sun would be rising. As the sun rose in a slightly different position each day, the plants had already made the adjustment in advance, knowing that they would not capture the maximum sunlight at yesterday's angle of the sun but needed to make a micro-adjustment each day in order to maximize the levels of energy that they were going to absorb."

Q. 2: "Wow."

F: "Exactly. So the point is made regarding the plants: conscious-energy is functioning. Now, when that flower 'dies' and 'rots,' is that the end of the elements?"

Group: "No."

F: "Consider the birds, trees, plants, eggs, nest, Spanish moss, etc. Are the same elements at play in all?"

Group: "Yes."

F: "So do you see that any supposed 'difference' in the things depicted in the painting is just an error in perception?"

Group: [Several pause. A few answer.] "Yes."

F: "Back to the orchid. When the oxygen circulating through that plant is released at the time the plant 'dies,' does that oxygen end?"

Group: "No."

F: When the energy vibrating throughout that plant is released at the time that the plant 'dies,' does the energy end?"

Group:"No."

F: "So the elements rejoin the elements...dust to dust. The 'breath' of the plant, the air, joins the universal air. The energy, which can neither be created nor destroyed, joins the field of universal energy-consciousness. Now, consider this: is there even the slightest possibility that the exact same elements and the exact same conscious energy could manifest again at some future point to make that same plant again?"

Group: [Laughter] "No."

F: "You laugh, but a few weeks ago, some of you were willing to fight to the end to defend your belief in that lie. Ha. [Mild laughter] If another life form, like a cow or a human, eats that plant, is the life-force / conscious-energy of the plant 'lost'?"

Group: "No."

F: "Might a portion of that conscious-energy be 'recycled' and manifest in some other space?"

Group: "Yes."

F: "So when you understand the infinite cyclings, do you understand why there is no 'birth' and no 'death'?"

Group: "Yes."

F: "Do you understand that there is no 'creation' or 'destruction'?"

Group: "Yes."

F: "Applying all of the current understandings to the human space, do you now see how unwarranted all body fears are and how inane all desires for body continuity really are?"

Group: "Yes."

F: [Silence] "Let's pause for a few minutes as you focus on nothing but that painting and its message regarding the cyclings." Please enter the silence of contemplation.

THE SEVENTH DEGREE
OF MOVEMENT TOWARD REALITY:
THE NON-BEINGNESS, PART FIVE

F: "So, we've reached the point in the process where it's time to begin our review. It's time to put all this together and get the 'big picture' in order to understand the functioning of the Totality. To Realize fully, you must understand the functioning of all that is taken to be the 'comings' and 'goings' … these manifestings and unmanifestings of conscious-energy and this interplay with the elements. We covered thoroughly the false. Let's return to the part of the vision where Truth is introduced. [Picks up paper and reads] ' … you crash through a veil of sorts and find yourself in a mostly dark, crystal cave.' The point?"

Q: "What struck me when you first read that was, it's in this 'spiritual realm'—or whatever we might call it—it's there that we can truly find ourselves. That didn't happen earlier in the vision, even while the eagle was witnessing everything in the material realm and seeing that it was all illusion."

F: "Excellent. Let's continue: 'You stop abruptly and then are swooped into an upright position, floating near the ceiling of the cave'."

Q2: "I noticed something in that passage when you read it the first time."

F: "Go ahead."

Q2: "You're 'swooped into position.' It didn't say, 'You swoop yourself up' or 'You place yourself in an upright position.' It's like the 'You' has no control over any of this, and isn't trying to take control anymore. Like she said, [pointing at Q.] it's more about understanding that it's all just happening."

F: "Yes. [Returns to paper] 'You feel at this moment as if you are exactly between nowhere and . . . nowhere. Never have you known such peace. Sensing yourself in only the vestige of a human-like form, you drift toward a lake below that covers most of the bottom of this huge cavern. [Moving further down the paper] To your left and to your right drift millions of forms, and on closer inspection, You see that they are ... You! Each looks to be a clone—maybe a transparent clone but a clone nevertheless—of You! As You near the water, You automatically pivot so that Your back faces the opposite shore. Sinking shoulder-deep into the water, You feel Your feet rise. Your entire body stiffens momentarily, Your feet rise further, You float onto Your back and then You bob on the surface of the water.' The peace of just going with the flow, so to speak, is shown. Let's see where we are at this point in the vision in terms of the cycles. This is the 'going,' the unmanifesting. Did you understand how this stage is the same in the 'coming'?"Q.: "As the conscious-energy manifests and begins its interplay with the elements, that stage takes place in the water of the womb. Then the child—the 'new' space—passes through a 'tunnel' and enters the 'material realm'."

F: "Exactly. This stage is the same, whether 'coming' or 'going.' Every stage is the same, whether 'coming' or 'going.' Living in this relative existence in the I Amness with the Full Understanding is as peaceful as that period in the womb. But at some point, even that existence becomes uncomfortable. The 'more perfect' rest was even prior to that. Let's continue: 'Now relaxed, You begin to be moved along, gently propelled toward the opposite side of the cave. Your movements just happen, no effort on Your part required. The music of the organ—ethereal and heavenly—sounds softly, beautifully; the waters are now calm and warm.' What's your take on that, anyone?"

Q2: "When you were reading that part originally, I felt that I was actually in the water, floating on my back, and I finally understood how I could allow things to just happen."

F: "Who's allowing?"

Q2: "Right. It just happened. Anyway, when you talked about a shift that occurred with you when you stopped teaching and just watched teaching happen, I didn't get it. When I heard that part of the vision, I got it."

F: "More accurately, 'I just watched teaching happen...or not.' What happens, happens. What a person thinks should happen...often won't. What a person tries to make happen...often doesn't. What does not happen does not happen, so more than 'allowing' or 'letting something happen,' you merely witness whatever happens...or not. Early on, you might consider 'accepting' to be a helpful tool, but the peace of the I Amness is not even about accepting. Who would be doing that 'accepting'? Some Religious or Spiritual Giant, maybe? Accepting still requires persons who think they are doing something and think they are choosing to do that something. The beingness and non-beingness are about merely being or not being. Let's finish this part. [Reading again] 'You float with millions of Your likenesses, or so it seems, flowing toward gigantic, granite steps cut amphitheater-like into the opposite wall of the cave. Yet the likenesses aren't likenesses at all. They Really Are You!"

Q3: "When you were reading that the first time, I was sitting with my eyes closed and at some point felt that I was actually in the cave, and when I saw myself looking around and seeing that everyone was 'me,' it was astounding, almost like I knew for the first time in my life what love truly is. That idea of 'unicity' became clear."

F: "Ego is believing that there's a vast multiplicity arranged in a hierarchy and that you're the pinnacle; humility is knowing that you're nothing, no-thing; love is knowing that You, with a capital 'Y,' Are everything." Please enter into the silence of contemplation.

THE SEVENTH DEGREE OF MOVEMENT TOWARD REALITY:
The Non-Beingness, Part Six

F: "More exactly, whatever It Is That You Are, That Is also What All Is, so in that sense You Are That Which Everything Is. But even that's an 'identity' that must dissolve. Resting in that understanding, where's the opportunity for any 'hierarchy'? Where's the chance for 'different' or 'separate' or 'dual' or 'multiple' or 'better than'? Having made that point, I'll remind you that 'ego,' 'humility,' 'love' and even 'the unicity' you mentioned are also concepts. Contemplate the I Am and the I Am That until you eventually have no need to contemplate anything."

Q: "I thought knowing the absolute 'oneness' was the ultimate goal."

F: "You knew that at the 'True Self' stage. It's just another phase in the movement to understanding the functioning of the Totality. It's not a Final Truth. Science has identified the circumstances in which matter and energy can be the same. A door looks like 'matter.' Know that which is below the outer appearance of the door and see the functioning of the energy. Since all exists in a unified field of consciousness, even to say 'That is oneness' is to imply that 'All else is not-oneness.' It's like saying, 'This is what's real and that is illusion.' While that might be a handy tool for the Teaching, no words can say Truth, so even to try to label the Reality is useless. Lao Tzu wrote: 'The Tao that can be stated is not the Eternal Tao'. I can only point toward the Absolute Reality."

Q: "Which leads me to something you said earlier, even before we got to the painting."

F: "Go ahead."

Q: "You mentioned 'Selflessness.' From my understanding of the Teachings, if we cross this 'borderline' between being and non-being that you're talking about, we should know we are the Infinite Self, the Supreme Self, right?"

F: "Correct."

Q: "But it sounds like you're saying that when we finally know the Absolute, we know there is no self or Self."

F: "Correct."

Q: [Questioning look]

F: "Any words I speak can be both true and false, depending on where you are in the journey, so you must toss the words and Know. You must Realize. Then, after Realization, you should even toss that concept. In the relative existence, the misery caused by not knowing what you already know can end. The elimination comes by knowing it all and then watching it all dissolve. It's all concepts, all to be tossed aside like thorns that were used to remove thorns."

Q: "I thought I had the understanding yesterday, but I'm hearing contradictions today."

F: "See if this helps clear up the seeming contradictions: suppose we're on a journey together, traveling in a car. I have the map and you're steering the car. I might tell you at one point that the truth is that you must turn to the right at the next intersection if we are to reach our destination. And you ask, 'Are you absolutely sure that's the truth?' And I answer 'Yes'."

Q: "Okay."

F: "So you turn right. Then, later, I tell you that the truth is that, to reach the destination, you must turn left. You ask again, 'Are you absolutely sure that's the truth?' And I answer 'Yes.' Then you question me and ask, 'But wait a minute. You told me before that I absolutely had to turn right to get to the destination.

And I say, 'Correct.' And you say, 'But now you are telling me that I must turn left?' And I say, 'Correct.' At the time that I told you what I told you, it was correct for you. At this time, I can tell you something else and it will also be correct for you. I've had students read Maharaj's early words and become totally confused. They want to point out every passage that seemingly contradicts something he said in an earlier passage."

Q: "That's exactly what happened to me when I read that book!"

F: "Maharaj, being Fully Realized, could listen to a visitor for a minute or so and know if he was 'wet charcoal,' 'dry charcoal,' or 'gunpowder.' He would never offer to a beginner—the wet charcoal—a pointer meant for one at the 'gunpowder' stage...ready for a few exact words to allow the Truth to 'explode' into awareness. [Pause] Back to our car ride. As we near the destination, I might tell you that you need to make one more right turn or one more left turn or that you need to steer straight ahead for a while longer. All that I speak is true and not-true. Ultimately, the Truth cannot be spoken, only pointed toward. All prior to where you are right now on the journey was a pile of thorns being used to remove thorns, concepts used to remove concepts. Now, it's time for no concepts. The non-beingness points to the no-Self Reality. Does this make sense to you?"

Q: "Yes ... and no!" [Laughter]

F: "Now you see! That's it! Yes ... and no. Remember, 'The Tao that can be stated is not the Eternal Tao.' My words, my directions to turn here, turn there, go straight ... all those were helpful, but the goal is to arrive at the final destination, the final understanding. Eventually, You'll know that there was no journey and no destination. We made it to the destination on that car ride as a result of everything that happened and because of every turn taken, but those have no significance now. When the thorns are removed, toss the thorns used to remove them as well as the thorns that were embedded. Toss it all."

Q: "None of that helps me to understand the 'no self' and 'no Self' that you're talking about."

F: "Does 'beingness' imply 'selfness'?"

Q: "Yes."

F: "Then wouldn't 'non-beingness' imply 'no selfness'?"

Q: [Pause] "I guess in a way it does."

F: "Not 'in a way.' It does. When persons say there is beingness, they take that to mean that some kind of 'self' is being. 'Self' is defined as 'individuality' or 'personality.' There is no Supreme Individuality or Supreme Personality.

'Not-being' suggests that a self that once was being is no longer being. It's a 'no-longer-being' or a 'non-being self.' But you were told that What You Are is beyond both beingness—selfness—and non-beingness—non-selfness. Peace comes when the last identity of any kind goes. Watch every concept dissolve, then for now, just be."

Q: [Longer pause, then ...] "Whoa!" Please enter the silence of contemplation.

THE SEVENTH DEGREE OF MOVEMENT TOWARD REALITY:
The Non-Beingness, Part Seven

F: "Whoa indeed."

Q: "That's the first time I've ever heard it explained that way."

F: "It's the first time I've ever heard it explained that way, too." [Laughter] Use any words you want. Use the traditional words to talk of an 'Infinite Self' or a 'Supreme Self,' or use modern words to point to what 'That' is, or use scientific terms to define it...it matters not. When I reached this point in 'my own journey,' I knew what I was not and I knew what I was told I Am, but I soon had to ask, "Who wants to be a 'Supreme Self'? Who is making the dual claim that 'I am free of all concepts' alongside 'I Am the Supreme'? Now, if you want to get into being the Supreme Self, rock an' roll, as long as you get out of being the 'self.' I Am That, and you can call That my 'Self' or 'Supreme Self' if you like, but in truth 'That' is beyond a self that is being, beyond a Self that is being, and is even beyond a self or Self that is not being any more. Understand that non-beingness: if you make a pot of clay, it is still clay...it is not 'pot.' In the analogy, the 'pot' is an appearance, but the real is the clay. The pot can be pulverized and all 'potness' disappears. But if you know the clay that remains after the shattering of the pot is still clay, would you claim that it is not clay but that it is the 'not-pot' instead? That would be insane...out of touch with reality. The next thing I know, you'd be telling me that you've traced the history of that quantity of clay and found that it was used once to make a statue, was used before that to make a vase, and was used before that to make a bowl, so now to be accurate you want me to know that the clay is really not only 'not-pot' but is also 'not-statue,' is also 'not-vase,' and is also 'not-bowl.' How out of touch with reality would that be?"

Q: "Now that made sense." [Laughter]

F: [Shakes head, jokingly] "Prior to now, this consciousness may have manifested in a plant, in an animal, and now in this space called 'floyd.' Is that to say that 'floyd' must be defined in terms of all three? The 'not-plant,' the 'not animal' and the soon-to-be 'not-floyd'? Or is the truth that nothing more than a cycling of conscious-energy was at play? Let's return to the vision to see what it can teach about the non-beingness and beyond: You begin to ascend the steps, leaving the water behind. You, and millions of Yous, walk in exactly the same fashion, moving toward the narrowing peak that leads to the door of the dome. As All near the door, All seem to dissolve into a form of light being drawn inside. As You approach, You feel the last remnants—remnants of whatever You had formerly thought yourself to be—gradually fading away. The dissolving seems to be occurring in slow motion, and you feel ecstatic. It's almost as if You are feeling blissful as your beingness seems to be dissolving into non-beingness. So you see the beingness dissolving into the non-beingness. But the vision continues because you were told that You Are beyond even the non-beingness. Finally, You merge with the All, into the light, and it seems . . . it seems over. It seems as if everything is over, is finished, is very near complete. Then some degree of consciousness seems to linger after this additional degree of separation fades. Even without a physical body or an earthly mind or a spiritual body, a subtle body detects a series of chambers leading to other universes. As the manifested consciousness evolves into its Unmanifested 'state,' we see this: All then fades into light. It is sensed that nothing represented in the vision is the Real. It is understood that only by peeling back all the layers of false identities—including the body, the mind, the spiritual identity, the child ignorance, the witness, even the True Self—could That Which One Really Is be known. It is understood that what You Really Are Is That, That which is often removed from awareness through many degrees of separation. In the fading moments, as beingness transitions into non-beingness, You come to know that You Are That common building block of All in this universe, in All universes. Then, before fading...your last consciousness is of the process that had moved That Which You Are from the rest state in the Absolute, past the non-being and into being, and then into whatever that True Self was. You see how you came to witness, how the learned ignorance corrupted the pure consciousness of the child state, how spiritual and religious roles were assigned, how mental identities were accumulated, and how dominated the existence was by the physical body's fears and desires. You KNOW. And then, even that dissolves. THAT is all there is. Consider that content again in light of what we've discussed since you first heard the vision. Is it possible that finding 'the Great Reality' happens when the conditioned consciousness is freed of all of the insane beliefs that leave a person out of touch with reality? We saw that the relative existence has been made miserable with desires for rewards, with fears of dread around potential punishment, by an endless quest to get the 'good' label and avoid the 'bad' label, and with belief in the concepts of birth and death and the subsequent longing for continuity of the body-mind-personality triad. Imagine the level of peace available to you at this moment if You know the Truth of the vision: that the desires and fears have no basis; that working all your life to earn the 'good' label and to avoid the 'bad' label is totally inconsequential; that your concerns about the fate of a body and mind and all your personas are completely irrelevant. How much peace could you enjoy in The Now if you let go of all that? How much relief could come, if relieved of all the lies and superstitions and dreamed-up beliefs and false ideas and faulty programming and corrupt conditioning?" Please enter in the silence of contemplation.

THE SEVENTH DEGREE OF MOVEMENT TOWARD REALITY:
THE NON-BEINGNESS, PART EIGHT

Q: "How many can pull that off ... to just let go and accept the complete dissolution of the body and mind and personality?"

F: "To know 'how many' are realized should be irrelevant to you, but even asking the question shows you aren't yet capable of 'pulling that off.' [Pause] You awoke this morning. Did you ask, 'I wonder how many other people awoke this morning'?" [Laughter]

Q: [Sour expression]

F: "At bedtime when you're exhausted, do you long for sleep, or do you fear the peace of sleep and try to avoid it because you might not awake into your body and mind the next morning?"

Q: "Good point."

F: "Why thank you very much. Ha. [Laughter] How old are you?"

Q: [Long pause, thinking. Finally...] "I have no age; however, I—the consciousness—have been manifested in this space for forty-five years!" [Laughter]

F.: "So now you want to prove how awake you are! [Laughter] If your body is forty-five, that means, let's see ... [pause] you've sought the 'loss' of consciousness some fifteen or sixteen thousand nights without concern. Witness the unmanifesting of consciousness the same way you've experienced that 'loss' of consciousness each night. Then understand that it's never 'lost.' Asleep, you are still conscious, just not aware of being conscious. Fully realized, You will even be aware that you're sleeping, but that's not the pointer for now. We know consciousness is still in existence even in your sleep because if I entered the room and shouted your name, you would sit up and answer. You go to sleep, but consciousness remains forever. If you're in deep sleep and unaware of being, then later cross the border-line and are awake to your beingness, what does either state matter, ultimately? Both are transitional 'phases' in never-ending cycles. You're beyond both. The real remains; the temporary fades away. What's to fear? In that knowing, who is 'afraid to accept the complete dissolution' of the body-mind-personality triad?"

Q: [Nods in understanding]

Q.2: "If you speak of Selflessness, then what does it mean to say that you're 'Self-Realized'?"

F: "It means nothing. I am not Self-Realized and I have no Self-Knowledge. Currently, there is no self and there is no Self. Even 'I Am That' is only a pointer, the truth being made clear when Lao Tzu said: "The name that can be spoken is not the eternal Name." Every word written or spoken by me, and every word in any of the Teachings, should be in italics or quote marks to show that the words are pointers and not The Truth, either. Both truth and freedom come in the silence. The truly Realized become very quiet. The shift is more and more toward that silence."

Q2: "I thought 'That' identified the Truth."

F: "Ultimately, 'That' is just another name. [Pause. Points at body.] There's this clustering of chemicals and a component of conscious-energy that's tempo-rarily manifested in this space. The body must have plant food regularly to replenish and sustain the consciousness that manifests and becomes 'usable' via plant functionings. This [points at body] is nothing more than a food-body. There is this conscious-energy that has manifested via a natural process and there is That energy-consciousness which is a potentiality but is not currently drawn into any manifestation. They are not two. 'Drinking water' is 'drinking water,' even if no one is drinking it at the moment. H_2O that is 'free' in the sky and H_2O that is 'manifested' in the space of my body is still H_2O. And even that water in the body will cycle out and be 'free' again. If a person looks at this food body and sees anything other than elements and energy, then that person is not in touch with reality. If you think this [points at body] is not primarily space, then visit a funeral home and ask to see the size of the urn that my remains will one day fit into prior to scattering. Manifested, I Am, but that's still about beingness. Beingness with pure, de-conditioned Consciousness, yes, but being-ness nevertheless. I Am prior to beingness, prior to consciousness, and even prior to non-beingness. I've passed eternity being That, joining with other waves and particles of energy during some temporary cyclings into manifestation. One can say 'That which is even beyond the non-beingness is Me,' but anything said in not the Final Truth. [Pause] The consciousness has manifested in this space for slightly more than five decades, but I've been the Absolute infinitely. I continue to be That, and I shall forever be That. No other continuity exists. But in the end, forfeit all concepts, all names, and all labels. Persons reside in limited, restrictive, semantic domains, in the world of 'spouse' or 'boss' or 'stud' and even 'The Supreme.' The world is in them…is in their minds. I am neither in the world nor of the world. I Am That infinite potentiality, temporarily manifested. I Am not in the Absolute…I Am the Absolute. I Am That Absolutely pure and nameless force. I Am prior to the contamination visited upon the manifested conscious-ness via conditioning and programming, but all words and names and labels are useless in the end. Know all that, then Realize, and then you too shall be stunned into silence." Please enter the silence of contemplation.

THE SEVENTH DEGREE
OF MOVEMENT TOWARD REALITY:
The Non-Beingness, Part Nine

F: "Before we end these sessions, you should come to know that That Which I Am is a conscious-energy that vibrates at a particular frequency. The tree you see out the window is the same conscious-energy, just vibrating at a different frequency. The consciousness I Am acts automatically and spontaneously and naturally, and a race of humans can result; the consciousness the tree Is acts automatically and spontaneously and naturally, and a forest can result. The only reason that there seems to be an appearance of difference is because of the condi-tioning that consciousness undergoes in persons, blocking the inner awareness of What They Are and What that 'tree' Truly Is. [Pause] You knew the unicity at one time. The child in a 'state' of Child Ignorance knows no differences, knows no strangers. That child hugs them all. That child hugs those of its 'own race' as indiscriminately as it hugs those of a 'different race.' It hugs 'males' and 'females' equally. It hugs without fear. It hugs in the early going without any desire to get anything in return. That's as close to 'loving' as most will ever get because, at that point, the child is totally removed from the narcissism that it—and those around it—will suffer some day. It has no identity, not yet having been programmed to believe it is a child, a boy, a girl, a 'good' boy or a 'bad' boy, an 'American,' an 'Indian' on a reservation here, or an 'Indian' in a temple there. Knowing What You Are is the key to being in touch with reality. The fact is that nothing needs to be taught or learned about that. Persons need but remember what they already know."

Q: "But knowing the Oneness is key, right? You said that love happens when we know that Oneness, correct?"

F: "Correct at the time I said it. Now, for you, it should just be seen as another concept. Persons think they want to love. Persons think they want to be loved. In actuality, the love-to-be dominates personas. Ego will fight to the death to sustain its image. It is the assumed roles' love-to-be, not love, that drives persons to joust with windmills for their entire relative existence. Remember: delusion ended when you realized that the seer, the seen and the seeing were one. What does that tell you about the lover, the loved, and the loving? Understand that and then you'll see why that which persons call 'love' is a total illusion. Understand that this thing that persons call 'love'—which they search for, work for, spend for, kill for, and often die for—is rooted in attachment to illusions resulting from their enculturation. The consciousness has been so warped that most accept that something involving money and killing and dying and desiring and fearing can really be 'love.' In fact, it is only personal desires and personal fears that are being mistaken for 'love.' [Pause] Persons take the image of another person to be real, idealize that persona/image, give to that image their 'love,' seek to get love in return from that persona, then spend some time with that personality and find that the image had been false all along. Then, they hate that person. Look at the pattern: from acquaintance to friend to lover to spouse to enemy to one who should die. Yet something with that kind of history is what most still want to call 'love'? [Pause] See Truth, then this concept called 'love' can be experienced in a non-destructive, AS IF mode. Knowing that, you may experience the remainder of your manifestation reveling in the feeling of love while suffering not at all from the emotion of love and all the emotional intoxication that comes with it. Or none of that might happen, but peace can still remain. Take duality to be the truth and you'll spend all your days analyzing why you feel separate and 'apart from,' experiencing cycle after cycle of 'falling in love' but then 'losing love.' Know the reality and 'love' will happen or not, in peace. I am loved? Okay. I am not loved? Okay. No desire. No fear. No agenda. No manipulation. No effort to try to control. No effort to try to make happen what a persona wants to happen. Peace. Call it 'bliss' if you like. Ultimately, it's all concepts, and you know what to do with concepts." [Note: An inquirer after this session asked, "Why wouldn't 'true love' just happen, after realization?" Persons will fight for their belief that "I do too love him/her!" "She / He does too love me!" The answer regarding "true love" was: "You are wise to use the word 'true.' What is true and what is false? All which is relative is false and only the Absolute is real or true. The relative is taken to be the real after the conditioning of the 'mind.' The Absolute is unconditional. The relative is limited; the Absolute is limitless. The relative is marked by 'if's' while the Absolute has no qualifications. The relative is temporary; the Absolute is permanent. Thus, to use your term, 'true love' could not happen if any element such as 'I'll love you if you do this but not if you do that' or 'I'll love you if you believe this but not if you believe that' is present. True love, to be real, would have to be (a) without any conditions at all (b) would therefore have to be unconditional love (c) would have to be limitless (d) and would have to be permanent. 'True love' would have to be absolute, not relative. How many instances of 'love' have you experienced or witnessed that met all those qualifications?" If you look ahead to the section entitled "REALIZATION: No Mind, Part Four," you'll see that Absolute means 'complete,' 'uncontaminated,' 'unconditional,' 'unqualified,' 'unlimited,' 'supreme,' 'certain,' 'sure,' 'entire,' 'whole,' 'unadulterated,' and 'unambiguous.' 'True love,' therefore, would have to be 'complete love,' 'uncontaminated love,' 'unconditional love,' 'unqualified love,' 'unlimited love,' 'supreme love,' 'certain love,' 'sure love,' 'entire love,' 'whole love,' 'unadulterated love,' and 'unambiguous love.' If that is the form love takes, call it 'true love'; otherwise, anyone believing that anything less can constitute "true love" is—to use Krishna's word—a fool. Is the "Oneness" known? Are all illusions of "separation" gone? Or is there a perceived "a" trying to relate to a perceived "b"? "Love" and a belief in the duality of "subject-object" are mutually exclusive. In the relative, feelings can be felt without the intoxication of emotions that only come from personas. Now, with that understanding, the transcript of the exchange will continue.]

Q: "That almost sounds like you don't want to love or be loved."

F: "Want. Desire. Fear of not getting what is wanted. What a needless pain. [Pause] I explained that peace came in the work situation when I reached the understanding that 'Teaching happens...or not.' So too is the understanding about love: 'Love happens...or not.' Only in that 'state' of not attaching to outcome—of not working to control and manipulate...only then can peace happen. Know that love is a concept. Experience it or not in the AS IF mode. What happens, happens. [Pause] What persons call 'love' is the most magnificent experience of all; it is also the most horrendous experience of all. With such duality, how can that possibly be taken for the real? Recall the earlier pointer about experience: all experience is about the five-sense, phenomenal existence, which is a mirage. As for feeling or emotion, if love happens as a feeling, take the ride and watch the feelings rise and fall; if love happens as an emotion— being experienced by a person in an ego-state—prepare for war." Please enter the silence of contemplation.

THE SEVENTH DEGREE OF MOVEMENT TOWARD REALITY: THE NON-BEINGNESS, PART TEN

Q: "But I've read many sages who spoke of love as something real."

F: "First, the only 'thing' that is real is the conscious-energy. Secondly, I've explained throughout these talks that sages offer many concepts at certain points that are to be tossed later. [Pause] What was your last lengthy car trip?"

Q: "Hummm, we drove to Eureka Springs."

F: "On the trip from Texas to Arkansas, did you find the directional signs along the way to be important?"

Q: "Yes."

F: "Did they assist you on your journey?"

Q: "Of course."

F: "On the way, were you sometimes focusing on the directional markers more than on your surroundings or even the destination?"

Q: "Yes."

F: "And then when you arrived at the end of the journey, did you give even a single thought to all those signs along the way, to the stops along the way, to any problems or pleasures along the way?"

Q: [Nodding head in understanding.]

F: "Once you arrived, then every sign and event and experience along the way dissolved. It all left your consciousness completely. You lay on the bed in a hotel and relaxed. Nothing was 'on your mind,' and certainly nothing that happened along the way was any longer in your consciousness."

Q: "Okay. I got it. Very clear."

F: "Take 'love' to be 'that which the True Self knows after realizing the Oneness,' but then move on. Most strangers in this western culture will not give you a hug if you explain that their aloneness can end when they know the all-oneness, as you do. [Laughter. Pause] When a black bear entered my campground one night in Arizona and began foraging about for food, I knew the Oneness, but I didn't try to blend some mystical mindset into that relative experience. I didn't try to hug the bear while telling him about the wonders of knowing that I was At One with him. [Laughter] Christ walked about the Middle East region saying, "Before Abraham was, I Am' and "When you speak of me, speak of me as I Am." And what was their response? 'Get a cross and some nails.' [Laughter] These sessions are not advertised. Fully realized Advaitins do not proselytize. Few persons have 'receptors' that are developed enough to receive all that the field of consciousness can reveal. [Pause] Being in touch with reality involves getting real in whatever remains of this manifestation, and here's part of the reality of what persons take to be love: the 'love' that they think they are experiencing is nothing more than a natural chemical reaction of a food-body. The brain, and sometimes a 'mind'—which is something altogether different—determines what persons do after a chemical reaction is triggered. [Pause] The conditioned consciousness develops the love-to-be. A bird with manifested consciousness, when alarmed, flies away to protect the food-body. The difference is that a person loves-to-be what it is not and loves its false identities since those are taken by the corrupted consciousness to be real. The bird just loves-to-be, period. As quickly as a person is capable of loving, just as quickly is that same person capable of hating. Where's 'love' or reality in such mutability? Knowing the Real, I am free of the hate-love duality and all other perceived dualities. That Which is complete, which is All, seeks nothing."

Q: "But why not advocate seeking love? I mean, wouldn't love eliminate all chaos?"

F: "Ha. First, I advocate nothing. I offer nothing. I take all away, for those who can hear. Next, all in this manifestation is chaos if you consider 'chaotic' to be the opposite of 'stable.' All in the manifestation is in flux except that which is real. All cycles. All is flowing into manifestation or flowing out of manifestation. During the cycles, entropy happens naturally during manifestation. Entropy, happening naturally, guarantees change. Change guarantees uncertainly in the relative for those who are not certain about what is real. If it's entropy and chaos and change you find unacceptable, then know that You Are the Absolute. Know that You Are fixed, immutable, ineradicable, constant, invariable. All that you take to be variable is perceived wrongly, merely fiction imagined via your variable mind. See reality and the illusions of change dissolve. You may think that on this journey you've changed: body to mind to spiritual role to a child in ignorance to the True Self to the beingness to the non-beingness and to the reality beyond. Realize..nothing changed except your wrong perceptions. [Pause] So, we've focused on those misconceptions that have separated us from reality or on concepts that have now helped us glimpse reality. Now, it's time to look at that which we sought and know for certain what we have known all along but had forgotten. Then, it's time to see what life in the relative is like for the realized." Please enter the silence of contemplation.

ADDITIONAL POINTERS ON THE NON-BEINGNESS

For a final clarification, here are three considerations for you to take into the quiet:

1. "How can that which is illusion, and therefore has never been, possibly be thought to 'be'?"

2. "How can that which is illusion, and therefore has never been, possibly be thought to 'have been at some time'?"
and

3. "How can that which is illusion, and therefore has never been, be thought to 'not be' now?"

Consider this relative existence experience: when "floyd" was married, a discussion about baby names took place. It was determined that if there were a female child, she'd be named "Ashley" and if there were a male child, he'd be named "Kyle." Only a daughter was born. We can now talk about Ashley, if you like, but can we talk about "Kyle"? Would you take Ashley to "be" but Kyle to "not be"? To that end, the non-Realized will (mistakenly) take Ashley to be "a being" and would have to (mistakenly) take Kyle to be "a non-being" as of now. They would also take "floyd" as "a being" now but, post-manifestation, to be a "non-being." (That can be a simple version, yes, but not the most accurate.) As Advaitins for ages have noted, all such talk would be no different from discussing "the child of a barren woman."

The reason that Krishna discounted the beingness and the non-beingness (ultimately making them both a moot issue) was because the Absolute Truth is beyond any relative existence illusions about (1) something "being" or about (2) something that "had been" but is now "not being" any more. If that which "has only been imagined to have been" via the warped consciousness is and was only imagined, then why speak now of something that never was as now "not being"? It's really simple, isn't it?

Is there is a point on the "journey" when the seeker must be introduced to such pointers? Of course. However, the only use of any terms or concepts along the way is to point to the various stages by which the consciousness was warped and thereafter to point to the steps that must be transcended in reverse in order to be free of the relative effects of the warped consciousness. Post-Realization, all of the terms or concepts are to be cast aside, including beingness and non-beingness as well.

An e-mail on Tuesday quoted an author who had written the following:

"The Absolute has an unawareness of self."

The response was:

To suggest that "The Absolute has an unawareness of self" would be tantamount to saying "The sun has an unawareness of the mirage in the desert." Okay ... and??? The fact is, fusion is just happening and the sun is not aware or unaware of anything. Use of the word "has" in "the Absolute has" is equally invalid. (To suggest that "the Absolute has" is to reveal that, at some subconscious level, the writer is still identified with something with personal attributes that can have or gain or possess something. Can the sun "have" anything, including an "unawareness"?)

The author was likely trying to offer the pointer that the Absolute is not aware of anything since no self or Self exists post-manifestation to be either aware of or conscious of anything. Yet this fact remains: Awareness Is, without awareness of awareness, so discussion of "unawareness" is useless.

Another accurate pointer could be that "post-manifestation, there is no self or Self that can be aware of or conscious of anything." Syllogistic reasoning can them be used uncover the facts regarding this topic:

(A) the Absolute is beyond both beingness and non-beingness;

(B) the Absolute is that which is real; therefore...

(C) neither the beingness nor the non-beingness can be real.

Understand that and you might understand why "the world" is only in you and that You are not in the world and why the illusions of beingness and non-beingness are also in you.

[PLEASE NOTE: The beingness and the non-beingness are discussed on the Advaita website in far more detail than was done with this particular group. For more detailed explanation, visit that site and search the two terms.]

REALIZATION

REALIZATION:
UNDERSTANDING "THE COMING," PART ONE

F: "How did our seven-step journey begin?"

Q: "With debunking body identification."

F: "So we know that a person cannot be any farther removed from reality than when in that limited identity. Fixed in that false identity, the body becomes the focus of all. It's given status, becomes a tool used to manipulate others fixed in body identification, and becomes a source of egotism. All in life becomes geared toward assuring body continuity. One is set up to believe in the most far-fetched teachings imaginable if the teachings include a plan for body continuity. Some of the longest-standing myths and superstitions deal with where babies come from. From those earliest fabricated explanations came the notion that children are 'gifts from god.' Rather high status, yes? Quite the source of ego, yes? We've seen that all misery in the relative existence is rooted in what I've referred to as false identities, personalities, personas or ego-states. From lack of knowledge come ideas and beliefs; from ego comes the drive to cling to the false ideas and beliefs. The ego-states of 'Super Parent' and 'Super Child' are rooted in such lack of awareness. Thus, the first of the seven steps on the journey to Realization must address the error of body identification. If persons cannot become free of the misconceptions about 'how they got here,' then they'll remain in the ignorance of body identification—as far removed from reality as can be. [Pause] So we began the journey by debunking, as you said, the myths and superstitions about 'how we got here' and by inviting protégés to find the answer to this question: 'How did this food-body come to be?' If one cannot get free of the myths and arrogance around this 'coming,' then the journey never even begins. The Realized know the answer. They know how this food-body 'came' to be. [Pause] Maharaj said that science would one day prove the accuracy of the philosophy that he taught. While science is not necessary for the understanding, the awareness already being within, it does now provide exactly what Maharaj predicted. We now understand scientifically that in most cases it is sunlight's interaction with plants that allows the process to begin, the exception being certain organisms thriving at the bottom of the ocean that obtain their energy from thermal vents rather than sunlight. With plants, the process of photosynthesis results in the separation of water molecules, the production of oxygen and glucose, and a means by which energy manifests in organisms that obtain their conscious-energy indirectly rather than directly. Plant-eaters acquire their energy by consuming plants. Carnivores receive their energy by consuming animals that ate plants. [Pause] These scientific explanations aside, one can understand how this food-body came to be by meditating upon a simple question: "Where were You in the days prior to conception?" Let me read a piece I've written for a book that will be entitled "The Twice-Stolen Necklace Murders." In an interview that will be included at the end of the novel, I offer the answer to a question asked by the editor: "How did you come to know that you are not the body and not the breath but are the conscious-energy alone?" The answer I gave is [begins reading] I did what my teacher suggested. I meditated on where I was in the days before conception, before the body began forming, before the oxygen began circulating. I determined where I was, via contemplation, during the days before being manifested in a mother's womb. I traced my 'roots' back to where I really came from in order to know What I Really Am. Anyone with a brain functioning without damage can do the same. If you are 35 years old, let's say, then count backwards. That is how I reached the pre-conception state and the awareness of What I Am. Literally say out loud, 'I am 35; I will now go back. I am now 34; I am now 33.' Try it." Please enter the silence of contemplation.

REALIZATION:
Understanding "the Coming," Part Two

F: "I mentioned earlier that the process of photosynthesis allows plants to use the sun's energy to produce sugar via cell respiration and to convert sunlight energy—which is non-usable by humans—into chemical energy that is usable. In the late 1940's, two people consumed plants that automatically formed sperm in one's food-body and formed eggs in the other's food-body. This space called 'floyd' followed a natural act of friction that triggered a natural chain of happen-ings. How, but via ego, can an act of friction have taken on such noble status? How has such pride come about when the fact is that friction occurring during a physical act resulted in the union of a sperm and an egg? Birds and worms accomplish the same. The arrogance regarding friction and conception dissolves when it's understood that the seven billion cells that make up this food-body derived from natural happenings following an act by two food-bodies. It all happened automatically. Should any legitimate claim of accomplishment be made for something that happens automatically? Humans ate plant food. They engaged in an act of friction resulting in conception. They continued to eat. A space developed inside a food-body, exactly as happens with a tumor. One is considered a 'blessed event,' the other a 'tragedy.' It's all about faulty perception. [Pause] This food-body was ejected from another food-body. That's it. What's the source of any self-importance about that process? Only from the conditioned mind of a 'self' can self-importance come. When the last 'who' disappears, the understanding of That appears. The question is not, "Who am I?" The ques-tion is, "What am I?" The 'who' always deals with a persona. The 'what' is the impersonal conscious-energy. So what is the source of the unbounded pride that persons take in the fact that conception sometimes follows acts of friction? One source is the belief by persons that they have created, or the belief that they have worked in equal partnership with a supernatural power to create. Another source is ignorance of science. Neither matter nor energy can be 'created.' No one has ever created anything. Trillions of trillions of food-bodies have 'come' and 'gone' on the planet. None of those happenings involved any 'new' or 'created' matter. All matter involved was already present on earth and was being recycled, and any energy involved in all those happenings was merely cycling as well. Only the ego—only a false personality—prefers to assign supernatural status to naturally-occurring events. The realized find the truth in contemplation, so let's return to the exercise begun yesterday. I said, If you are 35 years old, let's say, then count backwards. That is how I reached the pre-conception state and the awareness of What I Am. Literally say out loud, 'I am 35; I will now go back. I am now 34; I am now 33. Now, let's go on: Continue to count until you reach 'I am one year old'; then say, 'I am 11 months old, I am 10 months old,' etc. Then, 'I am 30 days old, I am 29 days old,' etc. Then 'I am 23 hours old, I am 22 hours old,' etc. Then, 'I am 59 seconds old; I am 58 seconds old,' etc. What happened with my countdown was, I got to 'I am one second before conception, I am conceived.'

I anticipated originally that the count would stop there, but it continued. 'I Am one second prior to conception; I am two seconds prior to conception. Where Am I? I Am minutes, hours, days before conception. Where Am I?' The answer came. Any sperm present in a man was not there much more than 'x' number of days earlier, sperm having a 'shelf life' inside a human male body. Plant food (or plant food consumed via animal food) was consumed and sperm cells resulted automatically. The 'I Am exercise' took me to a plant. Continuing the count took me to where I was before being absorbed into the plant. So it went like this: From 'child born' back to 'child in a womb' back to 'egg fertilized by sperm' back to 'sperm delivered' back to 'sperm' back to 'plants being eaten' back to 'the plant' back to 'the conscious-energy in the plant' back to 'the field'—the field of energy-consciousness. I AM THAT." Please enter the silence of contemplation.

REALIZATION:
Understanding "the Going," Part One

F: "If you review the last passages of the vision, you see how easy 'the going' is: As All near the door, All seem to dissolve into a form of light being drawn inside. As You approach, You feel the last remnants—remnants of whatever You had formerly thought yourself to be—gradually fading away. The dissolving seems to be occurring in slow motion, and you feel ecstatic. It's almost as if You are feeling blissful as your beingness seems to be dissolving into non-beingness. Finally, You merge with the All, into the light, and it seems . . . it seems over. It seems as if everything is over, is finished, is very near complete. All then fades into light. In the fading moments, as beingness transitions into non-beingness, You come to know that You Are That common building block of All in this universe, in All universes. You KNOW. And then, even that dissolves. THAT is all there is. After Realization, the 'staying' can be as easy as the 'going.' In both cases, what is given up is the body-mind-personality triad. It dissolves and the Ultimate Peace manifests. Why not allow the triad to dissolve now and experience the peace now?" Please enter the silence of contemplation.

REALIZATION:
"The Going," Part Two

Q: "So why is it that we're raised to believe that death is a tragedy?"

F: "Because the programming and conditioning, especially in Western cultures, is in the hands of the ignorant. Because the programmers are persons who believe the ancient myths about 'supernatural things' and who look to their superstitions to explain totally natural happenings. Because those who established the Western cultures had forgotten the cycles and believed in a timeline with their concepts of birth, life, death, judgment, and heaven or hell. Because the programmers are so identified with the food-body that they try to preserve it even after the consciousness is no longer manifested. [Pause] Look at their practices to understand the degree of their confusion: they put preservatives in the remains of a food-body, and they apply makeup to the remains to make them look good. They dress the remains up in their finest attire. They box the consciousless space in multi-thousand dollar containers, and they buy special pillows for the heads of consciousless food-bodies to rest on until the dust and mind supposedly re-form for eternity. They buy multi-thousand dollar plots for storing the container. They buy multi-thousand dollar markers to indicate the plot and container location. They decorate areas along the roadways where the consciousness was last manifested. Those who identify with the body obsess over their own bodies and the bodies of others."

Q: "But isn't it natural to feel grief on such occasions?"

F: "I've already made clear: feel whatever is felt. The insanity results when persons have so little understanding of the functioning of the Totality that they are wishing for that which would destroy all life as known on the planet and would end all the cycles."

Q: [Questioning look]

F: "Consider the billions and trillions and trillions of trillions of people and other life forms that have walked on or flown over the planet. If no one had died, no one could live, but then again...no one is dying in this wished-for scenario. What a conundrum."

Q: [Questioning look, again]

Q2: [To Q.] Of course! Don't you see? If the trillions of trillions of bodies were all still alive, the earth's surface would be covered in people stacked in mile-high piles, one on top of the other."

F: "No one could eat since no plants could live. Water and oxygen would disappear. You, on the bottom of the pile, would be starving, suffocating, and writhing in pain, but you wouldn't die...if most persons had their way. Soon, the hidden agenda among all persons would become obvious: 'OK, I want everything to cycle in and out except the few that I really care about.' [Laughter]. So much for 'love.' So much for knowing the Oneness. [Pause] The conscious-energy cycles, yet persons want to stop the natural and inevitable and inexorable cyclings. Such a desire would require a huge ego, and that's exactly what body-mind-personality identification produces: ego...the scourge of the planet, as far the relative existence goes. [Pause] Back to the topic at hand: to understand the 'going,' merely see the 'coming' in reverse: to 'come,' from the field of conscious-ness, energy manifests. That which had no 'beingness'—that which we can point to with the term 'non-beingness'—after nine months results in what is called the 'beingness' or—in the case of our species—what persons choose to call a human 'being.' A 'True' Self emerges—that which is manifested consciousness that has not yet been conditioned or contaminated and does not yet believe in 'the false.' Soon, an infant begins to witness, without opinion and without making the type of judgments that separate and that form the foundation of duality. Pure Witnessing occurs. Next, witnessing occurs with a subject-object perspective, establishing duality as a 'false reality.' Then, the Child Ignorance stage begins but gives way as roles are assigned. Child innocence is lost as a 'mind'—the contami-nated consciousness—results. Lies and superstitions based in the ancient myths are presented as fact, so religious or spiritual identities are assigned and assumed. A 'gift of God' identity is accepted and ego flourishes. Over the next twenty years, the mind is programmed to accumulate. 'More,' rather than 'less,' becomes the standard. Working to accumulate and maintain 'more' dominates the existence of persons. Self-Inquiry seldom occurs; thus, persons pass their manifestation absorbed in self—in false self identifications. Darkness prevails. Accurate 'seeing' that occurs with the benefit of light never happens, so the mistaking of the rope for a snake persists. No enlightenment happens. Perceptions rather than reality dominate the body-mind-personality, so fears and desires drive the personality through a series of sometimes pleasurable, but most often miserable, experiences. So consumed with efforts to try to satisfy the food-body and the variable mind and the sundry personalities, persons become obsessed with seeking the 'good' label and avoiding the 'bad' label. All of those efforts are to insure that the body and mind get all the rewards they want in 'this life,' get the 'ultimate reward' in an afterlife, and avoid the punishments that come if the 'bad' label is applied...'now' or 'later.' The dream of the planet, or the nightmare of the planet, becomes the very abnormal 'norm' for those walking about in their sleep. You are among the few who will ever be exposed to the opportunity to abandon the imprisonment of a timeline and concepts and body-mind-personality identifications. Know the cycles and be free of it all. The freedom of no longer believing all the lies, and of no longer being driven by all of their nonsense, and of knowing the truth...that is the bliss during this manifestation." Please enter into the silence of contemplation.

REALIZATION:
Understanding the Functioning
of the Totality

Q: "When you were talking about how persons who are identified with their bodies also obsess over the consciousless bodies of others, it reminded me of the 'ice cube metaphor' you used. Nothing is really 'lost'."

F: "Exactly. In fact, let's use that for a review. [Pause] The process begins at the core of a nuclear reactor called 'the sun.' I told you that this universe began with one hydrogen and one helium atom interacting. At the core of the sun, four hydrogen nuclei fuse together to form one helium nucleus, and that happens over and over. The part of the energy which that process releases as light travels in particle and wave form and, in the case of this planet, either reflects off a surface or manifests in plants. The water and oxygen provided via plant photosynthesis sets the stage for another cycling of manifested energy-consciousness. Then, we can look at the cycles of water and see the similarity with the cyclings of consciousness. Let's pick up with a cycle where water is evaporating. It can appear to be steam or vapor, then cloud, and then rain which can fall into a river or lake. There, the water can be drawn out, processed, conveyed to the outlet in a house, placed into an ice tray, and frozen into a cube shape. As a cube used to cool a drink, water can then cycle through the body and into a waste system, into a treatment plant where some of it can evaporate into steam and form a cloud, and then the process cycles again, ad infinitum. A configuration of two hydrogen atoms and one oxygen atom can manifest, and observers can assume that the varied 'forms' or 'appearances' are real and different, but we know now that they're all the same...all one. Clouds, rivers, lakes, steam, ice...all one thing—all $H2O$ clusters—but all appearing to uneducated observers to be unique and different. Similarly, conscious-energy can manifest and observers can assume that the varied 'forms' or 'appearances' are real and different, but we know they are all the same ... all one. Females, males, trees, cars, pianos...all one thing—all conscious-energy, merely vibrating at varied frequencies—but all appearing to uneducated observers to be unique and different. In the end, whether 'ice' or 'human,' none of the spaces or shapes or forms remain. What they truly are remains. The appearance of supposed uniqueness was really illusory all along."

Q: "Clarity came when you explained before that we don't 'create' anything when we think we 'make' ice cubes."

F: "Yes. So you understand that nothing has ever been created or destroyed."

Q2: "Clarity came to me when you explained that nothing was 'lost' and so nothing was 'gained.' It was all a natural process of automatic cycling, all just happening. Now, it's like, 'If I have a cube for my drink, okay; if I don't have a cube for my drink, okay'."

F: "Ha. That's as clear an expression of what "AS IF" living in the relative looks like as needs be offered."

Q3: "You've used that term 'as if' before, and several here seem to be familiar with it, but I'm not."

F: "We'll get to that in an upcoming session. For now, stay with the cycles. "

Q: "The cube analogy helped me get free of some misconceptions about reincarnation as well."

F: "In what way?"

Q: "Well, here's what came to me in meditation after you discussed that in an earlier session. Say I have a cube and I melt it in a glass and then pour that water into the ocean. Then, if I immediately scoop up that water, I might get some of the water used to make the original cube and some water from the ocean that was not used before. Then, I can take that water home, freeze it, and make another cube. Part of that water that took the shape of the original cube is in the 'new' cube, but not all of it. The 'new' cube might have some water that had 'cubeness' before and some water that had never left the ocean before but is now manifested into the space or shape of a cube."

F: "Hummm. Exactly. It seems the teaching can now happen via another space. [Light laughter] What you described as that temporary 'cubeness,' that's the case with the consciousness that appears as this temporary 'Amness.' Part of that 'new' cube is made up of other atom clusters that had been manifested in a cube shape before but is also made up of atom clusters that had never been manifested as a cube. So it is when conscious-energy is drawn from that field of consciousness and into manifestation."

Q: "So don't people who think they're going to recycle as 'a human' or as some other life-form get upset if they hear that explanation from you?"

F: "I've told you that it's none of my business what others think of me. None I know who offer the Advaita Teaching try to recruit. All of you found these sessions; I didn't seek you out. In fact, more and more, the silence calls me. More sessions may happen...or not. [Pause] As for being upset, if the knowing is known, there's no one to become upset. Always ask, 'Who is upset? Who is assuming a label or a role that feels threatened by these words?' Find the false-hood of that posturing and that role assumption and the upset ends; don't, and it will continue. Whatever. [To Q.3] Take that as your first pointer toward 'As IF' living. [To the group] If the knowing is not known, then 'upsets' become the rule, not the exception. If this functioning of the Totality is understood, the Realized can witness and feel, but no illusions shall be taken to be the real and no attachments to images or false roles shall be assumed. No offense can be experienced since no person is available to experience. [Pause] All sense of loss involves memories of things in the past that were seen to be a certain way—but that were not that way at all; or, a sense of loss can involve picturing a future that will not be what a person desires it to be or fears it will not be. Timelines are the trap; knowing the cycles frees you from the trap. Believing in 'time' at all is a trap. Freedom can only happen NOW. Truth is NOW only. The past is an imagining, generated in a mind—which is nothing more than contaminated consciousness. The future is an imagining generated in a mind...in corrupted consciousness. The Realized are free of all concepts, including the misconceptions of 'imagin-ings' and 'time' and 'mind.' So let's discuss 'NOW'."

Q: "At this time? Ha." [Laughter]

F: "It's time for you to leave." [More laughter] Please enter the silence of contemplation and meditate upon 'past' and 'future' and 'NOW'"

REALIZATION:
Knowing the NOW

F: "A woman in one group reported that she had suffered for years from a perceived loss. The man she claimed to love had left. She suffered most, she said, when she thought of the 'wonderful' times they'd shared and all the things they'd done that they would never do again.' She mourned the future events that would never take place. So our conversation went something like this:

F: "So those are your thoughts about past events and future events. Would you be willing to set those aside temporarily in order to consider something I can offer?"

Woman: "Sure."

F: "In spite of all the suffering you speak of, I want to know this: right now, at this very moment...are you okay?"

Woman: "Yeah, I guess so."

F: "No. No guessing. Right now, in this very instant, aren't you actually okay?"

Woman: "Right now, for this second, yes."

F: "Fine. So what about now?"

Woman.: "Yes, for now I'm okay."

F: "And what about now. Are you still okay right now?"

Woman.: [Beginning to laugh] "Yes, right now I'm okay."

F: "What about the future? Are you going to be okay?"

Woman: "I don't have a clue."

F: "Well, I do, but you never will, unless you realize. You can never have a clue about the future, for it's the false imagining of a corrupted mind. But leave that for a moment and tell me...aren't you still okay, at least for right now?"

Woman: [Laughing] "Enough!"

F: "Enough? Are you sure? [Pause] Do you understand?"

Woman: "I understand your point. The only time I can feel okay is right now, never when my mind is thinking about the past or the future."

F: "Go home and sit in the quiet with your last words. Stay with those words. Don't seek a super-conscious state. Stay aware of those words and contemplate upon them."

Woman: "I will. Goodbye."

F: "That's paraphrased, but it's close. Is the point clear?"

Group: "Yes."

F: "Then your invitation is the same: Don't seek a super-conscious state. Stay awake, stay aware, stay conscious of those words and contemplate their truth. Let's enter the quiet." Please enter the silence of contemplation.

REALIZATION:
No Mind, Part One

[Note: The full treatment of this subject is available in the book, There's No Such Thing As "Peace of Mind" (There is Only Peace if You're Out of Your Mind]

Q: "I'm certainly not sure that I get all you've offered, but why do so few 'get' this Teaching?"

F: "Manifested in only a few food-bodies is a 'level' of consciousness that is immediately receptive to receiving awareness of awareness...the awareness of the reality of the conscious-energy that flows throughout this universe. Those are called the sages or gnanis."

Q: "That's you?"

F: "Ha. Hardly. Next is the consciousness that is like gunpowder, ready for awareness to explode into consciousness after first challenging all beliefs and ideas. Then, there's the 'charcoal' that can burn after much effort. Lastly, there's that mass of contaminated consciousness that has been compared to 'wet charcoal'—never likely to 'light up.' Why is there such debate about who deserves credit for having 'invented television'? The consciousness of the science required to make possible the functioning of 'television' manifested in the consciousness of three men on three different continents within micro-seconds of each other, so all three have been given credit. Just as a whale's sounds can vibrate through a thousand miles of ocean and be received by another whale that comprehends the message contained in the vibration, so too can the manifested consciousness in certain food-bodies comprehend the flow 'into and out of' the unified field of consciousness which travels infinitely across infinite space. In addition to that lack of awareness are the other obstacles we've already discussed: rigidity, closure to influence, arrogance, conditioning, programming, enculturation, ideas, 'faith,' concepts, and the belief by personalities that what is 'in the mind' is 'their truth' and 'their reality.' Persons trapped in their ego-states refuse to challenge their beliefs since those attitudes are the very basis of what they take to be 'who' they are—their false, assumed roles."

Q2: "What about archetypes? Aren't they in the mind, and aren't their effects real?"

F: "First, if they're 'in the mind,' they can't be real. An archetype, by definition, is an image, right?"

Q2: [Long pause. Smile, then...] "End of that, huh?"

F: "Not really. Let's use that to move to the next pointer. [Pause] Are the brain, the consciousness, and the mind all one?"

Q2: [Long pause] "Consciousness and mind are one. Brain is different."

F: "If consciousness and mind are one, does that mean that your 'mind' is forever?"

Q2: [Pause. Thinking, then...] "Nevermind." [Laughter]

F: "Is that a pun?"

Q2: "Ha. Maybe, but I didn't mean it that way." [Laughter]

F: "So, what's your answer? Is your 'mind' forever?"

Q2: "Definitely not. When the food-body dies, the mind ends."

F: "And the brain?"

Q2: "The same."

F: "Is the consciousness forever?"

Q2: "Yes. As a form of energy, it can't be destroyed."

F: "So the difference in the mind and consciousness is?"

Q2: "One is eternal; one is temporary. One is real; one is not."

F: "What else? How about you?" [Pointing at a participant]

Q3: "You said earlier that mind is 'contaminated consciousness'."

F: "So let's get to the point in our review. The brain, the mind and the consciousness are not synonymous. For the purpose of our discussion, consider a brain and the consciousness to be 'concrete'; consider a mind to be 'abstract.' Consciousness is rooted in the Absolute. The brain is rooted in the elements. The 'mind' is rooted in wrong programming and faulty conditioning and lies and concepts and ideas and superstitions and falsehoods." Please enter the silence of contemplation.

REALIZATION:
No Mind, Part Two

F: "The fact that 'mind' is rooted in wrong programming and in lies and concepts is why I told you early on that, in order to be sane, you must be out of your mind. I told you that the Truth cannot be stated. Take the converse of that point to realize that any words said are the false. Every comment you hear as you move about your society in the coming week will be false. Listen objectively and see that every statement you hear will reveal how far removed the speaker truly is from knowing the truth. Everything that I say is to be used to get rid of another false belief until all ideas and emotional intoxication and beliefs are gone and nothing remains but the unstated understanding. Only then can the constant churning and re-churning of the false beliefs of the corrupted mind finally cease. It's that constant movement of contaminated consciousness that results in the variable, obsessive 'mind' that can find no rest. The intent of those using substances that can result in what is wrongly called 'a loss of consciousness' is not to 'lose consciousness.' It's to lose, to escape from, that troublesome, restless mind. All means of escape but one will provide only a temporary respite, at best. These Teachings are the permanent solution. Why? Consciousness is not 'lost' at the end of excessive drinking or drugging. Awareness is missing. Consciousness of consciousness is missing. The consciousness remains, but as in sleep, the person is not aware of being conscious. Recall, we know the consciousness remains because if we enter the bedroom and shout the name of the sleeper, then the sleeper will become aware and answer. Such is the case with persons. They are not aware of being conscious, of being consciousness. You can shout their name, 'You Are That!' but they will not answer because of the deep state of sleep that their programming and conditioning has lulled them into. The only movements in consciousness that they are conscious of are the movements of contaminated consciousness. The pure consciousness is not known because they are so far removed from the 'Pure Witness stage.' They will also be pre-empted from knowing, even asleep, that the consciousness remains; therefore, they'll not realize that when that 'final sleep' comes, the consciousness remains then as well. The true solution is to recognize all the false, discard it all, and then remain in the bliss of pure consciousness."

Q3: "I'm still lost in terms of one aspect of the consciousness."

F: "Specifically …?"

Q3: "I guess I'm most confused about the movement, from the 'field' you talk about to the manifestation in a plant and then into animals, humans, etc."

F: "Do you understand the archetypes he [pointing at

Q.2] mentioned earlier?"

Q3: "I know what archetypes are, yes."

F: "What are they, basically?"

Q3: "Well, Jung felt that, passed down as a result of the totality of human experience …."

F: "Excuse me. Most basically. In one word. What's an archetype?"

Q3: "You said it earlier … it's an image."

F: "Right. Now, how are those images passed down to humans?"

Q3.: "Genetically."

F: "So those images come from this huge 'field' of 'human experiences' and are passed down by particles of material that we'll call genes, right?"

Q3.: [Pausing] "Right."

F: "So particles can carry images?"

Q3.: "Right."

F: "Can energy move in a particle form?"

Q3.: "Sure. Light has a wave-particle nature."

F: "And obviously light moves, so focus on the particle part of the nature of that energy. Is consciousness energy?"

Q3: "Yes."

F. "We talked about using the EEG to measure the patterns of electrical activity in the brain. Let's go back to that. Various 'states' of consciousness can be measured and logged using the instrument. But if the equipment denotes a 'flat EEG,' does that denote death of the food-body?"

Q3: "Some would say so."

F: "Does it denote the end of consciousness?"

Q3: "No, because what's being measured is electrical activity, and conscious-ness is an energy form, and energy can't be destroyed."

F: "So consciousness is in movement when manifested, and its 'range' of movement expands as consciousness eventually returns to the field. You Are That which is forever. The food-body that allows the consciousness to know itself is temporary." Please enter the silence of contemplation.

REALIZATION:
No Mind, Part Three

F: "Now, before we leave the discussion of genetic messaging completely, another point needs to be made about the impact of the archetypes that you brought up. What we called the 'True Self' has nothing to do with any genetic self or encoding, but that 'genetic self' is another obstacle to realization. The collective unconscious might provide, via genetic transmissions, certain images that result in behaviors that are useful for survival of the food-body, but adults must eventually get free of the influence of archetypes as well, if realization is to happen. For example, a child might look over the edge of a tall building or cliff and get that automatic warning, that alarming 'jump' in the gut. The signal might prevent a fall, but as one seeks realization, the influence of archetypes must also be abandoned."

Q2: "Why should their influence be abandoned if they're natural? You said it's natural living that's supposed to happen in the relative existence."

F: "Archetypes aren't natural. They're the result of experiences, and only a body-mind-personality can have an 'experience.' I have no experiences. The consciousness merely is. Furthermore, to experience fear when not in danger is not natural. Billions have looked over the edge of the Eiffel Tower and had a fear-response triggered, but they all knew full well that with a protective screen of wire guarding the perimeter that there was no way they could fall over the edge. That genetic messaging is at the heart of seeing a snake in a rope, and we've agreed that 'wrong perspective' prevents seeing reality. [Nods] Archetypes are based in duality: 'up' is good and 'down' is bad; 'dark' is bad but 'light' is good. So the messaging goes. The tendency to moralize and judge and separate is implanted via archetypes long before a child receives its first lesson from a person or book that's claimed to be 'holy.' The point is, all that coding is about the person—about a food-body-mind-personality triad that works constantly to perpetuate the body—and is not even remotely about the Real. In fact, that coding contributes significantly to the desire for eternal body-mind continuity since the purpose of the coding is to aid in perpetuating the continuity of the food-body. That instinctive desire to be—to survive as long as possible in this world and then eternally in another—can convince a person that the impossible is possible and that the body-mind can last forever. The person's love-to-be is reinforced by that coding, so the messaging is another obstacle on the path to realization. The archetypal imaging, as is the case with all images, ultimately blocks the awareness of the Real."

Q2: "I don't get that at all."

F: "Consider this: it's only that slight vestige of uncontaminated consciousness that occasionally inspires a person living in one or more ego-states to say, "This in not who I really am. Who or what am I, really?" The genetic encoding, on the other hand, contributes to our not knowing who we are because it inspires further body identification and preoccupation with 'saving' the physical body. To understand exactly how you arrived at a dead end street, a street that is so far removed from the major highway that you must journey on to reach realization, is the prerequisite for returning to the main road and reaching your destination. When you began these sessions, you were all stuck at a dead end and not knowing where to go. Why? Because you didn't have the slightest clue how you ended up there, being completely lost. Now you know all the wrong turns that resulted in your being lost in all those false identifications: the obstacle of genetic coding that automatically sets up dualistic thinking, the programming and conditioning, the enculturation, and all those contributors to the 'storehouse' of lies and ideas and concepts and beliefs that corrupted the pure consciousness and resulted in the illusions of your restless and variable 'mind'." Please enter the silence of contemplation.

REALIZATION:
No Mind, Part Four

Q3: "You still haven't clarified the movement of consciousness that I asked about."

F: "Okay. You agree that conscious-energy can manifest in a plant and then into a food-body, right?"

Q3: "Right."

F: "And you agree that when the food-body disintegrates, the consciousness is not destroyed, right?"

Q2: "It moves into the field."

F: "Yes. Moves. It moves to that field...it merges into the Absolute, just as a drop of water merges into the ocean. And 'absolute' is defined as...?"

Q3: "Pure."

F: "Yes, among other things. Let me read some definitions of 'absolute' that point toward the Absolute for us. [Picks up a notecard. Reads] 'Complete' or 'uncontaminated' or 'unconditional.' [Pause] Could we say 'unconditioned?' [Nods of agreement come from the group]. Also, 'not relative,' 'unqualified,' 'unlimited,' 'supreme,' 'certain,' 'sure,' 'entire,' 'whole,' 'unadulterated,' or 'unambiguous.' And know that 'supreme' is just one of ten or more words used to define 'absolute' and should not be taken to have more significance than any of the other words on the list. Nothing about the Absolute should be taken to be 'supreme' in the sense of being the 'greatest,' the 'loftiest,' the 'best,' the 'ultimate,' the 'sovereign,' the 'ruler,' the 'creator,' or the 'highest.' If persons believe they are to be all that someday, egotism will quickly convince them that they're all that now. Nothing about the Absolute should be taken to be a 'reward' or 'prize' or 'payoff.' Who would be in that field of consciousness to receive such? The food-body won't be available. The fictitious 'mind' won't be available; oxygen won't be available. Remember, the food-body is a combination of elements, circulating the breath if consciousness is manifested. At the point called the 'death' of the food-body, its elements shall move and merge with the larger pool of elements. The breath shall move and merge with the larger pool of air. And the conscious-energy shall move and merge with the larger pool of consciousness. When I realized the truth of that, an indescribable sense of freedom and calm happened. No eternal body to be concerned with, no eternal mind, no everlasting breath, no eternally-manifested consciousness, no re-manifestation of this body-mind complex that would have to do all of this relative 'stuff' all over again, no more fear of eternal punishment, and no more dread of having to spend an eternity floating about and singing and glorifying an obviously egotistical male god who wants worship and adulation. [Laughter] Freedom from all. Nothing more to work for, to dread, to seek...nothing to be occupied or preoccupied with. A blissful relative existence has followed. To realize is to understand the minimal, the tiniest, the most basic 'building block' that is and which is the commonality of all. It is to realize I Am That which is the least, not the most. No 'different from' exists. No duality exists. Where is the room for separation and division and arrogance—for concepts such as 'better than'—when that truth is known? Persons seek to accumulate more...more roles, more stuff. Persons desire to be more, to be greater, to have more power, to earn great rewards now and to earn some 'Ultimate Reward' later. The Realized desire no more, accumulate no more, and know the 'less-ness' that is Real. Nothing is smaller than That Which I Am,

yet nothing is as limitless. While manifested into this "Amness," pure consciousness knows itself to be That Which It Is; thus, all other identities dissolve. In
knowing I Am the tiniest, the least, the most basic, I know the freedom of eternal
limitlessness. I also know the freedom of de-accumulation in the relative."

Q. 3: "The movement, please!" [Laughter]

F: "Who is seemingly wanting something so impatiently? Ha. [Laughter]
The stage is not quite set to understand the totality of the movement. Let me
offer another analogy. As with archetypes—images that can move about via
particles—energy-consciousness also moves about in wave-particle form. Pure
consciousness might manifest, but it doesn't remain in that condition for long
among persons. All humans could just be were it not for the corrupting of pure
consciousness. The consciousness can perceive itself, but programming convinces
the corrupted consciousness that it is not consciousness at all but is 'a boy' or 'a
girl' or 'a wife' or 'a husband,' or 'a good person' or 'a bad person,' on and on and
on. And all of those have agendas, defined and taught by cultures, and the goals
of the taught agendas demand constant effort. Religions and spiritual movements and other philosophies intend to make you a 'better' person or even a
'noble' person. Consider the actual aim of that: to make a better persona? You
may as well join me on my next trip to the deserts of the Southwest region and
try to work with the mirages that you think you see there and convert them into
'better mirages.' [Laughter] You laugh. A few months ago, that was your life's
ambition! Ha. [More laughs] You might as well try to 'save' mirages. You may
as well try to 'ennoble' mirages. You might as well tell mirages to 'be heartened,'
that you 'bring good news that they will not have to suffer the unbearable heat
for long but will soon be lifted up and rewarded with eternal existence in a cool
place, not a hot place.' What silliness. What arrogance. What delusion. [Pause]
Persons take abstractions to be the real. Since we know that light/energy has a
particle form, consider the real—the consciousness—to be concrete."

Q3: "I can't."

F: "Ha. Maybe you can. Let's try now to understand the movement to manifestation: if energy/light strikes something with an existing nervous system, the
light 'solidifies' and what some thought to be an 'abstraction' is actually 'matter-
form-energy-consciousness.' If the energy/light strikes something without a
nervous system, it's reflected; so either consciousness solidifies or reflects, manifests or doesn't, depending on whether or not it strikes something with a nervous
system that can interact with the energy in the form in which it arrives. On this

planet, the item that it strikes that has a nervous system that allows for manifestation just happens to be a plant. The energy does not arrive on earth in a fashion that is usable to humans with nervous systems because the human nervous system cannot process the conscious-energy in the form in which it arrives. Only after the energy changes form, via the process in plants, is it usable by humans. No plants? No manifested consciousness. No manifested consciousness? No humans or animals. An example of reflecting is found in what's called 'moonlight.' Moonlight is merely the light of the sun (or nuclear furnace) reflected off the surface of an object that has no nervous system. That which appears to be an emptiness of blackness and void around the moon is not that at all—the waves and particles of light are the fullness…they surround the moon and fill the entire space, but the eye does not see the non-reflected light since it's neither reflected from the surface of the moon nor manifested in a nervous-system-possessing-form." [NOTE: for further explanation, you may visit floydhenderson.com and read article number 2]. Please enter the silence of contemplation.

REALIZATION:
No Mind, Part Five

F: "Finally, here's the last understanding that you must 'get' to understand completely the nature of consciousness and its movement. [Pause] Let's go back to the ice cube. The ice cube is a system, really. A system is any complex whole marked by an organized arrangement. Organized arrangements just evolve as a result of consciousness. In this universe, an organization simply evolved…over a period of billions of years. As a result of the organization of the universe that happened to evolve, an organization on this planet also evolved…over a period of millions of years. At the root of that organization was hydrogen, oxygen and carbon and the helium mentioned earlier. The ice cube in our example is a system of two hydrogen atoms and one oxygen atom that, if organized into a particular space in clusterings, interact in a certain way at a certain temperature as a result of an organizing field of consciousness. That's the key to any system: the organizing consciousness is present. Put water into an ice tray and place the tray in a freezer and the process that results in what appears to be a 'cube' just happens automatically as a result of that consciousness. No one guides the process. The same happens when an oak tree ultimately results in a forest of oaks or when friction between two humans ultimately results in a race. Do you remember our earlier discussion of entropy? I made the point that entropy guarantees that all except the real shall change, but the change is only in appearance. When that ice cube melts, a change in appearance occurs, but the essence of the cube—the hydrogen and oxygen atoms—remains the same. So it is with food-bodies that come and go. The appearance changes...the essence remains. Later, as the cube undergoes the effects of entropy, then the field that organized that cube suddenly unmanifests from that place. It moves. [Q3 nods in understanding] As with electrical currents, it is not seen as it moves, but it moves and it's real, nonetheless. The organizing consciousness that allows all systems to function as they function, that consciousness itself, remains as a field or expanse that extends infinitely. It is not limited by time or space or form or shape. Consciousness might re-manifest if the circumstances are suitable but will not remanifest if circumstances are not suitable. 'Suitable circumstances' can include the circumstance that allowed for the formation of this universe when consciousness provided the organization of a system that allowed an original hydrogen atom to manifest in a perfectly-void vacuum. The consciousness guided that atom to split and eventually to fuse into a group of four which then formed a helium atom. When the two interacted, that act released an immeasurable amount of energy. That seminal function in the case of this universe is now the same system that is functioning at the core of what we call the sun. Understand the functioning of the sun and you understand the origin of this universe and all universes. That fusion process occurs at the core of the nuclear furnace that is supplying heat energy and light energy to this solar system. 'Suitable circumstances' can also include the circumstances that evolved on this planet that allowed for a system that organized plants and allowed them to flourish. 'Suitable circumstance' includes a system that allows photosynthesis to occur. That process eventually resulted in another system and another 'suitable circumstance' for consciousness to manifest in a plant that could be consumed and would eventually allow for the movement of consciousness from one space to another on earth. And a 'suitable circumstance,' namely the 'demise' of a food-body, allows for the unmanifestation and movement of that conscious-energy which will return to the field or expanse that extends infinitely and that is not limited by time or space or form or shape. Circumstances can also allow consciousness to re-manifest ... or not. [Pause] We've discussed the prerequisites for manifestation of consciousness on this planet, namely, plants and photosynthesis. We've discussed the prerequisites for the manifestation of consciousness into the space of a food-body. The prerequisites for contaminating the consciousness and producing the illusion of a 'mind' include words, letters, language, superstitions, traditions, beliefs, ideas, shared communications, efforts by persons to use all that to control other persons, the perpetuation of more concepts, the taking of imagined worlds as real, images taken to be reality, misperceptions, an imagined 'I' in the world, the 'I' taking desires and fears and needs to be real, faulty neurotransmitters, and chemical imbalances. All contribute to the constantly-in-motion thinking mind."

Q: "But if the consciousness that You Are has been freed of all contaminants, how can feelings of anger or joy happen? You admitted that you still have feelings."

F: "Feelings happen...via the food-body and the functioning of the brain. I don't experience them. They're witnessed, that's all. Pure consciousness is natural. Emotional intoxication is unnatural and is rooted in the agenda of false identities. Parts of the brain, via electrical and chemical functioning, can trigger fight-or-flight responses. So it is. That's natural at times and unnatural at times, depending on whether a threat to the food-body is real or imagined. Pure consciousness knows the real. Illusions are not even considered. When contaminated consciousness triggers a reaction based in the false belief that something harmless is harmful—consider the snake in the rope—that is not natural. A person can try to live supernaturally, driven by the illusions of magical thinking, and that is not natural; a person can live unnaturally, driven by the illusions of contaminated consciousness; or living can happen naturally when consciousness is freed of the contamination that results in the disquietudes of a thinking mind, when freed of the influence of concepts, when in touch with reality, and when freed of believing lies or myths or superstitions or any of the other insane notions set forth by persons in any culture." Please enter the silence of contemplation.

REALIZATION: NO self ...
NO Self ... NO SELF, Part One

[Note: This is typically where the nisarga yoga "loses" most seekers who have not already abandoned this yoga]

F: "Realization is marked by the abandoning of all concepts. On this seven-step 'journey,' we've used many concepts to remove concepts, not unlike the proverbial thorn used to remove a thorn. If you have something within you like a thorn, and you use a thorn to get rid of that which was within, that which was causing your misery, what effort need remain after the removal? The work is done; the tools required for the task—the thorns needed to remove the thorn— are no longer required. What further exercises could be indicated? Realized, You will not know any concern about any thorns from 'the past.' You will not long for any thorn to return. You will not save spare thorns just in case they might be needed in 'the future.' You will not work to maintain Your 'state of non-thorn- ness.' It's all gone, all dissolved. It just happened automatically when the last concept dis-appeared."

Q: "So there's not even one concept you believe in any longer?"

F: "Until the final concept is released, realization will not happen. If you have nine thorns in your hand, would you be free of all misery and pain if you removed only eight? All must go."

Q: "But how can anyone work a job, pay bills, meet responsibilities without some ideas?"

F: "We'll be discussing 'AS IF' living soon. For now, let's focus on one of the last concepts that persons love to cling to: the 'Supreme Self.' My teacher Maharaj made clear that the ideas of self and even not-self also eventually dissolve. Even those concepts, ultimately, are useless. Let's review the 'selves' that are discussed in the teaching: first, there's the 'personal self' that believes 'I am this' or 'I am that.' Via programming, the list of all the personas becomes very long: boy or girl, son or daughter, Christian or Hindu or Muslim or Jew, student, graduate, employee, young adult, friend, acquaintance, lover, spouse, enemy, mortal enemy, owner of this or that, adult, senior citizen, grandmother or grandfather, and finally 'the deceased,' 'the dearly-departed,' or 'the saint.' [Laughter] Again, you laugh. How many a few months ago were buying into one or more of those roles? [A few hands are raised; eventually, all are raised.] So that's 'the self,' the false self, the personality/personalities, the false roles being played. Shakespeare said that 'all the world's a stage and all the men and women, merely players.' If you complete all seven steps of the journey from that false 'I' to the reality of seeing all of the false and thus the truth, along the way you come to know the 'True Self.' You understand that Pure Witness, the consciousness freed of all the limiting contaminants that resulted in an existence that was dominated by beliefs in myths and lies and misperceptions. Some might call that 'the super-personal I Am'—beyond any identity with a person/persona. Some call it the 'I Amness' or the "Is-ness." Actually, we saw that the 'True Self step' was merely the platform from which we could see above all the illusions and glimpse what some call the 'Impersonal Absolute—The Unmanifested—The Supreme Self—The Infinite Self—That.' The problem is, when many perceive 'That' and begin describing themselves as 'Supreme Selves,' most have simply added another label, another concept, another thorn."

Q2: "How could it be a thorn to know the Ultimate Self? I thought that was the final goal."

F: "Tell me what your relative existence would be like if you know you are that 'Ultimate Self'?"

Q2: [Pausing] "I'm giving that some thought. I know it's a trick question. Ha." [Laughter]

F: "You've already failed. [Laughter] Who is thinking? Who wants to answer the right way? Who thinks she is now 'Supreme'? [More laughs] Let me answer for you. You imagine that if you know that you're a 'Supreme Self,' the remainder of the relative existence will be marked by your being much more…more loving in the awareness of the At-one-ment, a 'much better person,' a 'more helpful person.' In fact, I'll bet that you even become 'noble.' [Laughter] From that position, you would imagine that the world is a 'better place' as a result of your improving and that you could then change the world and eventually have a huge impact on the entire globe. You'll think that you can 'help people' and can guide them to become 'good' and 'better,' like you." [Laughter]

Q2: "That's not really the way that …. [F. frowns, smiles] Okay, it might be that way to some degree. [Laughter. F. stares, smiles] Okay, to a large degree." [Laughter]

F: "To realize is to know that the world was only in you, in your mind, and that you've never been in the world. It's to know that you can't be 'in the world,' for the world is an imagining in the mind of persons. As many worlds exist as there are persons to imagine the way things are. That Which You Are, and which all is, is that most basic 'building block' that cycles and recycles, or not. You're that invisible, infinitesimal, infinite, sub-atomic, sub-molecular speck of energy-consciousness that happened to find its way into a plant that was consumed and relayed via friction to an egg that evolved automatically into a food-body. That manifested speck of consciousness, once contaminated, believed itself to be a body-mind that has since experienced experiences for 'x' number of years. In truth, that speck is nothing more than the light in which everything seemed to appear. And the contaminated consciousness subsequently took every appear-ance to be real. Now, you want to take yourself to be a 'Supreme Self.' That's another want, another desire. Who is wanting? I've witnessed persons fighting for their 'Supreme Self' label as much as he [pointing at a participant] fought for his 'husband' label. Go right ahead with that identity, if you can know clearly that the unmanifested consciousness has none of the attributes associated with 'self-ness,' such as a form, a mind, an eternal beingness as a being, longing, desiring, or ideas about 'better than' or 'good.' Stop seeking more; know the bliss of 'less.' Persons seek everything; the Realized know the bliss of the nothing. The Void is all." Please enter the silence of contemplation.

REALIZATION:
NO SELF ... NO Self ... NO SELF, Part Two

Q: "I'm still having trouble with the point that no Supreme SELF exists."

F: "Who is having trouble ... with anything?"

Q: "But wait a minute. You named the personality by using the word 'self' and then told us it was false, so that was fairly easy to release. [F. twists lips and stares] Okay, maybe not so easy [laughter] but eventually released anyway. Now, it just seems that if the 'condition' or 'state' of 'Supreme Self' is named and you're now telling us it's false, then it's more difficult to let go of."

F: "And I will never tell you that any 'Ultimate Truth' can be stated. I will tell you that any label is ultimately false. I shared a quote earlier, explaining that 'the Tao that can be stated in not the eternal Tao.' [Pause] Once you look at a door under an electron microscope and see the microscopic elements, you know that the door is not what it appears to be, is not at all what they told you a door is, and is not what you've believed all your life that a door is. So the question again is, 'Who wants to be "The Supreme" instead of admitting that this food-body seated before me is just a temporary clustering of elements that for a limited time can serve as a space for the manifesting of the cycling conscious-energy that is permanent?' What is permanent is real; what is temporary and what is like a door—appearing to be something that it's not—cannot define What You Are. But once you see those sub-atomic particles that the door actually is, would you call either them or the door 'The Supreme' or 'The Ultimate'? [Laughter] Only an ego-state will fight for such titles. [Pause] I shared with you earlier some passages from the manuscript of a book that I'm writing. Let me read another section from that...the response to a question from my editor. [Thumbs through some pages...then reads]:

Editor: ...I know that modern science is confirming this teaching, as in the new revelations regarding the 'Field of Consciousness,' but is this understanding compatible with the newest teachings in physics, such as the 'strings theory'?

F: Absolutely. My Teacher said decades ago that science would one day catch up with the ancients' understanding and prove that the teachings are fact. Such is happening. Since strings are reportedly the lowest common denominator of everything, smaller than atoms, smaller than electrons, smaller than the mass of protons and neutrons at the core of electrons, then the understanding of the science of strings shows us that the only thing which makes you appear to be different from me—or from a piano, or from a tree—is the vibrational pattern of the strings. And since the strings are simply energy in motion, and since the strings know automatically what to do when they are manifested in a human as opposed to in a piano as opposed to in a tree, then the teaching of strings proves this Understanding, scientifically. We are consciousness-energy. We are all That, all the same, all one, with only appearances leading us to believe we are separate or different. We are not. Physics now proves that We Are That. It has proven that We Are All One. We are the strings or the smallest element or the tiniest 'whatever' that exists. Use whatever name you choose to refer to that one permanent 'thing' from which all is composed when manifest. More recently, the strings theory had been modified by some who now claim that the 'sparticle' might be even more basic than the string. No matter. What is Real is whatever that most basic, singular, non-dual 'thing' is, period. Now, call 'That' what you want, the truth is that Easterners have known for about 40,000 years that everything in the universe that is manifested or not is nothing more nor less than a manifestation or not-manifestation of That, of the one True That-ness. Call it 'strings' or 'That' or 'sparticle' or 'energy with consciousness.' That is All, and That is All there Is. [Quoted from The Twice-Stolen Necklace Murders, subsequently published in 2003]

F: "Only an ego-state wants to fight for the right to be considered 'The Supreme' or 'The Ultimate.' I speak to you of the no-self, no-Self, no-SELF Reality...that is all. All these terms are nothing more than words and concepts that are used to get you to the no-word silence and the no-concept bliss." Please enter the silence of contemplation.

REALIZATION:
NO SELF ... NO Self ... NO SELF, Part Three

F: "Granted, there's a period on the so-called 'journey' when SELF-consciousness was a prerequisite for losing self-consciousness, but now the understanding has matured. I'm no longer speaking to visitors who are at the 'wet charcoal' or 'dry charcoal' level. Consciousness is speaking to consciousness, and the consciousness to which I speak should be so purified by now that it's like gunpowder, ready for these pointers to ignite a degree of awareness that explodes away the final illusions and results in full realization. As we were taking the steps, of course discussion of the 'self' and the 'Self' and the 'Supreme Self' had to happen, but when totally in touch with reality, no concepts are given credibility any longer. No distinctions or labels are taken to be true. [Pause] You know now that you're beyond the 'being' and the 'non-being.' 'Being' implies a 'self.' A 'no-self' is implied by 'non-being.' You Are beyond both 'self' and 'no-self,' if you will. The 'Supreme Self' is a term used to point to that which is beyond both, but the Absolute—being at rest—knows neither a Self or a SELF. Only when consciousness is manifested can the I Am and the I Am That be known. That 'non-manifested state' is like the deep-sleep state. Consciousness is there, but consciousness is not aware of itself. Persons mistake the 'beingness' to be some body-mind-personality 'self' that is being. Recall that 'self' is defined as 'individuality' or 'personality.' There is no Supreme Individuality or Supreme Personality. There is no Supreme Body or Supreme Mind or Supreme Entity or Supreme Anything. Realized, all former imaginings of greatness give way to the reality of smallness. It is understood that the early programming to accumulate, and the years spent in endless effort to accumulate, resulted in dissatisfaction instead of satisfaction. That dissatisfaction set the stage for the seven-step journey of SELF-Inquiry that, along the way, revealed the false 'self' and the 'True Self' and the awareness of awareness. After realization, de-accumulation just happens, automatically. The fear-based and desire-based drive to work to be 'good' and to 'become better' in order to get a reward now and to insure the continuation of an imagined body-mind suddenly ends; religious and spiritual personas are seen to be 'transitional stages' rather than the 'ultimate state.' Realized, the relative existence is no longer dominated by fears and desires and emotional intoxication. The realized understand that What We Truly Are is beyond both the being-ness and non-beingness...beyond 'self-ness' and even beyond 'non-selfness.' The realized know the peace which happens in the impersonal relative existence after the last identity of any kind goes, and the realized know the non-relative, impersonal Absolute as well." Please enter the silence of contemplation.

REALIZATION: No Single Cause

F: "Upon realization, another duality disappears: the credit-blame duality. The realized know that assigning credit to one source or assigning blame to one source is to ignore the reality of an infinite chain of happenings. Here's a simple example that might be relevant. Last week, driving along the road that leads out here, the rear tire of a car ahead of me threw a pebble against my windshield and cracked it. You've all probably had a similar experience? [Nods in agreement] What caused that?"

Q: "The rear tire of the car ahead of you."

Q2: "Actually, the driver of the car was responsible. I think people who do that should have to pay for the cost of the repair."

F: "I'm glad you said that since your comment will let us see how wrong that type thinking is and let me offer the pointer about 'cause'." [Participant displays a mock frown. Laughter from group] As I passed that car and drove farther along the road, I caught up with a truck that was hauling gravel…and spilling it all along the roadway. The pebbles in the road, one of which was thrown into my windshield earlier, most likely came from that truck. Now who's to blame for my cracked windshield?"

Q2: "The driver of the dump truck."

Q3: "The manager of the hauling company who allowed the truck to haul gravel without a cover over the top to prevent slippage."

F: "The manager? Or could it have been the owner of the hauling company who was too cheap to provide covers or too negligent to be certain that covers were being used?"

Q4: "I'll play along: it was the fault of the highway patrol that is not efficient enough to pull over those creating hazards on the road." [Laughter from group]

F: "Or the legislators who misappropriated funds to their pet projects and underfunded the highway patrol? [More laughs] Okay, enough. You get the picture. A series of events evolved in a way that, at a particular moment, a particular set of circumstances also evolved that resulted in a broken windshield on my vehicle. And if we wanted to play this game a little longer, you've already shown that we could trace the cause back millions of years to the circumstances that resulted in a boulder being broken down into pebbles, one of which millions of years later struck my windshield. But billions of years before that, an atom appeared in a vacuum, maybe even spit forth from an adjacent universe. And that atom split and then split again and then formed a mutated atom and those two collided and…bang…that collision caused a chain reaction that resulted in our boulder being formed billions of years later. And then millions of years after that, the boulder atrophied into huge stones and then rocks and then pebbles, and because of that happening and because of a truck and an owner and a manager and a driver and a construction project and an inefficient highway patrol and a driver and a car ahead of me, my windshield broke. Ha. Look at the billions of events that had to occur over a period of billions of years in order for my windshield to be damaged. Yet arrogantly, persons want to claim that they know exactly what's causing any particular happening. Persons want to tell you the one cause that they think is behind whatever is happening. They want to credit one thing or one entity or one power. Or they want to blame one thing or one entity or one power."

Q: We're back to the pointer you offered before."

F: "Specifically?"

Q: "About over-simplifying the 'cause' of anything. You said something like 'the cause of everything is everything that's happened before'."

Q2: "And you said that if we don't realize that, we'll buy into the ancient myths about a single causer and a single creator of matter and energy. And you said that if one can imagine infinity beyond this manifestation, then one should be able to know the infinity before this manifestation."

F: "Well, that's not quite the way I put it, but your version is accurate enough. The point is just as you said: the cause of all is all that has ever happened. Forget seeking a prime cause. Who wants to know why a particular happening is happening? Who wants to be the one who understands it all? Who wants more knowledge and more learning and more information and more proficiency and more wisdom than others have? The Eternal Truth cannot be spoken. What's to know? What's to say? After the thorns have removed all thorns, who cares about any of the thorns? Enjoy the thorn-free relative existence of less knowledge, less learning, less…period." Please enter the silence of contemplation.

REALIZATION: AS IF Living

F: "I've mentioned five stages that can be transitioned if one takes The Seven-Step Journey to Reality. Persons are exposed to twenty years of programming and conditioning in their first years. In the Western cultures especially, the programming is to get, to accumulate. Afterwards, most persons pass the next twenty years in the second stage, consumed with the process of accumulating. Fears and desires mark their passage. Some few might ask, 'Who am I?' and move into the fourth stage as they begin a process of Self-Inquiry, investigation, and discovery. Most persons will never make that shift and will continue trying to accumulate until the relative existence ends. For the few who focus on the search for an answer to that critical question, some will complete all seven steps along the path and reach the fourth stage of realization. So what does the remainder of the relative existence look like for the realized? The fifth stage is AS IF Living. In the novel I'm writing, I've included these pointers [picks up papers and reads]:

De-accumulation is the mark of freedom from the early programming. After that, one can live AS IF, as if this life is the real but knowing it's not. The realized can then enjoy whatever remains of this relative existence, free for the first time—free of educational indoctrination, free of spiritual indoctrination, free of religious indoctrination, free of political indoctrination, free of economic indoctrination. Free. Independent. Period.

Let the exercises and concepts serve the purpose of bringing about an understanding of the differentiation in the true and the false, and then toss it all away and live simply and naturally, as if. To live AS IF is to know that THAT is all that is Real, but even the realized meet the requirements of a food-body and honor commitments made in the relative while the consciousness is manifested. Realized, You know that You Are Light, that I Am Light, but employment can still happen, merely without attachment. Responsibilities can be met and challenges will be handled, but without emotional intoxication."

Q: "As was the case when you were still employed to teach even after realization. You said that 'teaching happened' as opposed to 'you taught'."

F: "Actually, I said, 'Teaching happened...or not.' Sometimes it did, sometimes it didn't. So it was."

[Continues reading] Know that all which is believed to be observable is 'seen' in the flickering images of the light that plays before our eyes. It is not the Real, any more than the actors flicking across the screen of your television are Really there. They are but images in the mind. So is all that is 'seen.' Be aware that the Unseen, the Unseeable, is the Real. Be done with worrying about the false images of this manifestation we call our 'lives' or 'others' or 'self.'

Then, you'll enjoy the present moment, the Eternal Now, as long as the consciousness is manifest. And you'll have no expectations to meet nor any future rewards to long for nor any future punishments to spend a lifetime trying to avoid. Free of those, you are free of the control of those who dream up or pass along all those concepts that form the prison called 'the mind' that traps persons in fear, misery, depression, or all the addictive behaviors that follow those defects in an effort to try to escape them. As long as anyone tries to maintain a religious-spiritual image or role, he will be at the mercy of those who would manipulate him with religion or with spirituality. They'll tell him that a religious person does this and a spiritual person does that, and to keep his religious or spiritual image, he'll do what they say. Then, he's theirs. For some, both states can serve a purpose, but both are to be transcended. They are but bridges that allow us to cross the degrees of separation. In one does not transcend those, he is vulnerable, and thus in fear, and frustrated eventually as a result of being controlled by others. There is no freedom, and thus no peace, living in 'their' world with 'their' mind doing the driving. After transitioning those steps, the journey can continue to full realization and then to the peace of living AS IF, as if any of the relative existence is real but knowing that it's not." (From The Twice-Stolen Necklace Murders, subsequently published in 2003) Please enter the silence of contemplation.

THE FINAL SESSION

F: "So there you have it. Before we end this last session, I have some final considerations to offer. First, know that instability is a curse on 'relationships' in the relative existence. The realized have no 'relationship concerns' because there is no 'a' trying to relate to 'b.' Consciousness does not relate to consciousness. Consciousness is consciousness. End of story. The at-one-ment is known because it is known that I Am That and You Are That and all that is, is That. Differing vibrational frequencies that account for differing appearances suddenly mean nothing. For the realized, should a feeling like anger arise, it will be witnessed as it rises and falls. Such is the AS IF life in the relative. Realized, no ego-states exist that can trigger the emotion of anger that results in a reaction, and then in a reaction to that reaction, and then in a chain of reactions afterwards. For persons not realized, the instability of duality will continue until the consciousness is no longer manifested, and the relative existence will be marked by a series of actions inspired by ego-states and the subsequent acts of emotional intoxication. The realized observe with detachment the natural processes of entropy as elements disorganize and organize and disorganize again; persons not realized suffer the slings and arrows of the outrageous fortunes of the chaos to which they are addicted. Pure consciousness watches entropy happen; persons 'experience' chaos. [Turning to one participant] Imagine how different your 'experience' would have been when your wife left if you'd understood that some 'relationships' can even be affected by the law of entropy. You'd have witnessed the process of entropy rather than allowing the ego-state of 'husband' to drive you to suicidal or homicidal thoughts. 'Witnessing' vs. 'thinking.' [Participant nods in agreement. To group...] All instability occurs in the movement of contaminated consciousness. Impure consciousness can be known to be in chaotic movement because it's marked by the sense that 'I am close to some power' but later 'Now I am not as close to the power' or by thoughts that 'I am more fit at some times than others' or the idea that 'clarity has come but has gone' or 'I am better after that last experience' or 'after doing all my rituals I am far better than before.' With that constant movement, persons shift from the belief that they have 'got it together' to later deciding 'I don't have it as together as I thought and thus need to do some more stuff.' That's the result of the consciousness of truth 'coming and going' as the 'mind' fights to cling to its identification with the body-mind-personality triad while the 'True Self'—the pure consciousness—tries to answer the question, "Who am I?' If the relative problem centers in 'the mind,' then to be at peace 'the mind' must be stable. But a 'mind' can never be stable for it is the 'storehouse' of the very lies and beliefs and ideas and attitudes that generate chaos in the relative. 'The mind' cannot be stable for it is searching, always on the move, always looking for something to bring happiness by satisfying desires and alleviating fears, all of which are illusory. To abide in perfect, inviolable peace is to reach, and then be firmly stabilized in, the 'destination.' When we reach our destination on a trip, we stop movement, right? As long as we are 'on a path' or 'on a journey' or 'seeking with great effort,' or 'doing The Work' or 'regularly engaged in never-ending religious or spiritual exercises,' persons cannot realize that We Are the destination and What We Are is That, which is so stable that It has remained unchanged for infinity and will remain unchanged for infinity. Of course, some claim that all the 'exercises' were required in order to finally realize. Typically, they are just distractions. [Pause] Now, if you know that the manifested consciousness lacks that stability, then know that impurities remain. Certain vestiges of conditioning and programming remain. You are not completely out of your mind, which is not your mind at all but is actually theirs. They have co-opted the 'mind' that they created in the first place. The journey does not involve taking back your mind from them. The journey involves seeing there is no mind. There is only a collection of ideas and emotions and beliefs that are all lies. Peace doesn't come when you 'take control of' your thoughts and your mind. Peace doesn't come when you find 'positive' thoughts to replace your 'negative' thoughts. Peace doesn't come when 'right thinking' replaces 'wrong thinking.' All thinking is a lie. Peace comes when you realize that all that you've ever been told is a lie, when you realize that all thoughts and ideas and concepts are lies, and when all the lies are seen to be lies. Then, the 'mind' ends and its influence on your relative existence ends. Peace and stability come when the last belief in their concepts goes."

Q: "So if we can't continue to come here each week, and I know that the consciousness that I Am is not yet fixated in that state of peace and stability...?" [Lifts hands, shrugs shoulders]

F: "Then more 'work' is required before all 'work' will naturally end, but no more visits here can happen. What you needed to hear has been stated. Now, it but needs to be understood. Should the understanding not be fully established, then I have a cassette tape of the vision that I suggest you use daily until the realization explodes into full consciousness. Also, I'm writing a couple of meditation guides that lead the reader step-by-step to the full realization. You can get a copy of the manuscripts and use those on a daily basis until the understanding is firmly fixed." [Readers can see the reference by visiting the main website.]

Q2: "I don't want these sessions to end!"

F: "Then you've just told me that you need more 'work.' Use the tape and the guides. When it all ends with no attachment, that is the beginning ... the 'new' beginning. Then you'll know that there is no end and no beginning and only an uninterrupted continuum of cyclings. See the cycles, witness all that rises and falls, attach to none of it, and have fun in the remaining relative existence. Know that 'it don't mean a thing.' [Laughter] And in knowing it don't mean a thing, there too ends the search for 'meaning.' When all searching ends, true rest begins. Now, go, and just be, or do until you can just be … in peace." Please enter the silence of contemplation.

GLOSSARY OF TERMS

(NOTE: This glossary is for those in the stages prior to Full Realization. More is revealed about each term on the Advaita website mentioned on the copyright page. You may search that site for more details and for the explanations that are offered to seekers who are farther along the path.)

Person: Anyone not Realized; a persona; the outer physical self that is limited to self-identification with the body and with the mental roles dreamed up for the body to play; one who believes that the roles he/she plays actually identify who he/she is; one who believes his images are real; one who believes the images of others are real. [While the realized are free of ego and ego-states, persons are fully absorbed in false identities and are driven by the egotism that accompanies all assumed roles].

Realization: The understanding that results after completing the entire Advaita "journey" and being free of all personas (all false identities); the awareness or knowingness that results when one has been freed of the effects of programming and conditioning and no longer believes the lies that his culture claims are the truth; that "state" which results when the contaminated consciousness has been returned to a pure "condition" that is free of concepts, ideas, emotional intoxication and belief in the lies that had been taken as truth as a result of enculturation; the restoration of the consciousness That You Are to its pure "condition"; the "highest" knowledge (derived via meditation from within, never from without) that is the complete awareness of the unity of all things.

Persona: From Latin, meaning "mask"; one trapped in an ego-state, a false identity, a personality.

Ego: from Latin, meaning "I." Specifically, it is the pronoun used by those who believe any false identity to be real; the source of perceived separation; the source of fighting to preserve image; it follows assumption of a false identity, is used to defend false roles, and always propels a role to "super" status. (For example, as soon as one assumes the role of "a wife," she immediately becomes "Super Wife," deserves nothing less than a "Super Husband," and will expect to be treated in a super fashion. The case is the same with "husband" and the same with all roles. "Super Teacher" must have "Super Students" to survive, and "Super Teacher" will fight with non-super students as if a life-and-death struggle is under way, so thoroughly is the ego-state taken to be the real.)

Ego-state: that "state" in which a persona exists, taking false roles to be true identity. An ego-state is always identified by placing a word after "I am" (such as, "I am a spouse"; "I am a lover"; "I am an employee," "I am a teacher," etc.)

I Am, I Amness, Is-ness: The statement of awareness by Pure Consciousness which knows that it has temporarily manifested in a space, that it is the conscious-energy that is currently abiding in the state of Amness, but that also knows It Is That...the singular, most basic That Which All Is; the expression of Pure Consciousness.

True Self: the Pure, post-Realization Consciousness that witnesses purely and accurately as long as it is manifested, aware that no subject-object duality exists and aware of the Oneness. The Pure Witness.

Atonement: Not a reconciliation between humans and an imagined external power (conceived by man and bearing the image of men) but instead the aware-ness of the at-one-ment, of the Oneness, of the fact that all is only That and nothing more.

Witness: That impartial, objective observer that witnesses all happenings in the relative existence without attachment or reaction or emoting; in the early going, object-subject observation can happen. At the True Self level, Pure Witnessing happens without any subject-object delusions, with full knowledge of the lies of the relative existence, and with full awareness of the truth of the Absolute and the Oneness of all.

Subject-Object: A dualistic perception, believing that separates exist and can be seen, such as, "I" (subject) see "you" (object). The Realized, aware of the Oneness, see no separates and know that all is One.

Relative existence: The existence that persons take to be the real; unlike the Absolute that is completely pure and unadulterated and unchanging, all in the relative is marked by change and instability and misperception; persons taking the relative to be real live with a limited, three-dimensional perspective, focused only on five-sense experiences; persons in the relative live with no conscious contact with Reality and with no awareness of the sixth sense.

Absolute: The Ultimate Reality or the Great Reality, meaning simply...that which is real; that "field" in which consciousness is at rest; that "field" from which consciousness has been drawn into manifestation; that "field" to which consciousness returns once no longer manifested; THAT Which All Is; the conscious-energy Itself; that purest, unadulterated "whatever" that All Is; that lowest, tiniest common "something" which All in this universe and all universes IS, without beginning and without end ... never-changing; the conscious-energy that All Is, whether manifested or not.

Manifestation: Conscious-energy-light can be reflected off objects without a nervous system or absorbed (manifested) into something with a nervous system; on earth, the consciousness-bearing energy is absorbed into plants that can be consumed by humans/animals that are merely a space in which the consciousness manifests temporarily.

Programming and conditioning: The process whereby pure consciousness, manifested in what is primarily space but is called a "human" or "person" by the non-Realized, is contaminated with ideas, concepts, dogma, teachings, preachings, ad infinitum, all of which are false; the process whereby the ignorance of the masses (which they call their "knowledge") becomes the learned ignorance of their offspring.

"The mind": The storehouse of those contaminants of the originally pure consciousness; humans are born with a brain but not with a mind; the mind is that storehouse of all the lies and concepts and knowledge/ignorance that persons accumulate; once filled with the nonsense that persons dream up, it becomes the source of all misery, constantly in movement, constantly imagining desires/fears as a result of programming and conditioning. Persons each believe that they have what they call "my mind," but there is only "their mind," the mind that is created by programmers who pass along their ideas, their beliefs, and their concepts that the programmed then take to be their own.

Natural living: Living that happens without agenda, unfolding from a position of neutrality; it is the type of existence that unfolds for the Realized since they are free of all false identities and ego-states and thus are not driven to manipulate, to accumulate, or to control (or to seek and manipulate imaginary, supernatural power in an effort to control).

Supernatural living: Living that is based in magical thinking rather than fact, marked by constant attempts to bargain with or manipulate or appeal to an external power that they believe can grant their wishes or share power with them in their efforts to control; living marked by spiritual and emotional intoxication of the type that only ego-states can experience; the lifestyle followed by persons, so dominated by desires/fears and efforts to control people, places, things, and events that an imagined power (created in the imagination and the image of men) is endlessly sought and petitioned; a life lived by persons who are out of touch with reality; a life lived by persons who believe the Great Reality is a person (with supernatural powers); that which can be a transitional "stage," not quite halfway along the seven-step "journey" to Reality that can move persons from their belief that the "I" is real to knowing the Absolute Which Truly Is the Real; a lifestyle adopted by the masses during times of greatest fear or perceived attack; a lifestyle marked by rigidity and closure to alternative explanations; the type living that prohibits questioning and thus locks persons into believing in all of the false teachings of their culture; the type of living marked by beliefs that leave persons unaware of their inner resource and inspires dependency, especially on imaginary outer resources.

Magical thinking: Thinking based in non-fact, superstition, myth and belief in other-worldly powers; the belief that a micro-managing power in another realm (usually conceived as male in gender) is the single cause of all happenings on the planet; thinking inspired via religious or "spiritual" programming; thinking often inspired by abuse and trauma suffered in such a degree that a desire for rescue by some external power is wished or hoped for; thinking inspired by ego that wants control and therefore also wants a power at one's beck and call that can grant wishes; the fanciful thinking that leads persons to believe that they can petition a power in another realm that can then grant them control over people, places, things, weather, and all events; the type thinking that believes disasters are not events in nature but are punishments or signs delivered by an angry, other-worldly power; the type thinking that dismisses scientific facts and endorses blind, unquestioning faith; the type thinking that blocks all awareness of Reality and imprisons persons in the confines of the false concepts of "a mind."

Unnatural living: Living that is driven by the imagined fears/desires of persons who have taken their ego-states to be their real identity; in an effort to preserve their false identities, persons behave in self-destructive and destructive fashions in the relative existence; while That Which One Truly Is was never created and cannot be destroyed, persons are driven (though usually unconsciously) to destroy their false selves, those mental ego-states they take as their phony identities, and thus behave in a way that is contrary to the natural instinct to survive; among persons, the drive is for the false self to survive until the phony role playing results in so much misery that persons become driven to try to destroy the self (which can happen via Realization but more often happens through attack upon the body-mind that is playing the roles).

Self-destructive behaviors: Since persons take their bodies to be at the core of "who they are," and since they use their bodies to play out the false roles they accept as self-identification, it is the body that is usually attacked when persons become sick and tired of the phony roles and all the misery they generate; on occasion, the attack against the body is conscious and violent (as with suicides) but typically the attack is more subtle as persons try to destroy the body slowly with harmful habits, harmful foods, drinks, drugs, eating disorders, impulsive actions and risky behavior; self-destructive behaviors are also those behaviors that are typical of persons who are absorbed in false roles, who foster false images, and who sometimes know on some level that it is their assumption of their false identity and phony roles that is the major contributor to their misery. In truth, the false self can be abandoned (via the Advaita "path" to Realization) if one sees clearly it is false and then uncovers the Real, but most do not and thus try to destroy the body-mind that "houses" the false self; the desire to escape the false roles and all the chaos that they generate makes ego-states/ego a key source of addictive behavior that has at its core the desire to elude or shake off the misery of living the lies that all ego-states are and that all ego inspires.

Body-mind-personality triad: A triad is anything with three parts. Among persons, the three parts that they are conscious of (using their impure conscious-ness) are the physical body, the mind, and the personality (or personalities … the personas or roles that they are playing and take to be their true identity); believing in their "three-ness," they fail to know the unicity (that is, their Oneness with All); fixed in the delusion of a three-fold triad and not knowing the Oneness, persons believe in the multiplicity.

Multiplicity: The perception among persons that the world and the universe are made of multiple components rather than the one true THAT; the belief in the concepts of separate and different which, in turn, inspire judgment and sepa-ration, ego, superiority and inferiority, good and bad, right and wrong, better/best, and all dualistic thinking and wrong perceiving that prevents persons from knowing the unicity and being aware of the at-one-ment of all.

Unicity: The opposite of multiplicity; persons mistakenly perceive a multi-plicity of things that supposedly make up "this world"; in fact, all in this world is imagined, wrongly perceived. To understand unicity, understand the prefix "uni" ("one"). The universe is but One. All that exists is the one, single THAT; all does not have THAT in common but, instead, is in common.

Meditation (or contemplation): Originally, not the act of seeking the no-mind state but of seeking a quiet place and time to consider thoroughly any and all pointers offered by a teacher; it is during that act that all the false can be seen, all the truth can be known, the lie of duality can be seen, and truth of the unicity can come to light.

Duality: The great lie, the belief in separation (a belief that is rooted in false identity and the ego that always accompanies the assumption of ego-states as identities); the arbitrary and imagined division of all (which is actually One) into fictitious groups. For example, duality—taken only by persons to be real—results in a perception of separation based in superficial judgment followed by the cataloguing of all people and behaviors and things and events and places as either "good or bad," "right or wrong," "OK or not OK," "enough or not enough."

The Space: That grouping of elements that persons take to be "the body" and their "self"; the grouping in which the consciousness-energy manifests for a period. [To appreciate that what most take to be the body is actually mainly space, note the size of an urn that can contain all the remains after cremation.]

AS IF Living: The style of living that the Realized exhibit, seemingly living like persons but without persons' attachments, delusions, and emotional intoxication; the manner in which the Realized "finish out" the manifestation, meeting "responsibilities" and providing for the space while knowing full well that "this world" is nothing more than an imagining in the distorted perceptions of persons; a lifestyle that is unencumbered with attachment and emotional intoxication and belief in the lies of the culture; a lifestyle free of game playing and image perpetuation; a lifestyle unmarred by the emotions and emotional intoxication experienced by persons; a lifestyle during which the Realized can witness feelings rise and fall without any emotional intoxication, reacting, over-reacting, or setting off a chain of reactions (as happens with persons); a lifestyle free of the misery that is generated by the desires / fears of personas.

Emoting vs. Feeling: The Realized can feel without attachment and without a chain of reactions that result from emotional intoxication. Emoting, on the other hand, is what happens with persons—living in their false roles and ego-states—as they are perpetually intoxicated emotionally and constantly reacting and over-reacting to what they take to be "personal experiences" that are driven by desires/fears.

Desire/Fear: Two emotions experienced by persons that only appear to be different but always "appear" as one pair; both are based in illusion and both are actually the same, in fact. [To desire a mate is to fear aloneness or economic problems; to fear someone leaving is to desire that a false identity like "spouse" can be perpetuated. According to recent survey of 2000 recently-married men and women, the men married "because they were tired of the dating scene" and because "they thought they'd have more sex without the chase." Women listed as their top reasons, "He had a good job and income" and "His future prospects looked bright." Based in those answers, additional examples of the desire/fear link are seen: To desire a "wife" is to fear that the misery of "the dating scene" will continue; to desire a "wife" is to fear that too little sex will be experienced; to desire a husband is to fear their economic security will not happen or to fear they'll always have to provide that economic security for themselves; to desire a husband is to fear that one's economic future will not be secured. PS: Don't kill the messenger…just reporting the results of a survey that asked about "Why Men and Women Said They Married."] Thus, it can be seen that "desire" and "fear" are not two different emotions experienced by persons but are, in fact, inexorably linked. One will never manifest without the other, and neither will manifest without an ego-state having first been assumed; desire/fear is also one of the major roots of all co-dependency.

Co-dependencies: Co-dependencies are fostered when roles are assumed (since no role can stand alone). "Employee" needs an "employer" to exist. "Spouse" needs a "spouse" to exist. All role-assumption is accompanied by co-dependencies because no role can "stand alone" but must have another person assuming a counter role in order to sustain both roles; another source of unhappiness since persons with any dependency cannot be independent (free); thus, role assumption and its accompanying co-dependency rob persons of freedom and of happiness (and thereby are a main cause of misery as experienced by persons).

Understanding the Functioning of the Totality: "Functioning" refers to how all in this universe, and how all that is in all universes, has functioned and is functioning and will always function. "Totality" refers to every happening that has happened, is happening, and will happen infinitely. Upon Full Realization, the complete understanding comes of how all has happened and how all happens and how all will forever happen. How inclusive is that understanding? Among all that is understood are:

*** How this universe and all prior universes came to be;

*** How consciousness manifests in space containing a nervous system;

*** Where You Were prior to consciousness and manifestation;

*** What is relative and What Is Absolute;

*** Why no external power exists and why no truth can be found except within;

*** Why You Were never born and cannot die;

*** What happens when consciousness is no longer manifested;

*** How all cycles;

*** How the enculturation process puts persons to sleep even as they are certain they are awake;

*** The beginninglessness and the expanse of infinity;

*** The limitlessness;

*** Bliss via desirelessness;

*** The source of all suffering;

*** Freedom from the pursuit of meaning;

*** Infinite Cause;

*** The link between mind and fear;

*** Why "the mind" is a total illusion, and therefore

*** Why all perceived via "a mind" is false and is illusion;

*** Why you must be out of your mind to be sane;

*** Why all knowledge is nothing more than learned ignorance;

*** Why time and timelines are illusions;

*** How illusions are taken to be real by persons;

*** What the Oneness Truly Is;

*** What you are not; and

*** Who/What You Truly Are...to name but a portion of what becomes known.

The Drama of the Lie: When persons are programmed and conditioned to accept roles as who they are, they live the rest of their lives as if they are on stage, in the spotlight, and the center of attention. In accepting the lie as truth, they will live in a state of emotional intoxication, their ideas will be histrionic, and plagued by over-acting and over-reacting. Advaitins who teach by use of the original Sanskrit employ the term "lila," which means "play." Other definitions of the word "lila" include "pastime" or "amusement." The term "lila" is often used in conjunction with the word "maya" (meaning "appearance" or "illusion") in order to make the point that what persons take to be real is not. What persons think they are seeing and what they believe is happening in "this world" is nothing more than a play or a false drama. (Shakespeare made reference to the fact that persons sleepwalk through life and simply play the roles assigned to them by their culture when he said, "All the world's a stage, and all the men and women, merely players.") Persons, being asleep and thus unaware, take the play to be real and take their roles to be real when in fact it's all nothing more than an illusion or appearance. They are living the "Drama of the Lie." (Shakespeare later provided the antidote: "To thine own Self be true and it must follow as the night the day: thou canst not then be false to any man.") The Realized know that the entire manifestation in nature is nothing but an illusion (an appearance, a play, a drama) while also realizing that the absolute consciousness is the only reality. Persons "live" on stage, constantly playing one role after another and taking their roles to be their real identity. Just as an actor can take his part too seriously and internalize the role as an identity, so too can programmed and conditioned persons act out their roles so often and so seriously that they take the drama that they are a part of to be the real. That drama is really the "Drama of the Lie," wherein persons are behaving as if the play-acting they are engaged in is not play-acting at all; as if the roles they are playing actually define who they are; and as if the roles being played by others truly define who they are. It's all a lie. (One method used by some teachers to awaken those who are asleep to the truth is a psychodrama-type exercise called "The Theater of the Lie" in which a teacher will provide an opportunity for protégés to see all of the false roles they are playing, how their relative existence is nothing but an illusory drama, and how divesting themselves of all the ego-states they're using as assumed identities can clear the path for them to abandon the false self/selves and to know the True Self.

The Beginninglessness: Scientists in labs have now been able to reproduce the events that unfolded as this universe began: in a vacuum, a particle can simply manifest; other particles also form and then they all interact…being conscious of other particles. Eventually, in the case of this universe, the pace of their interactions resulted in an explosion of unimaginable force, followed within seconds by the formation of the first atoms (hydrogen and helium, which are still the most prevalent atoms in a universe that is like any body...mainly space). Those two interacted (atoms being conscious of other atoms) and began the chain of events that resulted in what is called "this universe." The particles had existed infinitely since neither matter nor energy can be created nor destroyed. Since no creation ever occurred, no creator could exist. Since All has always been, infinitely, no beginning happened and no end will happen. Infinity is infinity and was "as infinite" before the manifestation of the consciousness That You Are as it will "be infinite" following the unmanifestation of the consciousness That You Are.

The Expanse of Infinity: Many persons can easily imagine "infinity" after their "death" while at the same time ignoring the reality of infinity prior to, prior to all they perceive now. Infinite is infinite, not merely a "post-something infinity."

Infinite Cause: Persons seek to assign blame to one person or event or to one cause for "this" or for "that," pointing to a single cause. Those persons absorbed in magical thinking also want to claim the existence of a "Single or Prime Cause or Causer." The fact is that all happenings are caused by the accumulation of all prior happenings.

Discontinuity: Persons look one way on the outside (the image) but feel another way on the inside; persons feel "torn into pieces" and thus suffer the misery of discontinuity which happens when they try to combine the real with image. No image is real but is taken by persons to be real as a result of "not being true to Self." The illusion of discontinuity is especially taken to be real when a form that was once observable is no longer observable, such as happens when persons claim someone "died"; in fact, nothing was created and nothing was destroyed. All that seems observable is not what it appears to be at all. All appearance is illusion. The belief by persons that "appearances are real" will set the stage for persons to be trapped in the illusion of discontinuity and thus fail to know the unicity. From that perspective, persons will wrongly perceive that they are split, disconnected, separate and apart from. Sensing that they are disjointed and not whole, they will assume that they are in need of someone to make them feel whole or connected. Needs and wants and desires that always accompany fears will begin to drive persons. Destructive behaviors—that erroneously appear to persons in the relative to be constructive—will happen.

Infinite Continuity: Infinite continuity points toward a universe or universes that are limitless, unmanifested reality in which mass, events, and concepts like "time" seem to appear and seem to be real as the result of a belief in duality whereby imagined distinctions are assumed to be real. Infinite continuity makes clear that all is one, that reality/consciousness is all there is, and that nothing exists separate and apart from That Reality. There are no parts that are connected or interrelated. There are no parts at all. Nothing is relating. Conscious-energy is All there Is. The Realized, knowing that truth, only know the continuity; persons, not knowing the continuity, are trapped in their perspectives of duality and believe in separation and the judgment that always accompanies the belief that they are apart from. The result of the belief in being apart from is (a) the misery of feeling disconnected or (b) the ego/arrogance of being "good" or "better" and eventually "the best." Ego inspires more misery and all that persons call "relationship problems" in the relative.

"Death": A concept dreamed up by persons to label inaccurately the happening when something they thought they were observing is no longer observable. A concept dreamed up by persons who also believe that they (or others) have "created something" and "given birth to something" when elements simply combined in a process that happened automatically after an act of friction. In fact, what they thought they were seeing—regarding both "birth" and "death" and the "disappearance of other persons"—is not what was happening at all in reality. [Two examples: (a) Have you ever thought you really knew certain persons, only to find out that they were each showing the world a phony image and that image was not them at all? (b) Look at a steel beam with the naked eye, and then look at it with an electron microscope that allows you to see "below the surface" and see what's happening at an atomic level. The beam initially appeared to be one thing to you, but upon further investigation you can realize that it was not what it appeared to be at all.] Since nothing is created, nothing can be destroyed. Following the unmanifestation of the consciousness, the elements of a "human body" will return to dust; the breath shall return to the pool of universal air; the consciousness shall return to the pool of universal consciousness at rest. Nothing died in that process. All perceived forms merely returned to their original "state." The only thing that can be said to die (that is, that can be "given up") is the assumption that roles and appearances are real. To allow each belief in an ego-state to dissolve might be called "the death of ego" or "the end of belief in a false identity," but the identity was only imagined anyway, so no ego-state really dies either. All that is imagined or dreamed up by persons is false, a result of misunderstanding, programming, and not seeing clearly, as happens with the snake in a rope. "Snake in a rope" will be discussed in an upcoming post.]

Knowing the Unification / The Great Union—I AM THAT; I AM: The Realized understand that the "I Am" and the "I Am THAT" are "not two."

The "I Am" is the expression of manifested consciousness while "THAT" is the consciousness not manifested or at-rest. Some speak of "The Great Union" to point to that unification. Others speak of the manifest and unmanifest "at the borderline," but THAT is beyond both the "beingness" and the "non-beingness" (that is, beyond any "self-ness" or "Selfness").

True Self: Pure Consciousness, manifested; the Pure Witness, aware of Reality and the Oneness. Some teachers used the term to refer to "THAT," but the use inspires many Advaita students to assume that a "self" or "Self" or "Supreme Self" with "some kind of form" will remain post-manifestation.

self: (note the lower case "s"): The false self. Persons take the body to be the True Self when it is merely the false self. Beyond that physical aspect, the false self/selves also have a mental aspect since, in the "mind" of persons, the roles they assume as false identities also define "their self" or "who they think they are." The (false) self can also be referred to as the persona, the person, the personality, the ego-states, the roles, or the false identities. The false self is the false identity that results in persons being trapped in memories, timelines, ideas, emotions, beliefs, dogma, ritual, the misery of unfulfilled hopes and dreams, etc. The false self is so dominated by ego that it will believe in "others" and "others that are not as good as me" or "others that just aren't good enough." Those who have reached the third level of the "journey" to reality will claim that being religious or spiritual has given them humility to replace their ego, but "the religious person" or "the spiritual person" are merely two additional ego-states: the religious persona or the spiritual persona. Both, as with all ego-states, ultimately inspire persons to behave in a manner that "separates" them from all who they claim are not as "good" as they are, who do not believe what they believe, who do not behave as they behave, who refuse to accept their dogma or ideology, or who do not think as they think. Freed of all ego-states, no persona remains to think or judge or reject or believe that any can be "separate" from "others." Knowing the Oneness ends the delusional belief in separation and eliminates all the judgments and beliefs and thoughts that personas imagine to be true. Belief that the false self/an ego-state is a true identity is always accompanied by arrogance and ego to defend the role's image and to fight to give a sense of credibility to the false identity. That arrogance/ego generates self-consciousness (and prevents Self-Consciousness). In the relative existence, ego also inspires self-seeking; self-glorification; self-aggrandizement; self-centeredness; self-deception; self-destruction; self-indulgence; self-interest; self-will; and self-absorption.

Teaching Aids-"Clay in the Pot": When Advaitins speak of "the clay in the pot," the pointer being offered is that one can take a quantity of clay and shape it into a pot, a ball, a bowl, a vase, etc. Yet no matter what outward appearance or form the clay might take, the appearance or form is not what that really is which is supposedly being observed. Regardless of the appearance, it's just clay. So it is when consciousness manifests in what appears to be various forms: humans, animals, plants, things, "husbands," "wives," "teachers," "spiritual persons," etc. The outward form or appearance is never the real. It's a temporary form only. That which is forever is the consciousness. The pot, ball, bowl, and vase shall eventually disappear. The clay will remain. Similarly, humans, animals, plants, things, husbands, wives, teachers, spiritual persons will all disappear from the view of those who believe they are seeing those things correctly...but are not. Images and illusions will disappear. THAT which is unseen is real and shall BE forever, just as it IS and ALWAYS HAS BEEN. Realization allows the images and the wrong-seeing to disappear now and allows for the knowing of the Real to happen, now.

Teaching Aids-"Thorns Used to Remove Thorns": The Advaita teacher repeatedly extends invitations to protégés to cast aside ideas, emotional intoxication, beliefs, and concepts once and for all, yet the Advaitin teacher uses concepts during the entire process of guiding students along the seven-step "path" to Realization. How to resolve the seeming contradiction? Advaitins draw upon the ancient practice of using thorns to remove thorns to make the point. After a pain-causing thorn was removed from a hand, that thorn and the one used to remove it were both tossed aside. So it is with concepts used by Advaitins to remove the pain-causing concepts of persons. Use the Advaita concepts offered as pointers during the teaching process, but once the persons are Realized and thus freed of all concepts, then the teacher's concepts are to be among those tossed aside as well.

Teaching Aids-"Snake in the Rope": This analogy is used to help illustrate the notions of "perceiving wrongly" and of "images taken to be real" or of "seeing a thing as being other than what it truly is" or of how "enlightenment" works. Imagine students walking into a dimly-lit area and seeing a rope coiled up in a corner. Imagine them believing with all their heart that what they are seeing is truly a snake. Imagine the fear, the over-reacting to a mistaken image, and the emotional intoxication that seeing wrongly can inspire. So it is with concepts, with not seeing the truth but believing in something false. Now imagine the effect if a teacher takes the students back into the room and turns on the light ("enlightenment") and shows them that what was believed to be the truth was false. Upon seeing that the belief was false—that there was no threatening snake but only a coiled rope—imagine how quickly all the fear, the over-reacting, the belief in images, and the emotional intoxication will disappear. Realization springs forth that quickly when the light is cast on all false beliefs. Peace happens that quickly. When light is cast upon the false—making way for the truth to be seen—then all deception ends, reality is seen, and happiness begins.

Teaching Aids-Rope in the Snake: This is one I offer as another antidote to a miserable life in the relative existence when persons do not see clearly. As marred by misery as life is when imagining that every coiled rope is a snake, a relative existence can be equally miserable if one sees a rope in a snake. To deal with persons absorbed in their ego-states without seeing that they are projecting an image is to ignore a snake by thinking it's just a rope. The Realized do not take ropes for snakes or snakes for ropes and thus live an AS IF existence, free of the slings and arrows of living an outrageous life that happens when persons do not see the false, when they develop dependencies on persons who are asleep, and when they also fail to see the truth.

"Sleeping aids" are used by persons unconsciously as a result of programming and conditioning and enculturation. The "aids"—actually deterrents to awakening—keep persons asleep and prevent them from being awake, aware, and conscious. Most will never know Reality. Only a few will discover that Realization provides the solution to their relative problems. They will continue along the path that one described recently when he sent an e-mail saying, "I can't really take much reality at a time. I can only take a small dose at a time. I have to escape from reality and fantasize and daydream." He did not have a clue that what he's actually trying to escape from is not Reality but is the nightmare of his miserable experiences as a result of being out of touch with Reality. Following a recent accident in which the body suffered the breaking of eight major bones, countless fractures, displacement of the shoulders and hips, and abrasions over many parts of the body, it can be reported that the pain experienced by the body seems less severe when asleep than when fully awake. In truth, the pain is the pain. Being asleep might provide what seems to be a respite, but being asleep is not really a respite, the pain is there, it does not end because of being asleep, and sleep does not eliminate the cause of the pain. Why are most living their lives in a similar fashion? Depressed people seldom know, much less admit, that they are depressed. After being depressed for years, depression seems "normal." Most persons are offended if a professional asks to test them for depression or anxiety disorders and take offense at any who suggest their lives are marred by misery. Most will claim, "I have a pretty darn good life, really," though inventory would show the truth: few are truly happy and free. Some of the reasons include the following that block Realization:

Sleeping Aids—Memories: Recollections based in illusion. The "memories" that allow persons to experience the most misery are those involving the most assumed identities. Why do some "illusions of the past" seem to trigger more misery than others, if they are all illusions? Because some "memories" involve "recollections" of happenings that involved more false identities than others. Too, memories are distortions at their core. Persons did not see rightly in "the past" so they cannot possibly perceive "the past" correctly in the present.

Sleeping Aids—Hopes and Dreams: In a nation that refers to what it has to offer as "The American Dream," most consider it a sacrilege to address the illusions involved with taking dreams and hopes to be real. It is impossible for either to be real. In ignoring that truth, misery results. Hoping is about the future; dreaming is about the past or the future. Both past and future are illusions, and no one "living" in the past or the future has ever been happy in the present. Hoping and dreaming deal with wishing and wanting and desiring. Wishing and wanting and desiring are linked to fear, and no one being driven by wishes, hopes, dreams or fears can possibly be at peace, much less happy. Bliss can only happen in the NOW. Here are two recent examples that reveal why Advaitin teachers invite their students to give up the dream and see the real. First, an intelligent man said recently that he really had everything he needed but was still unhappy and asked for an Advaitin explanation. Several conversations revealed that a father with a doctor's degree and a successful practice had withheld praising his son, criticizing him for not earning higher degrees, for not being smart enough as a result, and for not having a job of the status of the father's. The father sent signals to the son all his life that he was not bright enough and not good enough. Of course the father's ego could only "love" someone who was an exact reflection of him. As in all cases, those assuming ego-states as identities can only "love" "others" who are an exact image or replica of them. Four decades later, the son is miserable. Why? The Advaita teaching makes clear: the son has a HOPE that the father will finally give a sign of love and acceptance of the son as He Is. He has DREAMED all his life that he could have that kind of acceptance from his father. The son will remain trapped in misery until he realizes that his hope that a father who is incapable of loving unconditionally will suddenly love unconditionally. He will be trapped in his misery as long as he clings to the dream that a father whose ego forces him to withhold praise and acceptance (and who can only "love" self) will suddenly know the Oneness and change his conduct when around the son. A father who does not know Who He Is cannot possibly know That Which The son Is and be at one with him. A father living in so many ego-states will automatically create a sense of "separation." In a second case, a man remained miserable for years after his wife left him. The woman had been raised by a cold, abusive father and by a mother who repressed all feelings and raised her daughter to do the same. Now more than fifty years old, the woman has never been told by either parent that they love her. The family has a "no-hugging" rule. Their daughter is therefore also incapable of loving unconditionally. The man involved with her lost his role as "husband" when she left. He mourned the loss of that ego-state for years, miserable in his HOPE that the woman would suddenly be able to love. He DREAMED of a tight-knit home and family. His hopes and dreams left him dependent on her image as "lover" and "wife" and "the key to fulfilling his dreams" and "creating a family." His misery did not end until he realized the truth: there is no hope that the woman will ever learn to love unconditionally, and if she does, he'll not be the object. His misery did not end until he realized that his dream was just that—a dream, the complete opposite of reality. While many tout the wonderful benefits of having hopes and dreams, the examples above illustrate that both are only beneficial to perpetuating false identities and continuing misery. Hope involves desire, and desire involves a perception of having unmet needs. Wrongly believing that one has unmet needs generates a false sense of fear. Desire and fear are never separate, and fear and peace never happen together. The examples above show clearly the fact that the failure to see reality—while believing in dreams and holding out for false hopes to happen—is the cause of misery in the relative existence. Hoping and dreaming always put the person hoping and dreaming at the mercy of "others" and dependent on "others" for fulfillment. If waiting for "another" to fulfill hopes and dreams, if trying to manipulate "others" to fulfill hopes and dreams, or if trying to force "others" to fulfill hopes and dreams, then peace cannot come. Focusing on hopes, dreams, and "others" fosters a belief in duality, and peace can never happen as long as persons cling to the illusion that dualities can be real.

Manifesting: The act of conscious-energy/consciousness entering into (manifesting in) something with a nervous system. As for human forms on earth, the conscious-energy "moves" from plants to humans or from plants to animals to humans. While the consciousness is eternal, the manifestation of consciousness is always temporary and will eventually unmanifest from the space (the plant or the plant-food body of insects, animals, humans, whatever) in which it is manifested.

Unmanifesting: The movement of consciousness (which was temporarily manifested into a space) back into that "field of conscious-energy" from which it came. Some speak of three bodies to help students picture the movement. Consider the gross body to be the space housing manifested consciousness; take the subtle body to represent something shifting beyond the personal, gross body; and take the causal body to correspond to the transpersonal stage that precedes total transcendence to the Unmanifest, to the no-body and no-mind Reality. (The erroneous beliefs in ghosts, angels, spirits, and an eternal life with a body were first given credence when the consciousness that was still manifested in some gross body became aware of subtle or causal stage manifestations of consciousness in the transition stage of unmanifesting. A woman who looked as if she'd seen a ghost approached me and told me her grandmother had just appeared to her and told her "everything is going to be OK." Fifteen minutes later, a call came that her grandmother had died fifteen minutes earlier. That event was nothing more than manifested consciousness being aware of unmanifesting consciousness. Rather than suggesting that some "magical world" exists out there or that "bodies last forever," that event merely illustrated that consciousness can know consciousness NOW. In fact, only NOW can consciousness know consciousness. Unmanifested from a space with a nervous system, consciousness is at rest in the "field of consciousness," and no exact same "cluster" of consciousness will ever remanifest in the same "clustering" again.) Only use the "three body stages" to help you picture consciousness not unmanifesting in a micro-second but fading out of the manifestation and into the unmanifest. Then, see beingness not ending in the flash of a micro-second but fading from a state of beingness, shifting beyond beingness, and striking a non-being state for a brief period until even non-beingness is transcended into the Unmanifest. [Some claim the weight of the consciousness-energy to be 21 grams, released at the time that consciousness unmanifests. That is probably more detail than is needed. Many persons claim that consciousness is "the soul" and that the soul will go to another world and remanifest there into the same body it was in on earth—along with the same "mind" it had at the "time" of "death." Of course that is impossible since dust does not regroup and since "the mind" was a complete illusion...the storehouse of all illusions.] To understand how the manifesting and the unmanifesting "fits into" the Functioning of the Totality, consider the following regarding the consciousness that has been manifesting and unmanifesting in the space called "humans" for millions of years: the formation of this universe happened over 14 billion years ago. On this planet in this universe, "human-like beings"—capable of making tools—roamed about at least 700,000 years ago. In fact, "human-like beings" have moved across the surface of the earth for something close to 14 million years (not the 6000 years that some claim). The manifestation of consciousness in what persons call "life-forms" began at the depths of the oceans where certain organisms thrive by obtaining their energy from thermal vents rather than sunlight. Over millions of years, the surface environment of the planet evolved in a manner that allowed for the formation of plants. The sunlight's interaction with plants led to the process of photosynthesis which results in the separation of water molecules, the production of oxygen and glucose, and a means by which energy can manifest in organisms that obtain their energy indirectly rather than directly. Plant-eaters acquire their energy by consuming plants. Carnivores receive their energy by consuming animals that ate plants. But since the earliest forms evolved at the ocean's depths, energy-consciousness first manifested there as far as earth's life-forms are concerned. Eight-legged forms—still the most common on the planet—left the water for brief periods until they were able to live above the surface as easily as below. On the surface, they thrived on the oxygen produced by plants and photosynthesis. Eventually, following one mutation after another, one especially-mutated branch of those eight-legged forms with outer shells evolved into four-appendage forms with inner shells (skeletal structures) and eventually came to be called "humans." Those who decry the suggestion that humans evolved from apes have not gone back nearly far enough to know that the earliest ancestors of "humans" were crustaceans. Humans are, in fact, the epitome of mutation, far from being the "glorious creation" that the ego and modern cultures would have persons believe. Rather than "O what a glorious piece of work is man," the fact is that "man" is the epitome of mutation and distortion...the most mutated and distorted of all forms in the history of the planet. No "creature" is farther removed from its original, natural form. His beliefs now make man not only the most physically distorted "creature" walking the planet but also the most mentally distorted. Thus, no creature is farther removed from living a natural existence with pure consciousness manifested, and "humankind" today is living with a level of consciousness more corrupted than ever before. Persons now live unnaturally and/or supernaturally as a result of the extent of all the distorting of consciousness. It is that corruption that drives persons to accept the ideas and beliefs of others that, in turn, always generate emotional intoxication and misery. Why know this? Only the re-purification of consciousness—via taking all seven steps of the "journey" from a belief in the false "I" as a real identity to knowing the Absolute That You Are can eliminate the misery. Awareness of humankind's actual status as the most distorted and corrupted form on the planet might facilitate the elimination of ego and ego-states that result in all the misery on the planet. The main pointer here is, energy-consciousness has been manifesting and unmanifesting in life-forms in general for billions of years but in human-like forms for at least one million years and possibly up to fourteen million years. The manifesting and unmanifesting of conscious-energy has been happening on this planet for millions of years, and the cyclings will happen until the sun expands to a point whereby it consumes this planet. Yet even then, the conscious-energy will continue, and it will continue to cycle…manifesting and unmanifesting eternally. Such is the Functioning of the Totality. Most significantly, know that What I Am and THAT Which We both Truly Are is beyond both the beingness and the non-beingness. Anyone believing otherwise has been fooled. If You Realize, You'll never be fooled again (by anybody or anything).

The End of Seeking: In cultures of accumulation, no peace can exist because the seeking of more is unending, unless Realization happens. The only possible result for persons who are programmed and conditioned to seek more is a guaranteed that they will never be convinced that they have enough. Persons never convinced that they have enough—enough money, enough respect, enough praise, enough "love," enough things—will never be content with whatever it is that they do have. Seeking produces misery, no matter how much is "gained" in the search. Peace comes via Realization, via the knowing that what one has is enough. In fact, Realization often reveals that—as persons—they already had too much and so de-accumulation begins. Then AS IF living happens. The Italians have a phrase used in a scene from the novel "The Board of Directors of Wars," available at floydhenderson.com:

Kirk then felt the peace that manifests when one knows "The Sweet Void," as he called it, when one can truly taste il dolce di fare niente—"the sweetness of doing nothing." Kirk even gained the level beyond that, experiencing what he called il dolce di Niente—not "the sweetness of doing nothing" but more simply "the sweetness of Nothing," period.

The Realized "live" between nowhere and nowhere, aware that what They Truly Are is the conscious-energy that is currently but temporarily abiding in the "I-Amness," devoid of all need.

The End of Identity: Via Pure Consciousness, the illusions of ego and personality dissolve. A multiplicity of ego-states are taken by persons to make up their identity. The illusions of ego, ego-states, separation and "separates" end with the awareness that comes when Realization happens. Realization is the purification of the consciousness that was contaminated by enculturation. Realization brings about an end to the assumption of false identities and to the beliefs and ideas that accompany them. As the assumption of false identities ends, those trapped in the level-three personas of "religious person" or "spiritual person" break free of those ego-states as they stop identifying with a super power, take the remaining steps on the "journey" to Full Realization, and live an AS IF life of authenticity as a result of the understanding that comes via pure consciousness. Misery ends and bliss begins.

Pure Consciousness: Unconditioned consciousness; consciousness not yet conditioned via enculturation or consciousness returned to its originally pure state after Realization removes all the contamination that results from enculturation.

Enculturation / Acculturation: The process whereby persons in various cultures contaminate consciousness by teaching knowledge (learned ignorance). A result of enculturation is an illusory "mind"—the conglomeration of the lies, ideas, concepts and beliefs of the persons in any given culture. The "mind," in turn, blocks conscious contact with Reality which is the source of all misery. Reality (the truth) can never be seen when persons are trapped in their "minds" (all the false believed).

Infinite Potentiality: Prior to this universe was an infinite potentiality that was unmanifested. From that unmanifested potentiality, a field of consciousness became the original manifestation in this universe and from that field all else manifested. Yet any manifestation is fleeting. The manifested consciousness becomes more and more limited when exposed to more and more programming. The limited state ends when the manifest becomes unmanifested or when the purified manifested consciousness comes to know Itself as the manifested consciousness and as the unmanifest, the Absolute, the Reality.

An Act of Friction: A vigorous act of physical union (practiced by a male and a female pairing among the various species) which can result in the release of male sperm with the potential of fertilizing an egg in a female. The act (if fertilization happens) begins another cycling of elements that persons wrongly take to be an "act of creation" (as in, "We made a baby." Magical thinkers claim, "We and the Creator worked together to make a baby" or "God sent us this precious gift.") In fact, the process is natural and automatic and is limited to only two contributing participants. The last thing on the minds of a human couple at the moment of ejaculation was the specific "child" that followed, and among the thousands and thousands of other species that enter into acts of friction, they certainly have no mind at all and are merely engaging in an act of friction that is inspired by a natural drive of attraction, pleasure-seeking, and release.

No Creation: One survey of U.S. adults revealed that 87% do not know "how babies are made." 87% do not believe that the process involves only two entities—a male and a female—but believe that a third party in another realm also plays a direct and active part in the process. Some believe in a physical intervention in which an other-worldly-male guides the swim-path of 40,000,000 sperm per second on this planet as well as the movements of all the eggs in females engaged in acts of friction. Some believe that entity provides a supernatural element while intervening and controlling the process and inserts some non-physical parts. So it is in a culture dominated by magical thinkers who have been conditioned to ignore the simple facts surrounding acts of friction.

No Creators: Why is nothing being created? All the elements involved in what persons take to be "creations and births" already existed on the planet, along with the air that will eventually be called "breath." Of the trillions of trillions of "humans" that have supposedly "come and gone"—and of the trillions and trillions of other life-forms that have seemingly "come and gone"—nothing really came and nothing really went. Every element involved in all those temporary cyclings was present on the planet then and is still present on the planet now. Appearances that are labeled "babies, children, adults, etc." are assumed to be something other than what they are. By comparison, a steel girder's appearance is taken to be what it really is, but looking at the beam under an electron microscope makes clear that it is not at all what it appears to be. So it is with all appearances. The only factor in the process of all the cyclings that arrives from outside the earth's closed system is the "energy." No creation or destruction happened. Neither energy nor matter can be created nor destroyed. No part of anything that has every manifested has left the earth's closed system, save the conscious-energy. Thus, there is no "birth" and there is no "death." Elements, air, and consciousness merely cycle. At the moment of what persons call "birth," the recycled elements' appearance is taken to be a body when in fact it is mainly space, and the form appears to change throughout the length of its manifestation because billions of cells are constantly being replaced along with a supply of conscious-energy, all via the intake and digestion of plants or via the intake and digestion of animals that have eaten plants. Nothing mystical, magical, or supernatural is involved with a very simple, natural process that unfolds automatically. Among humans alone, 40,000,000 sperm cells per second are being released (20,000,000 per instance of friction that results in an ejaculation) and two eggs are being fertilized per second as one sperm cell per instance "wins" the race to the eggs. Among all species, trillions and trillions of sperm cells are being released every second and billions of eggs are being fertilized every second. No "Prime Causer" or "Creator" is guiding trillions and trillions of sperm cells per second. It happens automatically, and nothing is being created. No creation equals no creator, including those assuming the roles of proud "parents." They merely entered into acts of friction that resulted in another cycling of elements, air, and consciousness. All that happens when an egg is fertilized happens automatically as long as the female consumes the plant-food that provides the elements and conscious-energy required for development of a space that will "house" consciousness. What persons call a "new-born" is simply a reorganization of the already-existing elements on earth into what is nothing more than a plant-food body/space with temporarily manifested consciousness. As with the eight-legged ancestors of "humans" that emerged from the water and later began to breath the oxygen in the air, the "new-born" that was in water in a womb will walk the surface of the planet and breath air until the consciousness is no longer manifested. Nothing mystical or magical or supernatural is involved in the totally natural process which begins with an act of friction that can trigger another cycling of three components—the elements, the air, and the consciousness—in combination, temporarily.

Cycling: Existing elements can combine, "un-combine," and re-combine automatically, so nothing has ever been created, nothing was born, nothing can ever be destroyed, and nothing has ever died. Only the seeming appearance of what is taken to be a "new space" happens. Only the disappearance of what was taken to be one thing (which was not that thing at all) has happened. Elements are simply cycling. The elements cannot be created nor destroyed, but in "minds" with consciousness that has been contaminated by programming and conditioning, the combinations of elements can be taken by persons to be different things when in truth they are only One thing. So, too, can consciousness cycle and re-cycle in spaces that have a nervous system. With the constant cyclings of the spaces called "humans," elements, breath and consciousness combine temporarily. Later, the elements return to the pool of universal elements, the breath returns to the universal pool of air, and the consciousness returns to the universal pool of consciousness-at-rest. The cyclings happen automatically and spontaneously, free of any "guidance" or "intervention" or any other magical factors that only personas believe.

Plant Body: A term used to make clear that what persons take to be "themselves"—their bodies—is really nothing more than plant food organized into a space that is circulating breath and temporarily "housing" the manifested consciousness which is the real. Plants are the vehicle through which non-usable energy from the sun is converted into a useable form on earth, allowing elements to combine in a way that results in a space (mistakenly called "a human body" or "an animal body" by persons) and allowing for the temporary manifestation of consciousness.

The Five Stages: An overview that shows how persons are programmed and what is required to reach Realization and AS IF living. To paraphrase the explanation offered in "The Twice-Stolen Necklace Murders" (available at floydhenderson.com): Stage One includes ages 1-20 when person are conditioned, indoctrinated, and programmed to accumulate, to get. Stage Two is ages 20-40 when persons unconsciously do what they were programmed to do, repeating what they were programmed to say, and believing what they were programmed to believe. Most never transcend that stage. For those who undertake "the journey" and follow the Advaita "path," they enter a Third Stage and begin Self-Inquiry. Some say, 'This life is shallow, hollow, unfulfilling. There must be more. I don't even know who I am—who am I?' If they find their True Self, they begin to de-accumulate in the Fourth Stage. De-accumulation is the mark of one becoming free of the programming. After that, one can live AS IF, as if this life is the real, and can then enjoy whatever remains of this life, free for the first time—free of educational indoctrination, free of spiritual indoctrination, free of religious indoctrination, free of political indoctrination, free of economic indoctrination. Free. Independent. Period. AS IF living means that the Realized know that this relative existence should be taken as nothing more than an amusement, not as anything that is really serious. Anything offered on this site is posted as a pastime, as an amusement, but never seriously as the Real.

On-going Advaita discussions are available at:

AdvaitaVedantaMeditations.blogspot.com

CONSCIOUSNESS / AWARENESS

THE NATURE OF REALITY BEYOND
SELF-REALIZATION
(PEACE EVERY DAY WHEN
ABIDING AS THE ABSOLUTE)

by
Floyd Henderson

CHAPTER ONE

THE AUDIENCE

THIS book is for those who have understood completely the teachings offered in FROM THE I TO THE ABSOLUTE and for those who have completed all seven steps along the "path" to Realization. If Self-Realization has not yet happened, and if an understanding of the Absolute is not complete, then you might want to read FROM THE I TO THE ABSOLUTE first. If you have Realized, then you are ready to begin a consideration of the pointers in this book.

This book is not for the novice, not for those at the "wet charcoal" stage, not for those at the "dry charcoal" stage, and not even for those at the "gunpowder stage." It is for those who have already experienced that "explosion" which reveals all lies to be lies and that blows away the belief in any and all concepts. It is for those who are ready for the Final Understanding.

Before beginning the book, the reader is invited to take into contemplation and consideration the following pointers on "Consciousness" and on "Awareness" that were offered by Sri Nisargadatta Maharaj (with some commentaries added). The contemplation can provide stimuli for considering far more about Consciousness and Awareness than most will ever consider:

ON CONSCIOUSNESS

"Understand then, that it is this conscious presence that you are, so long as the body is there. Once your body is gone, along with the vital breath, consciousness also will leave. Only that which was prior to the appearance of this body-cum-consciousness, the Absolute, the ever-present, is your true identity. That is what we all really are. That is reality. It is here and now. Where is the question of anyone reaching for it?"

Maharaj made clear that, if the Understanding comes, no "person" will remain who could try to meddle in the play of consciousness. He also affirmed that there is no omniscient creator that is meddling in the play. All is merely happening spontaneously. How did he define "spirituality" then? "Spirituality" is merely understanding that (1) a spontaneous play is happening, (2) recognizing the play is a fraud, and then (3) finding the basis of the play.

Maharaj was asked, "Where does consciousness come from?" He answered, "It never comes or goes; it just appears to have come."

He was also asked, "Where is the seat of consciousness." He replied, "In every particle of the juice of the body."

ON AWARENESS

"I told the consciousness, 'It is you who is suffering, not I'."

"Awareness is not aware of its awareness."

Maharaj explained that That Which He Truly Is was prior to consciousness. He made clear that there is no "he" to experience anything or do anything and that what persons take to be an experience is actually just the consciousness experiencing itself.

He explained that the Realized understand that the "world," indeed the entire "universe," exists in Consciousness alone. Neither "the world" nor "the universe" is real, and both only seem to appear in Consciousness. Knowing that, he was able to take his stand in the Absolute. In the Absolute, no Consciousness of the "I-Amness" or the "Beingness" or the "Is-ness" happens. In the Absolute, there are neither thoughts nor words nor deeds. The Absolute is prior to all of that…is prior to Consciousness.

Among the non-Realized, the consciousness has become identified with the space or form. A few move beyond body identification. Fewer still reach an understanding of what lies beyond the body-mind-personality identities. Even fewer will come to know "the source" that is beyond all enculturation, programming, and conditioning of the consciousness.

"I am really not manifested. Can you live like that, as the non-manifest?"

Now transcendence of the consciousness has also occurred. With the appearance of consciousness, the Absolute knows it is, 'I Am.'

Even this primary concept, "I-am-ness," is dishonest, just because it is still only a concept. Finally, one has to transcend that also and be in the nirvikalpa state, which means the concept-free state. Then you have no concept at all, not even of "I am." In that state one does not know that one is.

Full Realization, contrary to Self-Realization, is the same as Total Enlightenment, that is, understanding that You Are the Light. Not only does abidance then happen beyond the "I am" but it also happens beyond the "I."

CHAPTER TWO

AN OVERVIEW OF
CONSCIOUSNESS/AWARENESS

ALL is matter or energy. Neither was created. Neither can be destroyed. Thus, Consciousness was not created by anyone, nor was it created by any "Supreme One."

Just as a mirage is a phenomenal manifestation that can be witnessed by the naked eye, that which it appears to be can vary from one witness to the next. The identification of what a mirage is remains open to interpretation, depending upon the imaginings of the observer of the image. In the end, though, it really is just an image. The same happens when consciousness is perceived by the naked eye and is imagined to be something that it is not, such as "I am this body."

Does the body/space/form play a role in the manifestation process? Of course, but with no more significance than the space or form known as "a plant" plays a role in the manifestation process. Thus Maharaj's point that "the seat of consciousness is in every particle of the juice of the body." The body can be perceived, just as a mirage can be seen, but that does not mean that either is what it is perceived to be. Both are frauds, images only.

Thus, while seekers at one level can be told that "Consciounsess is all there is," at this highest level, another understanding is presented: that which is perceived is not That Which is Real, and even That Which is perceiving is not the Real, either. Maharaj explained that the Realized understand that the "world," indeed the entire "universe," exists in Consciousness alone; but since that which persons take to be "this world" or "the universe" is not the reality that it is taken to be via consciousness, then consciousness is the perpetrator of myths as well. If "the world" that the "I Am" takes to be its "place of existence" is a lie, then the "I am" is also a lie.

Since neither "the world" nor "the universe" is real, both only seem to appear in Consciousness. Knowing that, the Realized take their stand in the Absolute. In the Absolute, no Consciousness of the "I-Amness" or the "Beingness" or the "Is-ness" happens. In the Absolute, there are neither thoughts nor words nor deeds. The Absolute is prior to all of that…is prior to Consciousness.

Recall that Maharaj said, "Understand then, that it is this conscious presence that you are, so long as the body is there. Once your body is gone, along with the vital breath, consciousness also will leave. Only that which was prior to the appearance of this body-cum-consciousness, the Absolute, the ever-present, is your true identity. That is what we all really are. That is reality. It is here and now. Where is the question of anyone reaching for it?"

He said, "Awareness is not aware of its awareness." How dissociated was he from body identification., While that space was in the throes of the physical pain of debilitating cancer, he said, "I told the consciousness, 'It is you who is suffering, not I'."

Once consciousness manifests, the Absolute knows it is, knows 'I Am'," but among the Fully Realized, transcendence of the consciousness has occurred. Only when abidance happens as the Absolute can peace happen every day.

CHAPTER THREE

BEYOND SELF-REALIZATION

I F it is understood how the consciousness is corrupted among humans after manifestation, then it also becomes understood why seekers need a guide (or a guidebook with clear-cut directions, or both). As a basis for understanding Consciousness/Awareness, see why the seeker must transition seven steps in order to Self-Realize and only thereafter can reach the Final Understanding:

In the limitless expanse of energy called "The Absolute," that energy which has the ability to be aware of, if manifested, is uncontaminated, unconditional, unconditioned, unqualified, unlimited, pure, unadulterated, and unambiguous. When the consiousness manifests in the space called "a human," programming and conditioning and enculturation soon result in it being contaminated, conditioned, impure, adulterated, and ambiguous. That contaminating process results in seven degrees of separation from Reality, in seven degrees of separation from awareness of That Which the Consciousness Truly Is and from awareness of its original, unadulterated nature. Seven steps were involved in the-graduated-bastardization-of-the-consciousness process, so seven steps of re-purification must happen if the consciousness is to be restored to its natural, non-dual, no-concept, unadulterated state.

Only after Self-Realization can the movement to the next level happen, which is abidance not merely as the (re-purified) Consciousness but as the Absolute. This is often missed: even Self-Realization is not the end of the "journey." Thus protégés have been encouraged to understand the post-Realization Teachings as presented in this book. Why? Even after having read From the I to the Absolute and even after having completed the seven-step journey to Reality and even after Self-Realization, there is no guarantee of unwavering peace unless the Consciousness/Awareness is understood in order to abide as The Absolute for the remainder of the manifestation.

Even the Self-Realized, abiding as the re-purified consciousness, will experience instability since all manifested consciousness must necessarily involve some element of duality, conscious of-ness being inescapable in that abidance. Absolute stabilization can only happen via abidance as the Absolute whereby awareness happens without any "one" thinking there is someone or something that is present and able to be "aware of." Self-Realization is four steps beyond "The Religious One" and "The Spiritual One," and awareness is even beyond that One which knows the unicity and which knows the beingness and the non-beingness and which witnesses in a pure manner.

Abidance as the consciousness guarantees that duality will never be forfeited completely. Only the Awareness is "One" without any "one." Consciousness can know the "not two." Awareness is the absolute "not two." If you stay alert to the reality of "not two-ness," then for the sake of discussion you might take consciousness to be the essence of beingness, the re-purified consciousness to be the essence of non-beingness, and Awareness to be the essence of the Reality beyond both beingness and non-beingness.

Now, all that having been said, the basic pointer is this: in the no-concept, non-dual Reality, there is no "one thing as opposed to some other thing." Therefore, the Advaitin understands that the summative phrase "I AM THAT; I AM" can be stated and understood without any sense of duality at all. So can "Consciousness/Awareness."

A seeker asked, "Isn't consciousness all there is?" Yes, if you want to accept that there are levels of consciousness ranging from "pure and unadulterated" to "totally corrupted" and that there are modalities of consciousness ranging from "manifested" or "not manifested." Then you would consider some levels of consciousness to be "pure and unmanifested" and some levels of consciousness to be "manifest and soon-to-be corrupted." Next, you would likely speak of "the THAT state" as opposed to "the I AM state." If you take that stance, then you would also have to conclude that "sugar" and "sweetness" or "glue" and "stickiness" are the same.In the no-concept, non-dual Reality, the conclusion above can be valid. The discussion of Awareness/Consciousness is only offered in the last book in the series of Advaita books that are offered at www.floydhenderson.com because an understanding of Awareness/Consciousness is only "relevant" if it guides seekers to the total freedom (during the relative existence) which manifests if abidance happens not as the consciousness but as the unadulterated Awareness or the Absolute.

CHAPTER FOUR

THE BULB, THE LIGHT,
THE ENERGY

A seeker once asked, "Will you please explain consciousness as opposed to awareness."

In the no-concept, non-dual Reality, there is nothing "opposed to" anything else, but the terms can be used post-Realization to allow seekers to understand the nature of Reality beyond Self-Realization. Understand, however, that it is possible to abide as the Absolute Awareness during "the manifestation of consciousness" that is called the relative existence. The explanation will begin with this consideration for the reader:

From the third-floor balcony early one evening as a storm approached, the skies were seen to darken. Walkways cross the green terrace that leads down to the lake, and all along those paths, soccer ball-sized lights are mounted on two-foot posts to illuminate the way. As the remaining daylight was blocked by the heavy clouds, the bulbs inside the fixtures were seen to come on automatically.

As water puddled in the walkways, the lights began to cast diagonal reflections of themselves that appeared to be two to three-feet in length. Those golden lines of reflected light glistened in the water and appeared to become a thousand smaller lights, twinkling as the raindrops began to splatter into the gathered pools.

The invitation to the reader is to pause now, to consider consciousness/awareness, to consider the description, and to try to find a message in that description which might be relevant to understanding Consciousness/Awareness. [Please pause for consideration.]

Now, do you understand that the reflections were not the real light? Even the appearance of "a thousand smaller lights" was a misperception. If you the reader had been there and looked beyond the reflection, you would have seen the actual light fixtures in the background. Too, you would have understood that there was something even beyond that which was housing the light, namely, a form of energy. No one had to tell that energy how to behave in order for the light and reflections to appear. It just all happened automatically.

Recall that in the no-concept, non-dual Reality, there is nothing "opposed to" anything else, but the terms "Consciousness" and "Awareness" are pointers used in explanations of energy manifested, energy not manifested, pure energy, corrupted energy, and energy unmanifested. Know first, though, that since Reality is non-dual, Consciousness/Awareness is not two, just as I Am/I Am That is not two. That said, "attributes" can nevertheless be pointed to for the sake of discussion and understanding.

In that analogy, the bulb temporarily Is because of human behavior, just as an act of friction involving two humans made possible the temporary Is-ness of the short-term manifestation of consciousness presently being called "you." Because that bulb (consciousness) Is, the reflections seem to be. Yet neither the consciousness (bulb) nor the perceived reflections are real; that is, neither are That Which Is permanent. The bulb (consciousness) will someday not be as the elements combined as the space called "a bulb" will return to the pool of universal elements. When the consciousness (bulb) is manifested no more, then the reflections that only appear to be real will no longer be perceived at all. What remains? The energy that made possible the temporarily manifested conscious-ness (the lit bulb), which had made it possible for false reflections to seem real and which made it possible for the false "smaller lights" to seem real.

That Which Is behind and beyond the bulb—the Awareness—allowed the Consciousness to be temporarily manifested. The temporary manifestation of consciousness generated the temporary misperceptions. Thus: "Those alone who understand that I, the Absolute, am beyond the states of being and non-being realize my true nature, and all others are fools."

CHAPTER FIVE

GLUE, STICKY AND STICKINESS

U NDERSTAND that Consciousness is just a particular "form" of Awareness, made impure via programming and conditioning and enculturation. Awareness is the no-knower knowingness. Consciousness can be either (a) the not knowing, as with persons, or (b) the knowing which is assumed to be known by a "knower."

Another analogy might provide clarify for some seekers regarding the nature of Reality beyond Self-Realization. Take glue to represent consciousness and "stickiness" to be Awareness.

Consider glue sticks. Happenings by humans can result in elements being combined and temporarily manifesting as glue sticks. Glue can be described as "sticky" but, ultimately, "stickiness" is why it can be sticky. Similarly, Consciousness is what allows consciousness of to happen, but Awareness is why the Consciousness can happen. Glue is sticky—stickiness is why. Similarly, Consciousness is what facilitates knowing, but Awareness is why the known can be known. (To extend the metaphor and the understanding, Awareness is the "stickiness" that allows the sticky glue of Consciousness to happen. The sticky glue is temporary; "stickiness" is the nature of the glue that is eternal.) Consider these analogies:

sticky glue : stickiness as

the known : the potential for knowingness as

Consciousness : Awareness

Realize that glue, while a temporary combination of physical elements, has no independent and eternal existence apart from that fundamental background of "stickiness." Similarly, Consciousness, while manifested via a temporary combination of physical elements, has no independent existence apart from its fundamental background of Awareness.

Glue, even if not being used to adhere one thing to another, still retains its essence of stickiness. Even glue that is not gluing is still sticky. Like that, Awareness is the Fundamental Essence of Reality and the actual identity of That which temporarily manifests on occasion.

Stickiness is the fundamental essence of glue and is its actual identity when elements come together in a way that results in glue being manifest. Stickiness is the backdrop against which all individual forms of glue come about and adhere… by which adherence happens. You might get all caught up in a gluing process, get glue on your hands, stick all sorts of things together accidentally, and experience all sorts of chaos and anxiety and misery that might ensue, but the nature of the glue—the stickiness—remains undisturbed. That Which You Are is the "stickiness," not the glue which can lead to such a mess when manifested. Only if abidance happens in that fashion can an undisturbed relative existence happen.

To continue with the analogy, the capacity for glue to be sticky existed prior to any elements coming together and "making" glue. As the conditions and elements came together and glue took a physical form, its essence of stickiness manifested. The possibility for stickiness to manifest predated the glue.

Consider glue sticks and Scotch tape and Post-It Notes. While manifested, they can each exhibit the "attribute" of being sticky; but the Laws of Thermodynamics are constantly activated, so at some point those elements will return to the universal pool of elements. Then, what remains? Not glue sticks or Scotch tape or Post-It Notes but only…certain elements and "stickiness."

Now, please understand what can and what cannot happen with the Post-It Notes in order to understand what cycles and what does not. If you understand this, then you can be free of the belief in such nonsense as the Dalai Lama's claim that "New Orleans was struck by Hurricane Katrina because of the bad (dualistic) karma of the people." You can be free of belief in such dualistic nonsense as "You are going to cycle and cycle and cycle again, until you get it right."

To continue: it could be that millions of old Post-It Notes might be processed through a pulper that chops the paper into small bits and then heats them in a mixture that breaks them down into fibrous strands of cullulose (which is merely organic plant material). Then, the pulp can be screened and, if necessary, de-inked and color-stripped. After bleaching, the material can be processed in a manner that results in it again taking the form of paper which can once again take the form of Post-It Notes. But what really cycled?

The organic elements, not the same notes. Can these newly-manifested Post-It Notes possibly be taken to be the same Post-It Notes that existed before? Of course not. Will all Post-It Notes be recycled? No. Can their "form" end permanently? Yes. Can the organic material used to make paper be destroyed? No. Apply that to "forms taking form" and to consciousness manifesting and unmanifesting.

If notes are recycled, it is the same organic material which can cycle into a form that can appear to be the same, but that material could as easily take the form and appearance of a legal pad, a magazine, or a book. (That is how trillions upon trillions of "humans and animals and birds" have cycled into and out of manifested form on the planet while the planet has experienced zero-gain and zero-loss: organic material is merely being cycled, and it all happens with a speck of energy manifesting via plants. In the relative, you are what you eat and nothing more. It happens spontaneously with no master-control or Master-control involved. With condolences to those who take themselves or their offspring to be "gifts from God," what is really going on, and on-going, is a simple and natural organic happening, not a supernatural happening.)

Conscious-energy cycles (or not) in the same manner as the Post-It Notes. In the case of the legal pad, the magazine or the book, the attribute of "being sticky" would not happen, yet "stickiness" still remains though the original "sticky note paper" does not remain in its previous form. (Dennis Waite makes this clear by noting that those who are impeccable with their words will talk of "tably wood," not of a "wooden table.") Do you grasp fully the functioning of the totality? Do you understand completely what cycles, how it cycles, what does not cycle, what remains forever, and what is only temporarily manifested?

Similarly, "stickiness" exists, even after the elements that form the glue stick return to the original pool of elements. Glue, while manifested, is considered "sticky" as it adheres one thing to another (so it is dualistic in its very nature) but that which is independent and eternal is the glue's fundamental essence of "stickiness" (which is non-dual in its nature).

To review, take "sticky" to be a relative existence attribute of the elements combining as "glue" but take "stickiness" to be the underlying essence of glue; similarly, take Awareness to be the underlying essence of Reality that is beyond the relative and beyond attributes. Take "stickiness" to be the actual "identity" of the temporarily manifested elements called "glue," and take Awareness to be the actual "identity" of that which is temporarily manifested and called Consciousness.

Just as scientists discuss the various "forms of energy," take Consciousness to be a form of the originally pure, unadulterated energy which manifests and which then becomes impure and adulterated as the consciousness is programmed and conditioned and enculturated.

Fundamentally, the glue is not separate from the stickiness. It is the glue's root identity—pure, unconditioned stickiness, manifested, though temporarily. In fact, it is what the glue is, elements notwithstanding. (Understand what that pointer reveals about the "not two" and then it will be clear that the phrase "I AM THAT; I AM" actually points to the unicity.)

The glue has a molecular structure that is in motion, moving while manifested, active, bonding, etc. Stickiness transcends both movement and stillness. Glue is conscious of since "this" is forming a bond with "that," so manifested consciousness must involve duality; stickiness, to the contrary, is non-dual. Realize that glue has no independent existence apart from its fundamental background of stickiness.

Ultimately, stickiness cannot be defined and cannot know itself. It just is. From it emanates the ability of elements to combine and to be called "glue" and to bond. So it is with consciousness manifesting via a space of elements that can be called "humans" who "bond." But wherever glue appears, it is really just a reflection of its inherent stickiness, though the manifested glue is not itself the stickiness.

The glue may be gluing or not, but the stickiness still Is. It never ceases to be and makes possible all sticking that might or might not happen. When glue is gluing, there is a consciousness of—of the other molecules being bonded with. "Sticking" happens as a property of the elements and the way they function when combined in a certain manner, but there is no continuity to the manifested form of the glue. "Stickiness" happens with continuity beyond that physical combination. Glue is time-bound and space-bound. Stickiness is not.

Glue is a product of elements that have combined, originally protein colloids made from the tissue of animals. Proteins, such as milk and egg yolk, can be used to "make" glue, but glue is not being "created." Already-existing elements are merely entering into temporary combination. Proteins are often long, branching, stringy chains of molecules, and those molecules can be mixed into liquids to "make" glue. Chemical bonds form between molecules and intermolecular forces work spontaneously. Such is the case with elements combining temporarily to "make" bodies. Nothing is really being made. Temporary combinations are happenings.

As with Awareness/Consciousness, stickiness is the essence that makes the glue capable of doing what glue does. (The glue is certainly not a "do-er," so whatever happens merely happens automatically.) To compare, sugar is elemental; sweetness is not. It is the essence of the sugar.

A child eating a candy bar does not care about the elements but is simply enjoying the essence. That is the way the manifestation unfolds post-Realization as well, and that is the way that bliss can be enjoyed as well.

As in the case when that which is taken to be a "human" is believed to have "died," you can burn glue so it no longer retains its physical attributes; however, stickiness (the essence) cannot be destroyed. The stickiness in not the glue—it is what makes sticking possible when glue is manifested. Glue can be conscious of stickiness, conceptually. That is known because molecules bond with other molecules and "stick" and that process can be observed.

However, it is the pure stickiness by which all gluing happens, by which molecules can be conscious of molecules. The stickiness is behind all of the sticking that happens when the glue is manifest. The stickiness does not "make" the glue, but it makes gluing possible, temporarily. To label stickiness as glue is a misperception. Stickiness is the essence, not the material. Thus, to look in the mirror and to say, "this is me" is a lie. I Am the essence, not the temporary combination of elements.

Stickiness is unchanging and changeless. Glue is changing. Stickiness does not act and is not conscious of molecules. Stickiness just is. Glue is conscious of something, so "this" clings to "that." That involves duality, as exists when consciousness manifests. Stickiness is not aware. Stickiness does not act. That involves non-duality. Glue acts in the relative existence. It is dual in its nature. This is the difference between the stickiness which is not conscious of and the gluing process wherein conscious of happens.

Stickiness is the awareness that glue's consciousness is in, meaning that stickiness exists and "makes it possible" for glue's consciousness of something else to happen whenever there is an object…that is, when there is something to be "conscious of" and to stick to.

Glue is about duality; stickiness is non-dual.

Stickiness knows no thing, but manifested in the space called "glue," it allows the glue to be conscious of other molecules and to stick. Distortions happen when the common essence is ignored and all kinds of glue are considered to be different and separate and better than other types: fabric glue, super glue, wood glue, rubber cement, hot-melt glue, epoxy resin glue, acrylic cement, etc. They look different, but all are merely combinations of elements that share a common essence of stickiness.

The stickiness, the essence, of glue is simply everything about it, independent of the question of existence as a group of elements that have temporarily combined. After all the elements are no longer combined, the essence—the stickiness—remains in the background. The essence, or stickiness, of glue does not depend on anything else: it does not depend on any elements, it does not depend on whether the glue had manifested or not, it in non-depedent, period. So it is among the Realized. The essence is non-dual. Stickiness is the intrinsic, non-dual nature of the glue.

Such is the case with sticky glue sticks represernting the Consciousness and stickiness representing Awareness.

CHAPTER SIX

THE FOREGROUND
AND THE BACKGROUND

TO further illustrate, observe this picture taken from a window of the apartment used during stays in Tuscany:

In the foreground, preparation is being made to harvest crops; a new house is being built; some people are driving to work; down the road to the right, people are waiting to catch the local bus to the mercato in nearby Villafranca; someone in the white van approaching from the right is making a delivery. In the foreground of the picture, drivers are conscious of obstacles and intersections and traffic signs and lane markers. It appears that there are do-ers and it seems that they are doing. Take the background to include the portion with trees, mountains, clouds and sky. Beingness, rather than doingness, is the case in the background.

Now, you're invited to study the picture and (a) determine the ways in which the foreground might represent consciousness manifest and (b) determine what the background might reveal about Awareness.

Please review the picture. Next, for purposes of illustration, take the foreground in the picture to represent the I-Amness and the background to be the I AM THAT-ness. Take the foreground to represent consciousness and the background to represent Awareness. Note that consciousness involves being conscious of (something) so consciousness is always, ultimately, about duality: "this" is conscious of "that." (Thus, the seeker who thinks he/she is Fully Realized and is the unicity because he/she knows the True Self is mistaken. That seeker might be Self-Realized, but That Which Truly Is is beyond self-ness, Self-ness, beingness, non-beingness, and even Self-Realization. Reality is beyond "conscious of-ness" and is therefore a state of zero concepts and zero awareness. In that "state," Awareness is not even aware.)

But all of the happenings in the picture's background of unicity (as well as all of the supposed happenings that are occurring via the manifested, dualistic consciousness in the foreground) are only possible because of the energy of the sunlight breaking through the clouds in the background. Without that background energy manifesting via plants, nothing in the foreground could happen. (As Szent-Gyorgyi said: "What drives life is...a little electric current, set up by the sunshine.") Consciousness could not happen except for the background of Awareness, but Awareness IS, whether consciousness is manifested or not and whether consciousness of "this" or "that" happens or not. At the atomic and sub-atomic levels of matter/energy as "clouds" and "mountains" and "trees" in the background, Awareness IS. Yet there is no "one" that is conscious of anything. So it is when the temporarily manifested conscious-energy unmanifests and is subsequently "re-absorbed" into that field called "The Absolute."

Note too that in the foreground, many things seem significant: a delivery must be made on time; people must be at work on time; and food must be purchased in the mercato and consumed in order for the consciousness to remain manifested in the physical space. In the background, however, it is clearer that everything is merely cycling and nothing matters at all: clouds come and go; mountains that had formed will someday crumble; and trees that are rising will one day fall.

So it is when abidance happens as the Absolute: what happens will happen, yet "the insignificant" is never misperceived as "significant." "The foreground of consciousness" begins to unfold in the same way as "the background of Awareness." That leads to peace every day. Any faulty perceptions of the type that result in the insignificant being considered significant only happen via the warped consciousness, via the assumption of personas, and via the emotional intoxication that personas generate.

CHAPTER SEVEN

THE UNICITY BEYOND THE
APPARENT MULTIPLICITY

TO continue with the discussion of the picture, the doingness in the foreground is marked by consciousness and a sense of duality. Persons unaware
of the unicity believe that they are conscious of some "vast multiplicity" of things:
houses, roads, crops, intersections, buses, mercatos, etc. Being in the actual background of the picture, which includes trees and clouds and mountains and sky
and sunlight, there is no sense of duality. Why? There is no "one" to be conscious
of anything, yet there is Awareness. In what way is "Awareness without Conscious
of-ness" present in the background?

Observe that there appears to be a variety of "cloud" formations, but see that
"the clouds" are not The Real. What is "real," for the sake of this example, is H20.
A series of two hydrogen atoms are conscious of an oxygen atom, but there is no
"one" that is present to be conscious of anything. Consciousness (that is, pure,
non-personalized Consciousness) is just happening, so even though the talk of of
things manifested (clouds, tress, etc.) Awareness is not dualistic in its nature. It
is in that fashion, therefore, that the manifested, re-purified Consciousness can
remain manifested for a time but can function as Awareness…can abide as the
Absolute.

The H20 can manifest in various "forms" or "spaces" which persons try to
separate by using such labels as "rain, rivers, lakes, clouds, vapor, water, snow,
snowmen, snowballs, snow cones, snow flurries, snow flakes, snow piles, slush,
ice, steam, pools, waterfalls, streams, fog, ponds, hail, drizzle, floods, mist,
swamps, oceans, seas," ad infinitum, but it's really all one thing, all H20, merely
appearing to be different. (See why persons live in the delusion of duality? See
why persons are not "in the world" and why "the world" is in them…in their

wrongly-perceiving "minds"? See why they take what they think they see to be real and and how they try to support "differentiation" through labeling?)

Similarly, consciousness can manifest via the spaces labeled as "plants, animals, humans, birds," etc., and though it's really all consciousness manifested, it appears to the non-Realized to be multiple and different things. For any perception of rain, rivers, plants, or animals to happen, conscious of-ness must happen first, and as a result of inaccurate suppositions rooted in distorted perception, the illusion of duality manifests.

As with the "atoms as clouds," whereby awareness can happen without any "one" being conscious of, so it is as the Absolute. Awareness is, even though there is no "one" to be aware of. Thus Awareness involves no duality.

In both the foreground and the background of the picture, everything is merely happening; however, in the foreground where consciousness has been corrupted, consciousness takes itself to be something it is not and leads persons to believe that they are making things happen and that they are seeing separate things. Persons are taking themselves to be "do-ers," are lacking an understanding of the unicity, and are, therefore, strapped with delusional thinking generated by an illusory "mind."

CHAPTER EIGHT

THE SCIENCE, PART ONE

ANOTHER question raised by a seeker during a discussion of Consciousness/
Awareness was: I'll grant that the explanation of consciousness/awareness
over the last few days was clearer than any before, but I'm more inclined to seek
the scientific view, always. I read an article on one of your websites and it said
that Maharaj said that science would some day affirm the content of the teachings he offered. How about a bottomline explanation from that viewpoint.

In the expanse of space, energy can move via wave and/or particle form.
Subatomic particles of specialized energy exist and are moving through that
expanse freely. Because the expanse is so vast (limitless in fact), the particles are
not forced together into large-quantity clusters or groupings of energy within
that space. Consciousness only happens when large-quantity clusters or groupings of energy occur in compact spaces with nervous systems. Otherwise, the
background of Awareness IS and energy is moving without confinement in that
vast space labeled "the Absolute." Awareness IS, even when there is no "one"
to be conscious of...even when awareness of Awarenss is not happening. (That
is what peace every day looks like: being, without awareness of any concept or
anything.)

As the energy particles move, some enter the atmosphere of earth and strike
plants and begin to gather there. In that limited space, the particles of specialized
energy (energy able to be conscious of if manifested in something with a nervous
system) gather into "tighter" groupings as a result of manifesting in a limited,
confined space. Advaitins point to that happening as a step in "the manifesting
of consciousness."

Thus, the term "the manifestation of consciousness" really points to nothing
more than a spontaneously-occurring gathering of atomic and subatomic

particles of specialized energy into a compact grouping. Consciousness happens only when larger groupings of particles of this specialized energy come together in a "tighter" cluster and in a more confined space than occurs in the vast space of unmanifested energy-awareness. Here's another analogy which can illustrate the "different while not being different" aspect of the Consciousness/Awareness discussion:

Consider an ice cube "versus" water vapor. Really, the ice cube/water vapor is "not two," just as "I AM THAT; I AM" is "not two" and just as "Consciousness/ Awareness" is "not two." Yet "aspects" exists. When H_2O atoms are compacted and close together in a smaller space, water can take on the appearance of "a cube." When quantities of H_2O are subjected to intense heat, water can take on the appearance of "vapor" and will no longer appear to be compacted into a limited space as was the case with "the cube." The cube takes on an aspect of being fixed, confined, restricted. The "vapor" appears to be free. The "different" aspects become apparent depending on whether the H_2O appear to be limited by compaction or appears to be less limited by expansion. Similarly, the manifested consciousness in limited; the Awareness is limitless.

So the "vapors" are free to move about over a far broader area. The "cube" seems confined in a small space; the "vapors" seem free. Consider the manifested consciousness to be "the cube" (confined and compacted) and the Awareness to be "the vapor" (free and not compacted). That which is not limited is free and therefore at peace. That is also the only way that peace every day can happen: freedom is the prerequisite. The discussion of Consciousness/Awareness then becomes nothing more than a discussion about location and density. (Similarly, take a ball of clay, pinch a portion of it up into a flat shape that rises from the clay but remains attached. Is the raised portion different from the ball of clay, or is it just a matter of the pinched up portion's location and density?) The same is true of the discussion of "THAT" and "AM-ness." Located "here" with an aspect of density? Consciousness. Located "there" with no aspect of density? Awareness.

CHAPTER NINE

THE SCIENCE, PART TWO

THE essence (Awareness) is always in the background, even as consciousness is manifested. That awareness in the background can account for
the disconcerting notion generated by the "trapped" and "confined" manifest
consciousness that results in persons sensing that "I am not free" and "I need to
be free" and "I long for more freedom," all of which mark the relative existence
and that happen as long as consciousness is manifested and as long as abidance
is happening as that consciousness rather than as the Absolute. Are you understanding why the corrupted consciousness, and even abidance as the Self-Realized
consciousness, can never produce a sense of true freedom? The "journey" to true
freedom does not end at the point of Self-Realization, and to transmit that fact
is the only reason this discussion is warranted. Peace every day can only happen
even beyond Self-Realization.

So, Awareness is beyond both consciousness being manifested and consciousness not being manifested. Thus Consciousness is what allows consciousness of
to happen, but Awareness is why the Consciousness can happen. Consciousness,
while manifested via a temporary combination of physical elements, has no independent existence apart from its fundamental background of Awareness. (To use
an earlier example for emphasis here, does that ultimately mean that "sticky" =
"stickiness"? Or, is "stickiness" the essence of something that is "sticky"? "Sticky"
can only happen when physical elements temporarily combine. "Stickiness,"
though, is permanent and forever. Ultimately, it's all definition, all thorns that
can be used to remove thorns, and you know that the thorns are all to be tossed
eventually. All else could easily fall into the realm of "entertainment.")

When the previously pure energy manifests in humans, it is soon subjected
to programming, conditioning, and enculturation. "Minds" form and the endless
chatter of "thoughts" soon follows, all because specialized energy happened

to gather, accidently and spontaneously, into a limited space. The more that electrons accumulate into a natural coherence within a confined space and the more that conscious-energy takes itself to be "a human," the more frequently will abstract "thoughts" occur and the more frequently they will continue on a large-scale basis if personas are accepted as true identities. "The Abstract" is then erroneously taken to be "The Concrete, The Real" once Consciousness manifests and soon becomes corrupted consciousness. That generates false assumptions such as "I am a spouse" (or any other label that one might insert after "I am ...") when the abstract is taken to be the concrete.

By contrast, when single or elementary particles or coherent groups of energy-capable-of-being-conscious-of come together, smaller-scale abstract "thoughts" in consciousness happen. When the energy is totally "free" and is not gathered into large groups that are confined within relatively small spaces with nervous systems and is not bastardized with programming, then no thoughts occur...but Awareness remains. (That is the way that peace every day and AS IF Living happen: You Are, but there are no "thoughts," no "mind," no separation, no sense of confinement, no fighting with others who are not as "good" as your ego-states and egotism convince you that you are, and no chatter of a thousand monkeys inside your head.)

The manifested particles of energy can be freed of close confinement and compacting via the unmanifesting of consciousness. Prior to that, it is possible that particles of energy can be freed of the distorting effects of programming and conditioning and enculturation via the Full Realization process. Then, the energy can function in the pure and free and uncorrupted manner in which it functioned prior to consciousness, prior to manifestation, and prior to being corrupted.

Thus, Awareness Is, without consciousness of subjects and objects and without consciousness of any "thing" and without consciousness of some "thing." After "The Nothingness" is understood, You understand that You Are as You always Were, Are, and Shall Be: just being and just aware. The effects of compacted, manifested consciousness can be transcended and the manifested energy can function as pure, free, unconfined, unlimited Awareness instead. Voilà: peace every day.

We Are essentially That pure, unconditioned Awareness, NOW. We are not the consciousness that manifests and becomes corrupted into a "mind" that drives ego-states to experience emotional intoxication. As far as "floyd" or "you" are concerned, nothing more has happened than this, if Full Realization has occurred:

Bliss (which is nothing more than an undisturbed vibration) manifested and was subsequently personalized. That process has been reversed via Self-Realization so the de-personalization of bliss occurred; then, Full Realization and awareness of the non-aware Awareness followed.

CHAPTER TEN

THE SCIENCE, PART THREE

S O an attribute of conscious-energy is an ability to be conscious of, and that can happen whether manifested via a space called a "plant," a "bird," a "human," an "animal" or even if not manifested at all. Too often this is not understood: consciousness is, whether it is conscious of itself or not, yet it must be conscious of something to be consciousness. You might say, as was stated by a seeker, "I understand that conscious-energy can be conscious of itself if manifested in a space with a nervous system, but how—if unmanifested—can consciousness be 'conscious of' something without being conscious of itself?" To understand, consider the functioning of the subatomic particles of an atom:

One attribute of the subatomic particles at the core of atoms—the electrons, protons and neutrons—is that they are conscious of each other and function spontaneously in certain ways in relationship to each other...as do atoms as well. Electrons are conscious of a nucleus and swirl around it as if the two are dancing some subatomic dance together that is resulting from their "magnetic attraction" to each other. (The notion of manifested consciousness that the natural way for humans to behave when the consciousness is manifested via a "human space"— namely, to relate, to interact, to bond, and to break bonds, etc.—is subatomic in its nature.)

It's all automatic, it's all happening spontaneously, and it's all natural. No one teaches the electron to revolve around the nucleus...it's natural. No one need teach humans to be "attracted to" each other; no one needs to teach a human to masturbate; no one needs to teach two humans or two birds or two mammals to fornicate. It's all natural.

[NOTE: Only the bastardized "mind" (filled with all of its dualistic nonsense and the arrogant belief among persons that they have the right to manage the conduct of other humans and to control the bodies of others) will teach persons that it is unnatural to do what is natural: "Our dogma teaches that you can be supernatural (that is, super spiritual) if you do not do what is natural, because we believe that some natural things are actually unnatural!" Such a teaching provides an excellent example of how persons can be stripped of logic, how the consciousness can be programmed and corrupted, and how persons will end up behaving as fools if they unquestioningly listen to persons who have assumed position of "authority." Are you seeing how asleep persons are when programmed by their "leaders"? They can actually be taught that something which is completely natural is unnatural, they will then believe that something which is natural is unnatural, and then they will try their best thereafter to avoid behaving naturally. And in that process, they will be convinced that they are pleasing some supernatural entity by unnaturally avoiding the natural. That kind of learned ignorance, which bastardizes the consciousness and which thrives on blind faith, can produce either a nation of repressed, uptight and hypocritical persons or "an army of god" whose members are masochistic, sadistic, and suicidal. Such is the relative existence toll of corrupted consciousness and duality…and the subsequent unawareness of Awareness.]

Now, note the other ways that electrons reveal that they are conscious of: they can play a role in establishing chemical bonds, "A" being conscious of "B" and bonding with it. An ion from one atom can be transferred to another atom as all involved are conscious of each other. Electrons can also be shared between two or more atoms, so an electron in one atom can be conscious of other atoms, can interact with them, and can bond with them. (Yet the "not two" remains valid since this is all about energy / matter.)

Is any "one" directing an electron's behavior or orchestrating the way it conducts itself in relation to other particles about it? Of course not. Is consciousness present? Obviously. An electron can be conscious of an object (such as, in this example, the nucleus around which it is spinning). Is any "one" present within the atomic substructure to be conscious of a subatomic particle's consciousness of other particles? No. Even though no "one" is present to be conscious of consciousness, is consciousness present and functioning nevertheless? Obviously, yes.

At this very moment, there is a field of energy that can be called "the Absolute" in which acts of consciousness are happening even without any self-consciousness or any self to be conscious of. Take that to be a "pool" of energy or an "ocean" of energy or a "field" of energy or a "system" of energy. It doesn't matter what term is used to point to that field, but know that it is limitless and infinite and boundless and omnipresent. Understand that transferences of energy can and do happen between a "system" of energy and adjacent regions and understand that energy can also undergo transformations.

Thus, energy moves in wave or particle form "into" the field, moves throughout the field, and (sometimes) moves "out of" the field and manifests. ("Out of" is in quote marks since the "field" is all-pervasive.) In the meantime, the consciousness is still consciousness and is still conscious of, even though it is not conscious of itself when not manifested in some space with a nervous system. Compare that to the manner in which consciousness functions as it operates a heart and lungs even during an "unconscious" state of sleep. You are not conscious of your self, but the consciousness is conscious of. That is a natural function, not taught and not learned. AS IF living happens exactly like that. Peace every day can only come like that, too.

Also, see the examples on planet earth of such energy transferences and energy transformations: sunlight can strikes a human in a non-usable form, but if it strikes a plant, then the process of photosynthesis will transform that energy into a form that is usable by humans. That "transference" and "transformation" process facilitates the manifestation of consciousness.

The ability of energy to undergo transformation and transference sets the stage for (a) a plant to transform energy which (b) can be consumed and can thus (c) be transferred and transformed within a human space. The claim "we are what we eat," however, is only true to the degree that it makes clear that the body is a plant food body, though the body in not What We Truly Are.

CHAPTER ELEVEN

THE SCIENCE, PART FOUR

ALSO, understand that within that energy field referenced in the previous chapter, various atoms are moving, interacting, and being conscious of each other. Energy is moving in wave and particle form, so unmanifested Consciousness is not "at-rest" in the sense that it is not in motion. It is. The term "at rest" (certainly misleading on one level) merely points to the non-manifested status of the Consciousness at that point.

Moreover, do not think that there is some definable quantity of conscious-energy that is immobilized while in some larger system or field or pool of energy, "waiting" and positioned in a way that will allow it to be siphoned into some process that leads to manifestation or re-manifestation. Portions may manifest or re-manifest...or not. (Furthermore, as an example of the energy manifesting or not, note the difference in what happens when sunlight hits the surface of the moon vs. what happens when it hits the surface of a plant on earth.) Furthermore, the fact that some particles of previously-manifested consciousness might manifest again, and some might not, nullifies such concepts as "karma" and "reincarnation." I have not been born even once, so how could I possibly be "born again" or be born "multiple times"? Those two concepts are the result of body-mind-personality identification which always results in a desire for continuity.

So, at this very moment, there is a field or system of energy that can be called "the Absolute"—meaning the pure, absolute, conscious-energy. Within that field, there is movement and interaction...at this very moment; however, when conscious-energy is not manifested in a temporary grouping of elements with a nervous system, the Consciousness cannot be conscious of itself. Furthermore, do not take the Absolute to be some special "place." It is merely a "system" of energy—infinite, limitless, and omnipresent—from which quantities of energy might move to adjacent regions. If that energy becomes "caught up" in a movement of energy that happens to strike a plant, then it can manifest temporarily, yet there is no governing body or entity that determines whether such a chance happening might occur or not. To understand the cycling of consciousness "out of" or "into" a field or system, see what happens the moment that a bug is struck by the windshield of an automobile: much of the elemental structure remains on the glass (ash-to-ash, dust-to-dust); the air that was circulating as breath is instantaneously released and united with the universal pool of air; and the conscious-energy is instantaneously released into an omnipresent field … into that infinite pool of energy that can neither be created nor destroyed. The energy does not "go there" to some special place.

Next, understand that too much has been made of what is called "The Absolute." It is nothing more than an all-pervasive body or system or field or pool of energy, energy that is not currently manifested via a group of elements with a nervous system. Yet IT IS. In the process of trying to assign "supernatural" or "extraordinary" or "heavenly" or "special" attributes to a field of energy, (a) most persons now take the Absolute to be a mystical, supernatural location and (b) persons who believe that it is "up there" or "out there" do not understood that it is all-pervasive.

As a result of religious and spiritual leaders having glorified an energy field, the Absolute is imagined by many to be a place—even a geographic place in some teachings—that is not "here" but which is "there" instead. All such distortions attempt to place limitations on the limitless; yet even John Paul II, as programmed as he was, was aware enough to say that "we must correct the geography of Gehanna: there is no literal heaven or hell…they are mental states, and you are in one or the other right now." ("Gehanna" is also known as "Gehenna," "gehenom," or "gehinom.")

[NOTE: An editorial in La Civilta Cattolica, a Jesuit magazine with close ties to the Vatican, also said at that time, "Hell is not a 'place' but a 'state,' a person's 'state of being'." The pope and the magazine merely adumbrated what Christ the Advaitin had said: "No one will ever see the kingdom of heaven…it is within." Yet those who are programmed with religious dogma and who are enamored with their belief in the dualities of "good vs. bad" and "punishment vs. reward" as well as their desire for eternal continuity of body and mind and personality will ignore the later Advaita teachings of Christ regarding the fact that there is no heaven. They do that in order to cling to the desires of body and mind.]

With the widespread distorted thinking among persons, however, the Absolute has been misconceived as "heaven," as "the home of the gods or a god," as "a place where persons will go for eternal bliss if they are good," ad infinitum. The smashed bug is neither "at rest" nor enjoying "its place of final rest." Neither are any humans who have ever walked the planet.

CHAPTER TWELVE

PARADOXES, NOT CONTRADICTIONS

A NOTHER seeker said, There's all these contradictions. The part I don't
get is "there's only consciousness" but at the same time "in the Absolute
state there is no one to be consciousness of anything." Then Maharaj talked
about "even in the sleep state the consciousness still is conscious" but at the same
time "even in the Absolute state there is consciousness or awareness but no one to
be aware of it." Then, "neither matter nor energy can be created nor destroyed"
but "this is finite while that is infinite."

The reply was: there are no contradictions in the teachings but there are
paradoxes and there are seeming contradictions because Realization happens by
passing through specific stages. No teacher will offer a seeker at Step Two of "The
Seven Steps to Realization" the same pointers that will be offered to a seeker at
Step Six. That said, much confusion does exist regarding "awareness as opposed
to consciousness," regarding the nature of conscious-energy, regarding what "the
Absolute" is, and regarding what "The Absolute" is not, so some additional clari-
fications will be offered to try to eliminate the confusion.

First, everything in this universe (and in all universes) is energy/matter.
Consider energy and matter to be one reality, to be one in essence with two
aspects. Look at a steel beam under an electron microscope and you'll see that
the beam, considered by many to be only "matter," is a swirling mass of energy.
At the core of atoms are subatomic particles, and one of those (the electron) is
really a small particle of light. [The Advaitin Teacher of old did not say, "I am the
light." That speck of consciousness said, "I AM Light."]

Second, recall from any basic science course that neither energy nor matter can be created nor destroyed. There was no creation. There is nothing being created now. There will never be anything created. Furthermore, there is no destruction and there will be no destruction. Energy/matter merely cycles.

Third, to the confusion you reference in regards to the statement "in the Absolute state there is consciousness or awareness." Understand that the Absolute is the Awareness that Consciousness is "in," meaning that Awareness exists and "makes it possible" for Consciousness to happen whenever there is an object... that is, whenever consciousness manifests and whenever there is something to be "conscious of." One attribute of conscious-energy is just that: an ability to be conscious of something, and therein lies the basic flaw of consciousness: duality.

By definition, consciousness at its most basic level must deal with duality since an object has to be present in order for consciousness to be conscious of. During the manifestation, it is at the second witnessing stage of Pure Witnessing that such can be transitioned as the Oneness, as the non-dual reality, is understood. That only happens after the consciousness has undergone re-purification. So there are three pointers about consciousness, subjects-objects, and the eternal Subject that might help clarify what is often misunderstood:

[1] Manifested, consciousness can become aware of itself and that which it takes to be objects. [2] Unmanifested, consciousness can be conscious of particles of energy but not conscious of itself. For example, the electron can be conscious of the nucleus around which it is swirling even as the electron is not conscious of itself; or, the consciousness that was manifested and called "you" will remain as energy which can be conscious of surrounding energy or particles but cannot be conscious of itself after no longer being manifested. [3] Manifested and Realized, the re-purified consciousness can be conscious of the Oneness (of the unicity...of the eternal Subject) while no longer taking the illusion of "observed" objects to be real. [NOTE: This tip is for the advanced seeker: it is not that the tree is not "real," relatively speaking. It is that the tree is not that which the non-Realized take it to be.]

Next, take Awareness to be the original "state," prior to the manifestation of Consciousness and its post-programming, Subject-Object class of witnessing. See that Awareness is primary and that Consciousness is secondary. See that Awareness is antecedent and that Consciousness is subsequent to Awareness. To abide as the Absolute is to abide as Awareness, freed throughout the remainder of the manifestation from the machinations of the consciousness which was bastardized by programming and conditioning and enculturation. (Thus, it has been noted: "Ultimately, even identification with the Pure Consciousness fades as the Realized transcend and abide as the Absolute.")

Abiding as the Absolute—as the Awareness—You are aware of the functioning of the totality. You are not conscious of objects any longer, having understood that no "object" (which can supposedly be perceived) is actually as it appears to be. It becomes clear that nothing which can supposedly be seen by the eye is actually THAT; therefore, all Subject-Object Witnessing is transitioned and Pure Witnessing happens via the Pure Self (the Pure Witness, the True Self) for the remainder of the manifestation. More exactly, that is the only witness that remains…that Self-Awareness, which you can also take to be "unicity-awareness". (Yet there is that which is even beyond Self-Awareness that must be understood before Full Realization can hpapen.)

At that point of Self-Awareness, the Realized have been "re-membered," so to speak. You could, at that point, know THAT which You were prior to consciousness and prior to the corruption of the manifested consciousness. There never was anything other than the unicity, and upon Realization the unicity is understood and all assumptions of duality cease.

But keep it simple now as you revisit one set of the teachings that were a quandary for you: "It's all consciousness…there's only consciousness" but at the same time "in the Absolute state there is no one to be conscious of anything." Now you should be able to see from the example of the atoms that they are conscious of the presence of each other; that they move in relationship to each other; and that their movements influence the behavior of each other.

However, even as atoms were conscious of the presence of other atoms, there was no "one"—no "being" with a nervous system—that could allow the consciousness to be conscious of the fact that it is; nevertheless, the consciousness still IS, though it is not conscious of the fact that it IS. The same is the case with "you" prior to manifestation, and the same shall be the case with "you" post-manifestation.

It has been shown how consciousness IS even though there is no witness of that consciousness when unmanifest. Therefore, the consciousness was and is definitely "there," the atoms were and are conscious of the presence of each other, and they all acted and reacted and continue to act in a certain way as a result. Even in a pre-manifestation state, consciousness was functioning, even without any consciousness of consciousness. (So much for the concept of "sacred contracts.") The same happens each night as you sleep.

Even as you are not conscious while in deep sleep, consciousness continues to function and guides the brain and heart and other organs through their functions, automatically and spontaneously. You need not try to stay awake and be aware of your heart and lungs in order for them to work. Consciousness does that. Yet awake or asleep, you need not be conscious of the consciousness that is guiding the lungs to inhale and exhale and that is guiding the heart to contract and pump. That parallels abidance as the Absolute: as this manifested conscious-energy called "floyd" functions as consciousness that is conscious of, there is no "one"—no person—who is there and witnessing it. It's all just happening, spontaneously, by itself. Post Full Realization, all abidance happens as the Absolute Awareness.

CHAPTER THIRTEEN

RECONCILING THE "I AM" AND THE "I AM THAT"

TO review, one attribute of conscious-energy is just that: an ability to be conscious of something. By definition, then, consciousness at its most basic level must deal with duality since an object has to be present in order for consciousness to be conscious of. During the manifestation, it is at the second witnessing stage of Pure Witnessing that such can be transitioned as the Oneness, as the non-dual Reality, is understood.

Yet Awareness is that knowingness that knows no thing. Knowingness allows Consciousness to know, but the knowingness does not know. Some equate Pure Consciousness with Awareness since it is unadulterated by being conscious of any phenomenal concepts. Yet even Pure Consciousness must be considered to be conscious of something, by definition. By contrast, the Awareness is, but is not aware of. Only those attributes lead some to conclude that Consciousness and Awareness are not one, as if sticky glue and its stickiness could be separate.

The knowingness—the Absolute—precedes all consciousness while nevertheless being that which allows consciousness to happen. It is knowingness without knowing "this" or knowing "that." Even to declare that "I know I AM THAT" is an act in consciousness...an act made possible via knowingness, yet it is an act in consciousness nevertheless. That which precedes even the knowing of I AM THAT is THAT Which Is knowingness but that is unadulterated with any knowledge of any thing, with any concepts, with "the known." Ultimately, there is no knower. To say "I know the knowingness" is duality. To say "I know the knowingness but there is no knower" is still an exercise in consciousness and is thus dualistic.

Why do those that Realize the Reality function in ways that are considered

THE ADVANCED SEEKER'S SERIES

"moral" even when there is no belief…including any belief in definitions of morality? In the absence of a knower or "decider," there are no decisions made and there is nothing that is known. (In fact, that is exactly what is known: nothing.) From that stance, all that happens merely happens, spontaneously. With no concepts or dogma or body or mind or personality identification that is driving persons, there are no fears and no desires. In the absence of concepts and ideas and beliefs that generate fears and desires, no "others" are attacked out of perceived fears and no "others" are manipulated, abused, or used to fulfill imagined desires. Peace every day then happens.

This no concept, non-dual Reality results in the void and the nothingness. Italians have an expression: il dolce di fare niente ("the sweetness of doing nothing"). Since the teaching make clear that there is no do-er, then the Advaitin pointer could more accurately note, il dolce di niente: the sweetness of nothing, the essence of nothing. Remember the earlier point: sugar is elemental; sweetness is not. Sweetness is the essence of the sugar. A child eating a candy bar does not care about the elements. The child is enjoying the essence. Realization is about enjoying the essence, the sweetness, which is the essence of the void, of the nothingness, of the no-concept, no-thought, no-mind, non-dual Is-ness until the manifestation ends.

CHAPTER FOURTEEN

Reality

I RONICALLY, much of the "journey" along the path to understanding Reality is spent in focusing on that which is not real. Krishna said, "Those alone who understand that I, the Absolute, am beyond the states of being and non-being realize my true nature, and all others are fools." So Krishna suggested that fools can be known by these facts:

1. Fools do not understand that states-of-being (of believing that they .....
   are being "this" or being "that" and playing roles and accepting them as
   a true identity) are false.

2. Fools do not know that, post-manifestation, there is no beingness or
   even non-beingness. There is no false self that will be; nor is there any
   Self that will be, so there is not any Infinite Self or Supreme Self that will
   be either. Nothing with any identity or shape or defined space will be.
   No selfness or Selfness exists. Only That which is beyond both beingness
   and non-beingness shall remain. All that there will be is the unmanifested energy in the universal pool and the matter which cannot be
   destroyed. And those who do not understand that truth are fools (that is,
   they are persons who have been fooled by taking the dreamed up beliefs
   of other humans as gospel. As one famous social critic said, "There is no
   belief that has been dreamed up by men that is worth believing").

CHAPTER FIFTEEN

PEACE
(AND THEREFORE HAPPINESS)

S OMEONE said that the key to peace and happiness is acceptance. Tell that to the person sitting in prison. The key to peace every day, and therefore to happiness, is freedom. And what robs persons of freedom? Primarily, programming, conditioning, enculturation, under-functioning body organs, assumption of roles, and delusion.

Upon Full Realization, it is seen that all spiritual knowledge was nothing more than a part of that massive accumulation of learned ignorance which burdens persons with the heaviness of their "something-ness" rather than the lightness of the "nothingness." To fixate at that knowing stage—at the so-called "spiritual stage"—prevents abidance as the Pure Consciousness and prevents eventual abidance as the Absolute. Therefore, the final step of the "journey" is not marked by the gaining of spiritual knowledge but by an understanding of the functioning of the totality that happens in the absence of any "Understander" or any "Knower" or any "Spiritual Person" or any other "good" identity that is being assumed in order to replace former "bad" identities.

The re-purified consciousness will lead to de-accumulating, to understanding the bliss of the nothingness, to touching the validity of the void, and to being free of the insanity of the relative existence.

Since it cannot be stated, no one can share truth. Among the Realized, the "emptiness," the Void, the Nothingness is understood in the beingness; it is personas who engage in the doingness and who think that they are full of knowledge and intelligence when they are actually full of self.

When those roles are finally abandoned (and they—along with Self—are always the last to go) then the Void or Nothingness or the space can be understood and the true stillness of the de-programmed, de-personalized consciousness can happen. The corrupting process, and how to become free of corruption, was explained thusly to one seeker:

Seeker: And how has my consciousness been corrupted, according to you?

F: Via impressions—or samskaras—as my teacher called them. Here's an analogy: imagine you're at the beach, a few yards from the water's edge. As you walk, you leave behind impressions of your feet. Are those impressions real?

Seeker: For the moment, yes.

F: Really? What's real about those impressions? They are only space—nothingness, emptiness—that seems to your eye to be "something" when in fact they are nothing. Will they last?

Seeker: They'll last until the tide comes in and washes them away.

F: So are they an actual form, or just a temporary space that appears to have shape and form?

Seeker: OK...they're temporary.

F: So it is with everything you think you see. It's only an appearance, and appearances are distortions, and distortions trigger misery. You look at the body called "floyd" and all that is there is a space, but you think you are seeing some thing. It is emptiness...nothingness. Just a handful of elements with air and energy temporarily circulating through the space. If you remove the water that is within the body, then the elements won't even fill a small urn.

Realization is like the wave that can come along and sweep away all the false impressions imprinted on "the mind." Realization makes You aware that the nothingness that you've always taken to be something is not that thing at all. Those impressions were never real. You mistook an empty space to be something, and that's what persons do all day long, all month long, all year long, year after year after year. Most spend their entire relative existence convinced that their perceptions are the "right" perceptions when if fact they have never seen anything "rightly."

As a result, they will suffer from one false impression after another, not unlike all the impressions in your "mind." Footprints in the sand appear to have some shape or form, just as mirages in the desert appear to have a shape or form, but the reality is that all impressions and all mirages are just a part of the fiction of the "mind." To be "in touch with reality" is to be able to differentiate between what is illusion and what is real, between what is delusion and what is truth, and between that which appears to be dualistic as opposed to that which is One and truly Real.

If Realized, however, it is known that this beingness is temporary and that the non-beingness is the completely natural state (as opposed to unnatural states or supernatural states as adopted by non-Realized persons). Energy manifests and is aware of the beingness, then energy unmanifests and has no space or form by which the beingness can be known.

THAT is perfect peace, not unlike the delta-sleep state of brain movement during deep sleep. The non-beingness is that natural state with no body, no mind, no form, no space, no...anything. It is the Void, the Nothingness, when THAT Which Is does not even know that It Is. Call it "bliss" if you like, but the Realized know that bliss can only be known during the beingness if the Void and the Nothingness are Realized during the manifestation of consciousness. If one is at perfect rest during a deep sleep, that might appear to be a blissful state, but the human in deep sleep does not know that it is and is not conscious of "bliss."

Only when fully awake, aware and conscious can the bliss be known—if Realized. Bliss is the stuff of being manifested and Realized during the period of Amness. The non-being state that follows has no awareness of awareness. Having transitioned into the non-beingness, the Consciousnss Is, but it cannot know It Is. Enjoy it NOW, for no other opportunity exists. That allows for peace to happen every day. So does a clear understanding of what bliss is and what bliss is not.

The only thing "blissful" about re-absorption into the Absolute is the bliss of the Void, of the nothingness, of the no-mind, no-body, no-personality, non-beingness and That which is even beyond the non-beingness. If one is "wanting bliss," then it can be known now, but it cannot be experienced in the way that most want to experience it. Why?

Post-Realization, there is no experiencer. Actually, bliss is nothing more than a vibration that continues to vibrate without any disturbance. Any other definition that generates some unattainable experience is an obstacle to peace happening every day. Those who seek the state that persons mistake for "bliss" are being set up for disappointment by their belief in a concept.

If peace during the relative comes in the void (in the nothingness of sleep) and if peace awaits (in the nothingness of that void when unmanfested conscious-ness returns to its former "at-rest state") then how might persons find that void in the NOW and experience that bliss (a) while awake rather than in deep sleep and

(b) while the consciousness is manifested rather than unmanifested? The peace
of the void cannot be known by persons driven to seek more rather than less.

"Con" = "together," "with," or "together with." The very prefix reveals the
duality. Consciousness cannot be the non-dual reality. The non-dual reality is
beyond dualistic consciousness.

Awareness is thoughtless, unmanifested consciousness...is no-mind
consciousness. This is far beyond any talk of samadhi or its five types. Awareness
does not provide a temporary respite from thoughts and desires and fears.
Awareness is permanent freedom from the fictitious mind and the beliefs and
desires and fears that originate therein.

"Being in touch with Reality" is actually about being in touch with nothing...
freed from being in touch with anything that is not real, that is phenomenal, and
that is mind-generated or culture-generated. Awareness removes all identification with anything other than the void or nothingness, which means there is
no identification at all. Abidance as the awareness can happen even during the
manifestation of consciousness and is the unconditional "condition" referred to
by the terms Fully Realized, Enlightened, Liberated, Actualized, etc.

Essence is the attribute (or set of attributes) that make an object or <u>substance</u>
what it fundamentally is. The essence of a being is simply that which it fundamentally is, and happiness during the manifestation comes when aligned with
the essence. Thereafter, peace every day happens.

Earlier the pointer was offered that "the 'journey' to true freedom does not
end at the point of Self-Realization, and to transmit that fact is the only reason
this discussion is warranted." The Full understanding of Awareness must happen
for freedom—and therefore happiness—to manifest. It must be understood that
Awareness is but has no awareness of self, of Self...of anything.

Namkhai Norbu said this about Awareness: "This is the open secret, which
all can discover for themselves. We live our lives, as it were 'inside out,' projecting
the existence of an 'I' as separate from an external world which we try to manipulate to gain satisfaction. But as long as one remains in the dualistic state, one's
experience has always underlying it a sense of loss, of fear, of anxiety, and dissatisfaction. When, on the other hand, one goes beyond the dualistic level, anything
is possible." Including peace every day.

The Final Frontier" of the Advaita Teachings is transitioned when the Nature
of Reality is understood and when the Advaita Teachings are "applied" on a daily
basis even in the absence of any "Applier." The Nature of Reality cannot be

understood until the attributes of Consciousness and Awareness are understood. Understanding the Nature of Consciousness allows for abidance in the I AM, but what of THAT Which Is beyond, and that which is beyond the beyond?

Only abidance as the Absolute allows the remainder of the manifestation of Consciousness to happen in Perfect Peace.

The Final Frontier" of the Advaita Teachings is transitioned when seekers understand the attributes of Consciousness and Awareness, can define the exact Nature of Reality, can witness as Full Realization happens, can come to an understanding of the Functioning of the Totality, and can then fixate in a state of peace from NOW until the Consciousness is not longer manifest.

If not firmly fixed as The Nothing (as the Awareness that is not aware), then everything in the relative existence will be taken to be "something": a breakup, a traffic ticket, problems with school assignments, problems while seeking employment, problems with neighbors, problems with persons not accepting you in the fashion you expect, problems with persons behaving in a way that is not pleasing to you, problems with persons not properly "honoring you" in the manner your egoism desires, ad infinitum.

Even among those seekers who "find," who feel that they have Realized Fully, fluctuations have been witnessed. In cultures that program persons to "get," the value of absolute de-accumulation is usually given little more than lip service. In cultures where desires are a motivating factor—in homes, in schools, in churches, in jobs, ad infinitum—how many have any chance at all to actually desire... nothing? It is the very desiring, along with concern that all which is desired might not be attained, that perpetuates imagined fears.

When "desiring" is given such value in cultures, how many will be content with "nothing" (which is what allows all desires and all fears to end)? Enculturation programs persons to want something, not nothing. "Zero" is despised among persons, but only by reaching a state of "zero concepts" can peace happen every day.

Moreover, persons become so trapped in their desire for post-manifestation body-mind-personality continuity that they think they cannot be happy during the manifestation unless they also have continuity of all things: their spouse or partner; their home; their whatever—they want the temporary things in the relative to have absolute continuity. How can anyone ever be happy, living in such a delusional condition? One cannot.

"Peace Every Day" can only happen in the abidance that is "beyond conscious of-ness." The relative existence comparison offered by Advaitins is "the deep sleep metaphor" wherein peace happens beyond relative consciousness. (Again, compare the "beyond conscious of-ness" to the awareness of the body's need that automatically, spontaneously keeps the heart and the lungs functioning even as there is no "one" present to consciously "do" that. Also, understand the auto-matic, spontaneous functioning in order to understand how the relative existence happens with no illusion of a "do-er" being present and with abidance happening even beyond conscious of-ness. That happens when abidance as the Absolute happens.

It should be seen why it is frequently repeated that, ultimately, there is no "goal" of abiding as Consciousness. For full freedom (and then happiness) to happen during the manifestation of consciousness, abidance must happen as the Absolute.

Furthermore, peace cannot happen if body-mind-personality identification is not transcended because persons will continue to fear death and will desire continuity. Do you see now why the concept of "death" is given no credibility by the Realized, much less any "concern"? It is understood by the Realized that what persons call "death" is merely the unmanifesting of consciousness, is merely the releasing of compact groupings of energy that are just "ungrouping" and being "freed up" to move about in a wider, less-limited (actually infinite) space, exactly as prior to manifestation.

That "ungrouping" and "releasing" of energy from a confined space (called "death" by persons) is a totally meaningless happening except to the corrupted consciousness that believes in the distorted, dualistic concepts of "good" vs. "bad" and "right" vs. "wrong" and the subsequent "punishment" vs. "reward" of a body-mind-personality triad with supposed eternal continuity. In fact, only the energy is infinite and eternal; the body and "mind" and personality are illusory phenomena that are finite and temporary.

So that which persons refer to as "the moment of death" is really just the unmanifestation process whereby those larger groupings of energy particles in a confined space are freed from that space and enter into an expansive, unlimited energy field or space (called "The Absolute" in order to emphasize the pure and unadulterated state of the energy while in that space). By "relocating" from a confined space called "the human body," for example, those elementary particles can group together in that vast and expansive ocean of energy; however, they will group into smaller gatherings and into fewer configurations since they are not being compacted into a small space. The prerequisites for "human conscious-ness" are not met in that case. That is an ending of "prerequisites," not an ending of "life."

During the process whereby consciousness unmanifests, therefore, particles of energy are merely "spreading out" or "being freed from 'confinement' in a compact space." After being freed from the confines of a relatively small space with a nervous system—such as a plant or a plant food body (which persons dualistically call "a human" or "an animal" or "a bird")—the energy moves into the limitless expanse of The Absolute and the particles "move apart." In that freed-up space, the essence of Reality (Awareness) IS.

Now, are you also seeing that though the cycles are naturally happenings, the manifesting of consciousness is actually, on one level, a very unnatural event? Why? That which is normally and naturally free to move about in an unrestrained environment and in an unrestricted manner is temporarily not free to function in that manner. Manifested consciousness, as the physicist will understand, is actually "restricted" and "restrained" when compared to the "normal" state of particles of energy which move about in a limitless field or space. Compare (a) the unrestricted movement of light waves moving instantly from the sun to the moon and reflecting off that surface with (b) the restricted movement of conscious-energy striking one synapse after another within the limited space of a human brain.

Here is all that happens when a human "dies" or when a bug is struck by the windshield of a car: a temporary "association of" or "involvement among" certain elements and energy and air comes to an end. Though that particular association ends, the elements do not end, the air does not end, and the energy does not end. What did come to "an end" with the smashed bug (or a supposedly "dead human") was an ever-changing combination of elements, air, and energy which were in a constant state of flux but perceived by persons to have had conti-nuity. The fact is that no "same bug" will ever be again, and no "same human" shall ever be again, but the same elements and air and energy shall be forever.

CHAPTER SIXTEEN

PEACE AND AS IF LIVING

RECALL the pointer offered earlier: Nothing more has happened than this: the personalization of bliss (to the degree that "bliss" is an undisturbed vibration which was subsequently manifested and eventually personalized) became de-personalized via Self-Realization, Full Realization, and Awareness.

Once abidance as a body or mind or persona is transitioned, once abidance as a self or a Self is transitioned, once abidance as the re-purified consciousness is transitioned, then abidance as the Absolute can happen. Then, for the remainder of the manifestation, AS IF living can happen. Recall this pointer as well: That is the way that AS IF Living happens: You Are, but there are no "thoughts," no "mind," no separation, no sense of confinement, no fighting with others who are not as "good" as your ego-states and egotism convince you that you are, and no chatter of a thousand monkeys inside your head.

Peace and AS IF Living happen from a point of total "mindlessness." Peace and AS IF Living happen without identity. Peace and AS IF Living happen without concepts. Peace and AS IF Living happen from a position of neutrality. Peace and AS IF Living happen from the stance of Witnessing. Peace and AS IF Living happen when the Oneness is known. Peace and AS IF Living happen beyond self-ness, Self-ness, beingness, and non-beingness. Peace and AS IF Living happen when persons transcend all personalization and abide as the Absolute. Remember that Krishna said, "Those alone who understand that I, the Absolute, am beyond the states of being and non-being realize my true nature, and all others are fools." Peace and AS IF Living happen when the role of "fool" is no longer accepted and the unspeakable truth is known. Then, the truth speaks from within and the full understanding of the Functioning of the Totality happens. And once that happens, all attachment to the phenomenon is cast aside and the peace of the Noumenon manifests.

Peace and Light
Please visit
<u>floydhenderson.com</u>
and
advaitavedantameditations.blogspot.com

BOOK THREE OF FOUR IN
"THE ADVANCED SEEKERS' SERIES"

FROM THE ABSOLUTE TO
THE NOTHINGNESS

by
Floyd Henderson

Consideration

Regarding one character in a Michael Connelly novel: "He was long past believing in God—the horrors he had seen documented had little by little sapped his stores of faith and in those seemingly final days, as his own heart withered and tapped out its final cadences, he did not grasp desperately for his lost faith as a shield or a means of easing the fear of the unknown. Instead, he was accepting of the end, of his own nothingness. He was ready. It was easy to do."

CHAPTER ONE

THE AUDIENCE

[This book is for those who have understood completely the teachings offered in FROM THE I TO THE ABSOLUTE and in CONSCIOUSNESS / AWARENESS]

AS with those two works, this book is not for the novice, not for those at the "wet charcoal" stage, not for those at the "dry charcoal" stage, and not even for those at the "gunpowder stage." It is for those who have already experienced that "explosion" which reveals all lies to be lies and that blows away the belief in any and all concepts. It is for those who are ready for Understanding "The Nothingness."

Dennis Waite wrote, "As ever, in the philosophy of Advaita, the teaching is graded to suit the level of understanding of the student - and it is no use trying to 'jump levels' if we have not yet grasped the lower level principles."

Therefore, it will also be of no use for any seeker to try to 'jump levels' and understand the pointers in this book if he has not read and understood the pointers in the two books mentioned above that lay the foundation on which these principles rest.

Dennis continued, "All levels of identification must be transcended and this should be done in a controlled and stepwise manner that has been validated through millennia of teaching. Attractive though it might seem, it is not possible to jump straight to the end."

Rightly put. All levels of identification must be transcended, and this book will discuss the means by which such transcendence can happen.

Waite also explained that "in reality, there is no karma, no saMskAra, no puruShArtha because there is no person who could have them. They are all teaching devices used to bring the student to a realization of the truth by means of carefully gauged, progressive levels of understanding."

This book offers pointers on the final level of such understanding.

Finally, Dennis wrote, "It is the perennial problem of the teacher to be able to judge where the student currently is in his or her understanding and lead them onwards from there. This is why a living 'guru' is really needed, so that questions may be asked and answered face to face."

CHAPTER TWO

INTRODUCTORY
CONSIDERATIONS

ACCORDING to the earliest Native Teachings, that which is "true" is only the space between exhalation and inhalation. Advaita teachers agree that truth cannot be spoken. Because inhaling and exhaling is a meaningless occurrence involving a temporary combination of earth elements, it is in the silence between those actions that "truth" can be understood in the moment of non-action. Quiet meditation, therefore, was intended not to still the "mind" but to focus on the nothingness during that breathless span of freedom from body and "mind" activity, wherein truth can be realized during that empty moment.]

CHAPTER THREE

IDENTIFICATION:
Something, or No Thing?

THE content of this book is for those who have the same belief system as one seeker who reacted to a pointer regarding the fact that no true "identity" really exists:

No identity at all? Everybody is SOMETHING, and whatever that SOMETHING is, is our identity.

He was told, "First, the way in which you use the word 'identity' would need to be clarified, and there are likely some additional subconscious usages that you are not even aware of. Do you mean 'the distinct personality of an individual regarded as a persisting entity'? Realized Advaitins understand that there is no personality and that no entity persists.

"Or do you mean, 'the individual characteristics by which a thing or person is recognized or known'? Realized Advaitins know that 'the individual' is a bogus concept, that 'characteristics' are fiction since they deal with personality, and that persons/personas are nothing more than assumptions generated via corrupted consciousness.

"Or do you mean, 'That which describes objects in a manner that distinguishes them from other objects'? Realized Advaitins understand that 'one as opposed to others' is dualistic and thus false.

"You likely are not referring to 'the individual sense of importance in a social context,' but might you be referring to 'self-knowledge about one's characteristics or personality,' that is, to 'a sense of self'? Surely not.

"So consider: if you are referring to 'True Self-knowledge' or to 'a sense of True Self,' then you are still dealing with a false identity. How could that possibly be false? Because the terms 'True Self' or 'Real Self' are frequently misused (even by many Advaitins or would-be Advaitins). Many now use the terms to point to the noumenon or to the Absolute in an effort to support the existence of a Self-cum-continuity, even while agreeing that no self can have continuity.

"Likely, your stance is that, while the phenomenal is that which is physically manifested and observable by one or more of the five senses, some other sense is employed to recognize that an identifiable Self exists beyond physical manifestation. At the elementary level, when a protégé is taking the first steps on the 'path' to Realization, that idea is often allowed by teachers.

At the more advanced level, though, it is understood that the True Self is merely the second of two witnessing modes, the pure or re-purified consciousness that knows ItSelf and knows the Oneness (as opposed to subject-object witnessing). That Pure Witnessing Consciousness sees no 'others' and is incapable of any dualistic misperception, yet it's entire functioning is still dependent upon its manifestation. Thus, even that 'True Self' is limited and is not an 'eternal identity.'

"Further, that 'True Self' is not 'God,' though many who have morphed this philosophy into a religion will defend that Self-God concept as well. Instead, the True Self is merely that pure consciousness which can look to the phenomenon and know that it is not as perceived, which can know that no self is real, and which can understand that no noumenal 'Self with identity' exists either.

"The pure consciousness understands that when the pronoun 'I' is employed as the pure consciousness speaks, it refers to that which is beyond beingness and beyond non-beingness; therefore, it is beyond 'I-ness' and identity as well. Krishna was very direct in stating that any who do not understand that are 'fools.' That which is beyond beingness and non-beingless must also be beyond self, Self, self-ness, Self-ness, no-self-ness, and even no-Self-ness.

"Of course, that pointer about 'fools' is misunderstood by most, understood by few, and hated by many. For those still trapped in the egotism that is generated by accepting and defending an identity (whether that might be an identity 'now' or an identity 'later'), let it be said that they have at least been fooled and continue to function from within that condition. The primary consideration must be, 'How can the state of zero concepts be reached if the concept of 'identity' is still being clung to'?"

CHAPTER FOUR

NATURAL VS. SUPERNATURAL OR UNNATURAL

AGAIN, the content of this book is not for the beginner. Beginners cannot move from some point that is even before step one of a seven-step "journey" to Realization (that Realization coming at the seventh step) without understanding many paradoxes that are presented at each of the steps in between.

They will first see what they think they see; they must next understand that everything that they have ever thought they were seeing was not that at all; afterwards, they must see all of the false in order to prepare for seeing the Real; and then only can they finally fixate firmly in the no-concept, non-dual Reality.

Thereafter, they can be truly free while abiding as the Absolute; can abide as Awareness that is not even aware of awareness; and can thereby live in a natural, AS IF fashion...at peace for the remainder of the manifestation. The exhaustion of living unnaturally ends, as does the toil of trying to live in a supernatural fashion. Only if abiding as the Awareness that is not aware of awareness can natural (nisarga) unencumbered living happen, spontaneously. Disciplines and considerations end. Toiling and working and searching and seeking end.

Ultimately, to try to support any "identity" alongside "the no-concept, non-dual Reality" is itself contradictory. At the "highest level" of understanding, any identity is also seen to be conceptual. Preoccupation with identifying "what the generic THAT is" becomes another concern that can continue to disturb even those who have transitioned kindergarten spirituality, who have understood the I AM, and who know the True Self but are not functioning as the unaware Awareness.

"Bliss" is merely an undisturbed, unconcerned vibration. Preoccupations and concerns activate a disturbance when the natural vibrational pattern of anything is forced to shift. Apply what is happening to the phenomenal planet to grasp what can happen to the phenomenal body-"mind" under those conditions: because ice caps are melting as a result of global warming, a slight tilt is happening along the axis of the globe. That is triggering not only all of the physically-observable results on the planet but is also generating mental and emotional effects on life forms as well.

When vibrational patterns shift from natural to unnatural movements, phenomenal effects result because of the disturbance of that which is natural. Only the natural vibrational pattern of Awareness will allow "bliss" to happen (again, "bliss" being nothing more than that undisturbed, unconcerned vibration mentioned earlier).

At the "highest level," having understood the no-concept, non-dual Reality completely, WHO / WHAT remains to be concerned with any "identity" or to be disturbed by not being able to apply another man-made label to the man-made pointer called "THAT"?

Persons are so sure of all they believe. After being challenged to question it all and not being so sure, they nevertheless return to that state of being certain at the third step on the "path" after assuming religious or spiritual roles. Many at that point think that they have found the "Advaita Understanding." They have not. They have substituted one egotism-generating persona for others and have substituted several egotism-generating belief systems for another. They are mistaking the dawn for high noon.

The ultimate Advaita understanding is that there need not be any understanding. (Again, that pointer is not for the beginner.) Yet AS IF living (based in the no concept, non-dual Reality) is seldom modeled among "humans"; thus, one need not look there to find examples of such "living." Look to nature instead.

True AS IF living is a mode of natural living, modeled in nature by animals such as the deer, primarily docile and at peace…living a minimalist existence… accumulating nothing…believing nothing…never fighting for any "belief"… functioning quite splendidly without any "identity" even though sensing its presence…and either enjoying all aspects of the manifestation or tolerating all aspects of the manifestation in a no-attachment-mode, without any concern or disturbance at all.

How closely does your relative existence reflect that mode of natural living? Is it possible that you might also function quite splendidly, even without an "identity"?

CHAPTER FIVE

ONLY THE EGO WANTS
TO BE SOMETHING

MOST who read pointers dealing with zero concepts (as offered by some Direct Path Advaita Teachers and by some "Neo-Advaitins"), will feel as if they are dying or being robbed of their "true identity." Some will feel that their "true identity" is being minimized and not recognized for the glorious post-manifestation "SOMETHING" that it is…all "heavenly" and "celestial" and "splendid"…maybe even "saintly" or "godly" or "cherubic" or "spiritual" or "divine" or "holy" or "something" which they believe will be "even above and beyond" all of that.

Some resent the implication that their relevance, either during the relative manifestation or after the relative manifestation, is being decreased or diminished or underestimated. They hate the suggestion that to have taken themselves and their beliefs seriously for so many years was all nonsense. They hate hearing that their years of fighting for their causes were uselessly passed in vain and were steeped in egotism and efforts to support their false identities/ego-states.

They hate hearing that their entire existence is all much ado about nothing. They despise being told that they have been fooled. They hate pointers dealing with purposelessness and meaninglessness. They hate pointers which suggest that all of those times when they made mountains out of molehills was pure foolishness. They hate the notion of "nothingness" and thrive on all their concepts that deal with "somethingness." They hate hearing that their beliefs and their concepts are fiction.

They hate when their dualistic belief in their own eternal reward is exposed as a fraud or when their belief in an eternal punishment for their enemies is debunked. They bristle when it is pointed out that their "life-long" attempts to defend their various concepts have amounted to nothing more than a waste of breath.

They hate to hear that the energy spent in trying to make their views understood and accepted was for naught. They can become livid when it is noted that their actions (which earned applause from the masses who considered those actions to be "accomplishments") were for nil. They despise the pointer that no one has ever "made the world a better place" as a result of any action.

They are offended when it is suggested that the naming of streets after them, that the building of statues in their honor, and that the construction of libraries built to house evidence of their "achievements" amounts to just so much rubbish. They reject any suggestion that the desire to extend in perpetuity the memory of them and their "identity" is mere tripe.

Similarly, the following pointer was offered to the seeker who raised the issue of "SOMETHING" in defense of his "identity," desiring as he does to verify it and to be assured that it will be extended in perpetuity:

"Whether your identity is of a phenomenal nature or a noumenal nature in your 'mind,' your preoccupation with it is evidence of the fact that you hold in esteem either that which you currently believe you are, or that SOMETHING which you think you shall be forever, or both. In fact, when a 'state' of zero concepts is reached, it is understood that there is no 'identity' at all. It is also realized from that 'state' that there is nothing deserving any esteem at all, contrary to the tendency among the non-Realized to demand that they be shown 'the honor they deserve'."

The pointer offered earlier was that "there's no identity to be concerned with at all." Another pointer is offered for those seekers who would reach the "next level" of understanding and who are capable of reaching the zero concepts "state":

"Absolute," "THAT," "Brahman," "God," "energy," "energy-matter," "Consciousness," "Awareness," and "SOMETHING" are still man-made labels generated by persons; however, since Awareness is not even aware of awareness, what justification can be offered for being "concerned" with any of those labels, if Fully Realized?

The concept of "SOMETHING" blocks the understanding of what is most pervasive in this universe (and in all universes). What is most pervasive? Not something but…no-thing. The physical body of a human is neither "primarily energy" nor "primarily matter." It is primarily space, primarily a void, and can thereby serve as a microcosm of the universe which is primarily space, primarily nothingness, primarily no-thingness.

Similar to every bridge that will eventually be reduced to rubble, a couple of hundred pounds of "floyd" will be reduced to a few pounds of ash. That which is mainly "space" is misperceived by the non-Realized as being "something."

Typically, "the nothing" is neither seen nor understand as persons show deference to, and preference for, "something." Only for "the most advanced" is this pointer offered: if the nothingness is understood, then not an iota of attention is wasted with concern about the "SOMETHING" the seeker mentioned.

At "the peak" of understanding, it is realized that "concern" with a post-manifestation identity is just so much silliness. Persons who focus on "SOMETHING" become "concerned," and "concern" about anything will generate unnatural or supernatural thinking and living. All "concerns" prevent peace and natural living from happening. If an excess of energy is available, employ it to realize all that you are not if you would eliminate insane-like thoughts and words and deeds and relative destructiveness from an otherwise ego-dominated existence.

To focus on the concept of "SOMETHING" prevents seeing "The Reality of the Emptiness," "The Reality of the Void," "The Reality of the Nothingness." All "mind"-stuff attached to "somethingness" will preempt any understanding of the no-concept, non-dual, no-thing Reality.

Peace and happiness only happen (a) during the manifestation and (b) in the absence of a "mind" that focuses on any THING. So, would you rather be concerned with SOMETHING, or would you rather be at peace as a result of being concerned with nothing? Again, there really is no identity that you need be concerned with at all. All that you have ever concerned yourself with was really just much ado about nothing.

CHAPTER SIX

SIXTY YEARS OF MUCH ADO ABOUT NOTHING

A N e-mail was received from a man named Gulllermo who was a friend of a seeker who had attended an Advaita Retreat:

My friend Ricardo told me to write to you. I just want peace. I just want to be happy. Help. William (Guillermo)

The following response was written to him:

Hello, Guillermo. Since you are obviously just beginning the search for peace and happiness, understand that some come to the Advaita philosophy with high expectations. They are searching for immediate joy and bliss when that bar might be set too high for beginners. Realize that, ultimately, peace and happiness during the relative existence cannot happen unless it is first understood that all happenings are "Much ado about nothing." Meaning? Meaning that if you observe all events with a clear perspective, you'll see how the trivial is elevated to the status of "significant" by persons. Then, seeing how trivial it all really is, you might be able to assume a position of neutrality around all happenings. Then, you might at least attain a sense of contentment before pursuing joy and bliss.

If it is understood that the entire manifestation of consciousness is much ado about nothing, then those obstacles which interrupt peace cannot materialize … obstacles such as belief in dualistic concepts, attachment, caring, judging, involvement, emotional intoxication, desiring, fearing, needing, etc.

What does much ado about nothing look like? It looks as if important happenings are occurring, happenings that require a dualistic stance, either for or against. But those happenings are really just the various parts of a fable; however, the elements of a fictional story can only be reviewed objectively if one functions as a non-attached witness.

Then, by reviewing the elements of the fiction from a "distance," one can see clearly how it all amounted to nothing. Here are the elements in one tale with a 60-year span. It will show how much ado can be made about nothing when persons think the events in their relative existence amount to something important. This particular fictional tale included such elements as:

A young girl abandoned after her mother died in childbirth; that girl later kidnapped by a relative; a young man watching his brother being cut in half by a train; a chance meeting; "love"; a marriage; Germany and Japan are declared "the enemy"; war declared; separation as a result of a war; two bombs dropped; returning home; prosperity; pregnancy; birth; another pregnancy; another birth; parents were pleased; parents were angry; teachers were pleased; teachers were angry; children were whipped with paddles; palms were beaten with rulers; national crime rates went down; and ultimately, it was all much ado about nothing.

Germany and Japan are then declared "our friends" and communists are declared "the enemy"; bomb shelters were built; drills happened in schools, along with crawling under desks and putting books over heads; making friends at school; fighting with friends at school; Cuba was declared "an enemy"; and ultimately, it was all much ado about nothing.

a lack of prosperity; crime went up; a tonsillectomy; an appendectomy; a toe severed by a lawn mover; a rare Southern snow; intense heat; punishment for not being "good"; exposure to religious Occidentals and their nonsensical beliefs; fear when the promise of eternal fire and damnation were introduced; accepting "salvation" in order to please, but knowing it was hogwash; dating; championships won; graduation; college; another graduation; employment; bosses were pleased; bosses were displeased; Vietnam was declared "an enemy"; another war; being drafted; another war ended; graduate school; a Master's Degree and another graduation; low-paying employment; a meeting; "love"; a marriage; Vietnam was then declared "a friend" and "trading partner"; a divorce; and ultimately, it was all much ado about nothing.

too many lovers; a chance meeting; "love"; a marriage; high-paying employment; a Bush declares an Ortega "a friend"; plaques and certificates of achievement and paid vacations awarded at annual banquets; pregnancy; birth; a healthy child; a sick child; swings in the economy; low income; high income; a Rumsfeld meets a Saddam and declares him "our friend"; an apartment in Tuscany; months at a time in Europe; dream jobs that became nightmares; fortunes lost; fortunes earned again; huge homes purchased and filled with "stuff"; friendships with neighbors; fights with neighbors; pets bought; pets buried; repairmen scheduled; pipes OK; pipes burst; more contractors dealt with; and ultimately, it was all much ado about nothing.

vast accumulations; wealth; hurricanes came, trees fell, property "destroyed"; property rebuilt; property taxes increased; evaluations protested; fortunes lost; dream relationships became nightmares; hearing the word "cancer"; a spouse who got into her car and drove away the day before the scheduled surgery for cancer, never to return; a divorce; and ultimately, it was all much ado about nothing.

arranging a funeral for a parent who preferred burial; Republican rule; nations to the south were declared "the enemy"; glasnost; Communists are then declared "a friend" and "a trading partner"; a parent's stroke; more invasions and war; a declaration that "We must fight them in Central America or we'll fight them here"; secret U.S. death squads; meeting a U.S. sniper using drugs to try to suppress the guilt of assassinating 46 innocent civilians in Central America (including a teacher and a priest) who were declared "the enemy" by the U.S. for anti-U.S. speeches; illegal arms deals; Democratic rule; huge surplus in national treasury; Republican rule; a Bush declares an Ortega is now "an enemy"; two poorly-designed towers fall; a Rumsfeld and others who had declared a Saddam to be "a friend" said he is "an enemy"; another war; national treasury surplus gone, replaced by huge national debt; a declaration that "We must fight them in the Middle East or we'll fight them here"; nations to the south again declared "the enemy"; now, the health care providers no longer say "cancer," but last week one said for the first time, "diabetes"; but ultimately, it's all much ado about nothing.

To review those happenings from the perspective of the objective witness, Guillermo, is to see the insanity of all of the duality that robbed the players in that "Drama of the Lie" of peace and happiness: good and bad, satisfied and dissatisfied, pleased and displeased, reward and punishment, war and peace, enemy and friend, friend and enemy, rich and poor, sick and well, marriage and divorce, good times and bad times, chaos and stability, knowing who "the enemy" was then not knowing who "the enemy" was. Everything thought to be bad would eventually be thought to be good and everything thought to be good would eventually be thought to be bad. In fact, it was all dualistic fiction, all dualistic nonsense, all ego-based silliness, all ego-driven BS.

Then, searching began; seeking; doing; going; zooming; next, finding; understanding; awareness; and relaxing; and ultimately, it was Realized that it was, indeed, all much ado about nothing…all nothing more than a lot of sound and fury. Only when the addiction to the sound and the fury ends can the joy and bliss of the silence begin.

Those who believe in timelines would say those events covered "six decades in the life of one man." The re-purified consciousness sees nothing more than the elements of a fable…a series of happenings all based in idiocy. Again, the words of the Advaitin William Shakespeare apply: "Life is a tale told by an idiot, full of sound and fury, signifying nothing."

Signifying…nothing. The invitation is to look at all of the elements in that fictional fable and see that they cover only 60 years of happenings on one planet that is spinning away in a universe that has a 14-billion year history. The invitation is too look at all those happenings and to note how "very important" they were all considered to be when they were happening. The invitation is also to see that the happenings amounted only to so much sound and fury…with no importance or truth or reality involved at all.

To understand that whatever persons take to be "something" or "something really important" is actually just much ado about nothing will allow the nothingness to be understood. When the nothingness is understood, then That Which Truly Is Everything can be understood. When the functioning of the totality is understood, all things false are abandoned and peace just happens.

Relatedly, the Advaitin poet also wrote, "All the world's a stage, and all the men and women merely players. They have their exits and their entrances, and one man in his time plays many parts," and "Life's but a walking shadow, a poor player that struts and frets his hour upon a stage." And then? "Out, out, brief candle."

Enjoy the play, Guillermo, but know that the play is a play. Then and only then will you not be deluded and made miserable by the dualities of the relative existence. Then and only then can the peace you long for manifest and remain for the duration of the manifestation of the consciousness. For now, this likely sounds senseless to you. Borrow the books Ricardo bought from the site and begin the readings in the order he can show you. Best regards on the "journey."

CHAPTER SEVEN

WHO WANTS TO BE "SOMETHING"?

I N response to the pointer that "advanced" seekers can reach a "state" of zero concepts and thereby understand that "Absolute," "THAT," "Brahman," "God," "energy," "energy-matter," "Consciousness," "Awareness," and "SOMETHING" are nothing more than man-made labels and that since Awareness is not even aware of awareness, then there is no reason to be "concerned" with any labels at all some will say, "How dare you discount spirituality." Others will ask, "How can you dare to minimize the Pure Absolute that I AM?" Some will exclaim, "How dare you close the door to immortality by suggesting that there is no eternal reward...or punishment," or "How dare you suggest that all of my good works here will not be rewarded there."

Even among those who claim to be "Advaitins" and who claim to have "cast aside their ideas and concepts," many begin to cling to their newly-discovered Advaita concepts. They refuse to cast aside the thorn called "the Advaita Teachings" even after all other thorns have been removed.

The pointer has been offered that "to look to the universe and to focus on the concept of 'SOMETHING' prevents seeing 'The Reality of the Emptiness,' 'The Reality of the Void,' 'The Reality of the Nothingness'."In fact, "the entire universe"—no different at all from "this world"—is contained in consciousness as well. Many will reject the no-concept, no duality, no identity pointers being offered in this book. Some will claim that to even discuss "emptiness" is an affirmation of consciousness (and proof that consciousness is their true identity).

Those making that claim will suggest that denying consciousness as one's ultimate identity requires consciousness to be "a true identity" because the refutation itself proves that consciousness is present to make the denial. At the conceptual level, their argument is accepted.

Yet what of the "no concept" level? For a philosophy that invites seekers to find out all that they are not, an inordinate amount of energy is being expended in seeking the answer to "Who am I?" instead (even though the ones asking the question—or answering the question—are still assuming false identities: "The Spiritual Giant," "The Seeker," "The Religious One," "The Advaitin," "The Realized One," "The Guru," "The Non-Doer," ad infinitum).

The question ignores the simple fact that "there is no who to discuss or to find anything." At best, only a "what" can be legitimately discussed, and it could be asked, "Why discuss even that?"

At Advaitin seminars, seekers have asked such questions as the following:

"So who am I, really?" and "What is love?" and "What is permanent?" Another made the comment, "I'm sick of trying to 'get this.' I understand that I'm not those roles I've played all my life. Why is that not enough?"

The consideration was offered: "Maybe it is enough. If you were never to find the answer to questions regarding who you are, but you were able to discover everything that you are not, then the course of events in your relative existence would turn 180 degrees. If you were never to find the answer to questions regarding what love is, but you were able to discover everything that love is not but that is driving you nevertheless, then the course of events in your relative existence would turn 180 degrees.

Persons are driven by what they are not. That Which They Are will have no effect whatsoever on the only existence that they will ever be cognizant of, namely, the relative existence. (Again, the post-manifestation Awareness has no awareness of itself.)

Maharaj predicted that only one in a million will ever Realize That Which They Are. That miniscule percentage has never impacted the planet, has never "made the world a better place," and it never will. However, were all of the non-Realized on the planet to abandon belief in all of the personas which they have assumed as identities but which they are not, then the resultant ending of all ego-states and all egotism would assure that the remainder of the manifestation would happen with freedom and in peace. That will not happen on a planet-wide basis, but it can happen for a few. Freedom and peace come when the something-ness is ignored and when the "state" of nothingness is reached.

CHAPTER EIGHT

The "Non-Journey Journey" to a "Non-Place Place" Far from the Madding Crowd

The following e-mail was received from a visitor to the Advaita website:

IN my so far endless quest for enlightenment, my employment and my limited finances mean the quest is done only by reading books or free websites such as yours. I keep reading about people who have gone to India and been enlightened, people who have literally gone to a mountaintop and been enlightened by someone there, or people who went to the jungle and did exercises there and been enlightened. I can't do any of that, so is there really any hope for those of us who cannot travel around the world in our search for Self? Margaret

The response was: Yours is the second e-mail this week to ask that same question. Consider: the title of Thomas Hardy's novel Far from the Madding Crowd is taken from Thomas Gray's poem Elegy Written in a Country Churchyard. There is a natural appeal for the natural, the result of which is an archetypal drive among most to find a geographic place with some very specific traits for retreat (and re-treat), and that place is far from the crowd. That innate drive will support the belief that there is a place (or places) that people must travel to in order to find Self and freedom and peace and happiness.

Over a period of thirty-three years, nearly 5000 persons were polled during discussions concerning the movement away from the madding crowd. (Most of those polled, like you, did not have the option of arranging a permanent retreat from society.) Prior to the polling, the participants were told that most people have in their imagination a quiet place, a place that they would consider to have all of the attributes of "the perfect hideaway" or "the ideal area for escape."

279

It was explained that they were not to try to describe a geographical place that they have actually visited but were to tap into the recesses of their consciousness and describe that place which can only be visualized and that has always been within. Next, they were asked to list the words that best described the place and its surroundings.

In 95% of all responses, six common traits were always mentioned:
1. remote
2. quiet
3. a place of solitude because no other humans are anywhere near (meaning one can be alone there without feeling lonely)
4. water
5. the natural sound of the movement of water (waterfall, brook, stream) and sometimes the sound of a gentle breeze blowing through the trees
6. wildlife, esp. birds

A Cherokee grandmother used a term employed by the indigenous peoples to describe that "non-place place": she called it "The Medicine Place" or "The Healing Place," reached by conducting a "Spirit Journey" (hence, the title of the CD that you can order).

Do most require at least some time with a teacher to address one-on-one the seeker's questions? Often that seems to be the case; however, no expensive trip is required for you to reach that "healing place" where the True Self can become known.

After traveling the world on a quest that covered several continents—and that also included, yes, a trip to the mountaintop to sit with a sage as well as 25 months of solitude in the forest, all to no avail—the light came while reclined on a small sofa in the corner of the same house from which each of those futile trips had began.

Relatedly, this e-mail was received from a seeker in Iceland:

I try to make the best of the situation I am in. Advaita is in some way benefi-cial in seeing the false via insights. You once told me that you sat in silence and watched the light hit the darkness in you and it disolved. It's like that when I read clear Advaita texts. Sveinn

As for "hope for those of us who cannot travel around the world in our search for Self," note that enlightenment is about touching that Original Understanding which predated both language and world travel. There is an "inner guru" or "inner resource" that can be tapped into; however, programming and conditioning and domestication and enculturation have created such a barricade of blackness that more light is required to penetrate the barriers than most will ever muster alone.

Next, in order for Realization to happen (and for peace and happiness to continue thereafter), must one travel to a geographically-remote area and reside there in order to be removed far from the madding crowd? Of course not. Post-Realization, all is seen for what it is, and the madding crowd is recognized to be as grand an illusion as everything else that is misperceived by the non-Realized. A mirage in the road ahead can only be troublesome for those who are deceived and who believe that illusions are real.

Instead of having to take endless trips around the planet, yours must be a "non-journey journey" to the "non-place place" where the no-thingness awaits. The no-thingness? Yes. To understand that it is the nothingness that is found at the end of this "path" prevents most from ever even starting an Advaita-based "journey" that is marked by annihilation...not gain; by elimination of all of the learned ignorance that has been collected...not acquisition of more knowledge; by de-accumulation...not accumulation.

If that which awaits at the "end" of your quest is understood, you will know that there is no benefit, no one to benefit, no purpose, and no meaning. Know that and your quest will lose that frenzied drive that might be characterizing your current efforts. That will allow a calmer state to manifest, which is the only kind of state in which Realization can happen. Best regards on that "non-journey journey."

CHAPTER NINE

Il Dolce di Niente

EGOTISM drives persons to want to "be something" and to "be somebody." Programming and conditioning and enculturation and domestication convince the non-Realized that they "are something"…that they are, in fact, "many things." (Hence, "duality," "plurality," or "multiplicity.") Desires drive persons to seek states of rapture; fear, combined with a desire for power and control and continuity, drives persons to seek "the divine."

Ego always wants more; freedom from the bondage of ego results in giving value to less. Ego is about going and doing and zooming in order to collect more; freedom from the love of more allows the non-doingness (the beingness only) to manifest.

Thus, persons search for "the divine" and for an understanding of all that is "supernatural" when in fact there is nothing that is supernatural at all. That which is thought to be supernatural is contained entirely within the warped consciousness. Though the only style of living that makes sense in the relative is natural living, the fact is that persons either live unnaturally or think that they are living supernaturally as a result of their having been fooled.

The result of their having been fooled is an endless stream of desires and fears that create a constant sense of longing. A constant sense of longing generates a sense of emptiness…of not being full…of a lack of fulfillment. The desires and fears generate the adoption of one false self after another, so the non-Realized end up being "full of themselves"—meaning, mentally full of their false selves.

Since those selves are illusions without substance, the sensation of emptiness among persons is ever-present throughout the manifestation. The non-Realized never come to the understanding that it is only the emptiness that can be fulfilling during the manifestation.

Onone occasion, after securing the lines on the boat and then leaving the harbor, this exchange was overheard as one man asked another: "What have you got lined up for the weekend?" The second answered, "Nothing. Not a GD thing. Isn't that great?"

If an empty schedule for two days can be considered "great," imagine how wonderful such emptiness could be 24-7 for the remainder of the manifestation.

Yet who that has been programmed to accumulate more could possibility prefer de-accumulation and less? The answer is, "Only those who have tasted even the slightest bit of that sweetness of less…of nothingness."

A pointer that has been shared before will be repeated here since it is relevant to this discussion:

The Realized can taste what the Italians call il dolce di fare niente—"the sweetness of doing nothing." The Fully Realized will shift to a level even beyond that and will understand something even simpler than "the sweetness of doing nothing," namely, il dolce di Niente—"the sweetness of Nothing," period.

It has been asked, "If nothingness is the real deal, then why are words gathered into books or posted on a site? Someone is doing that gathering and posting." That comment indicates delusion. Consciousness speaks, but consciousness is without personal attributes or individuality or doership. Here, there is no person or being or consciousness choosing anything. All happens spontaneously. Words come automatically, without thought…without thinker.

Consciousness has neither body nor mind nor personality. It assumes no identity if pure or if re-purified. No matter how dedicated you are to finding an identity and "being somebody" and thereby "being fulfilled," the fact is that whatever you might claim your permanent identity to be, it cannot be any part of a non-permanent relative existence. You really aren't anybody.

Thus, whatever you would claim as your real identity must be void of self existence and void of SELF existence. Whatever you might think you are is actually beyond beingness and non-beingness and attributes. The self is a conceptualized mirage and the SELF is a conceptualized mirage. Not a single, spoken or written word conveys truth. Words can merely point toward the truth. The self is limited to the relative space, and any temporary, assumed selfness is just so much space. Post-manifestation, there is limitless, infinite space.

Maharaj explained the misunderstanding (and then the understanding) this way: "Now, consciousness has identified with a form. Later, it understands that it is not the form and goes further. In a few cases it may reach the space…."

CHAPTER TEN

REACH THE SPACE

A LL identities are limiting. Limitations restrict freedom. Restrictions of freedom prevent the manifestation of happiness during the relative existence. Preoccupation with finding identities and assigning labels has the same effect.

Nothing other than space is limitless. Should you identify with anything other than the limitless nothingness, then you will never enjoy the happiness that can only happen NOW, during the manifestation. If happiness is to happen, you must reach the space.

Bodies are limited; minds are limited; planets are limited; galaxies are limited; the boundaries of the universe, though expanding, are nevertheless limited; the self and the Self are limited. Even the Absolute is infinitesimal when compared with the limitless space. You may have reached the Absolute, but have you reached the space?

Planets are finite and their forms will end; all stars and suns are finite and their forms will end; galaxies are finite and their forms will end. Only space is limitless. Only nothingness is pervasive. Emptiness abounds, and during the relative manifestation, you will never feel "more full" than when you are truly empty: empty of identities...empty of preoccupation with self...empty of preoccupation with Self.

Yet that can be understood only after years of being imprisoned as a result of having been programmed to accumulate; after years of accumulating; after seeking "something" beyond the emptiness of collecting "stuff"; after years of serving self; after years of seeking Self; after de-accumulation; and after enjoying the freedom of less-ness. Only then can one understand the irony of this paradoxical teaching: the bliss which manifests after being aware of the fullness can only happen after understanding the reality of the emptiness.

Consider the moon and the surrounding space. Is the moon suspended in darkness and emptiness? Not at all. There is as much light surrounding the moon as is reflected from its surface. The surrounding light is not seen because it is not being reflected off a surface. That which appears to be the emptiness is really the fullness.

So it is during the manifestation: the non-Realized miss out on understanding the reality of the fullness, focusing as they do on their nagging sensation of misconceived emptiness. The sense of "emptiness" that they think they are experiencing results when their false selves believe that they have not gained something they have always wanted or when their false identities think that they have lost something that they wanted to have forever. Meanwhile, both gain and lost are illusion; therefore, their misery is illusion-based as well.

In contrast, the Realized enjoy a sense of fullness though there is no longer any body or mind or personality that is reflecting anything. Being emptied of the false, the fullness of being unencumbered and free results in a sense of freedom (as exhibited by the man mentioned earlier who was going to be free over the weekend because he had nothing lined up).

If you would be free, line up with the nothingness as well. Reach the space.

Next, "If there is no post-manifestation self or Self," some ask, "why is there any need to engage in any religious or spiritual activities?" Indeed. When asked if all spiritual disciplines should be dropped, Sri Nisargadatta Maharaj pointed out that "At the earlier levels you have to do your homework." Yet he also noted that "at the highest level, this is so." Drop the religious activities, drop the spiritual personas, transition that step, and complete the other four steps of the seven–step "journey" to Reality. Then relax and enjoy the remainder of the manifestation.

Fixating in either of those Step Three ego-states will cause the focus of persons to be on getting ... getting influence and control over the masses ... getting rewards now ... getting rewards later. The egotism that accompanies the assumption of ego-states as identities always generates a desire to get ... to accumulate. Among "accumulators," "something" is dualistically thought to be "good" and "nothing" is dualistically thought to be "bad."

Furthermore, those who believe in "getting" will dualistically believe in "losing." For either to happen, a self (some identity) must have been assumed. Again, the belief that there is a self that has lost something will result in a miserable relative existence.

To abide as consciousness or as the Absolute or as the Awareness does not mean that any concept need be believed. At the highest level, even the I AM THAT can be relinquished after giving up all identification with the I AM. Post-manifestation, there is nothingness as far as any you or You is concerned. So Why be concerned with … something? Why be concerned with … anything?

In fact, why even be concerned with nothing, ultimately? In the end, even the discussion of that concept of nothingness is conceptual. Maharaj said in this regard, "All my knowledge has gone into liquidation. I am unconcerned."

If you/You would be unconcerned, then all of your knowledge must go into liquidation. Has that happened? Have you reached the space?

NOTE: When excerpts from this book were being offered in one forum, a person challenged the observation regarding "loss":

"Easy for you to say that 'a sense of loss is illusion,' but if everything you worked for and earned during your adult life was taken away by an egomaniac, something so flippant might not be stated."

The following clarification in brackets was then offered:

[Actually, most of the material things that were worked for and paid for during a twenty-year period were taken away by an egomaniac. The money and those possessions are now being shared with another man by that person, so the pointer that you reference was not offered from within a vacuum. More to the point, though, is the fact that the bitterness that is implied in your message might be dispelled if you were able to understand this pointer from Maharaj:

Suppose somebody abuses you and you find out who it is. Is it the body? It is not the body. Then what could it be? Finally you come to the conclusion that it is spontaneously happening out of whatever that body is. You will not attribute it to any individual. When your individuality is dissolved, you will not see individuals anywhere, it is just a functioning in consciousness. If it clicks in you, it is very easy to understand. If it does not, it is most difficult. It is very profound and very simple, if understood right.

A thorough investigation of the background of whoever you think to be the most abusive person that you've ever dealt with will usually reveal that person to also be the most abused person you'll ever meet. Since there are no individuals, however, what you and "floyd" were really dealing with were highly warped specks of consciousness. An honest and objective look at what inspired you and "floyd" to attach for a time to those warped specks of consciousness would reveal equally warped specks of consciousness that were being driven to try to satisfy a desire or a fear. Also, an honest and objective look at what you think you've lost

THE ADVANCED SEEKER'S SERIES

would reveal that you haven't lost a thing. To the degree that you cast aside your self, to that same degree will both your illusory sense of "loss" and your bitterness be cast aside as well.

Some functionings in consciousness are entertaining. Some functionings in consciousness are not. So it is. If you shift beyond your identification with body, mind, personality and beliefs, you will be able to witness your feelings rise and fall without attachment and therefore without such bitterness. Freedom from emotional intoxication follows freedom from identification with body, mind, ego-states, and ideas.]

Sri Nisargadatta Maharaj explained to a seeker who was preoccupied with finding an identity, "You are asking, 'Who am I?' and you are not going to get an answer, because the one who will get the answer is false. You may have an idea, a concept, and you will think you have found yourself, but it is only a concept."

Understand that "the Self" is as much a concept as "the self." Both can function only during the relative manifestation, the self being the false identity that can only see the false and the Self being that which can see Reality. Yet all seeing—be it "True" Witnessing or "false" witnessing—can happen only during this manifestation. All labels—whether labels dealing with the phenonenal or labels dealing with the noumenal—are contained in the temporarily-manifested consciousness.

Maharaj said, "Brahman, Isvara, God, all these are names given to the consciousness when it is conscious of itself." Later, "Isvara is the manifest principle by which all activities are carried on. It has no form...."

He said, "If you have properly understood this knowledge, what will be your position at the moment of so-called death? That state cannot be described." He continued, "It is called Parabrahman, the supreme Absolute, but that is only a name for communication purposes."

"...The last traces of personality and individuality have left me. My dwelling place in the grosser world is gone now; presently it is in the subtler sphere, as in space."

"Give me a photograph of the meaning of that word 'I'. You can't. That principle has no name or form or shape."

So why are you trying to name it, to identify its form, to determine its shape? Why are you concerned with "something"? Why be concerned with anything? Maharaj said, "Words are the expression of space...." Reach the space.

CHAPTER ELEVEN

REACH THE SPACE

MAHARAJ also said, "This knowledge is for those who have no desires." It is obvious that the seeker who wrote about "SOMETHING" has a desire for an identity, a desire which inspired his talk of "something." Since he desires an identity, the content of this book will not likely appeal to him. Is one also desiring life eternal? Then the ultimate understanding is not for that person. Because persons want to be "something" (and something forever) then the ultimate teaching will likely have no appeal.

If you still desire to know who you are (and that is appropriate at the earlier levels), these highest level teachings will not be for you. It can be asked legitimately, "Then what is any of this about? Why are the teachings happening? Why does the consciousness continue to speak?"

Maharaj was asked that very question and he answered, "What is the worth of all these activities of human beings? It is all entertainment, just to pass the time. You get pleasure only when you forget yourself." So for ultimate pleasure, forget your self, and forget Your Self.

He said, "Liberation means what? It is no more there. [Flicking his cigarette lighter off and on.] This cigarette lighter is the body; the consciousness is the flame. Now it isn't there anymore; it is liberated. Where is the need to label it … ?"

"First I thought I was the body, then I experienced that I was not the body but I was the consciousness, then I got the experience that this consciousness is not really me, and there is no form, no individuality, no nothing."

It has been asked even by the more advanced seekers during satsanga sessions and Advaita Seminars and Advaita Retreats, "Isn't there something that you believe in?"

The reply: "Not only do I not believe in something, I don't even believe in nothing…no person, no concept, no form, no nothing. 'Something' is temporary and 'nothing' is also temporary—all fleeting aspects of an ever-changing universe that wasn't at first and that later suddenly was." (More on that in a later chapter.)

Wherefore your desire for permanence? Wherefore your desire for an "identity" when even before the "SOMETHING" that was referenced by a seeker, there was nothing? Ultimately, either your view of Reality involves no concepts and no duality, or your false sense of reality involves concepts (which, in turn, support duality and falsehoods).

Far more pervasive among persons who will never find a "true identity" are their distortions regarding all of the false, assumed identities which they are not but which they think they are. (And those are the "identities" that have a far more influential impact, relatively speaking).

If persons would be free of the suffering that is rooted in the ignorance of their ego-states—and the egotism that always accompanies their false identities—then freedom from identity (not more identification) is the solution. Most would do well to move even that far along any "path" to being truly free ... to being truly independent.

Among those with whom this part of the teaching has been discussed "face-to-face," the most frequent scenario has been: "I've got it! I've got! I've got it!" followed soon by "I had it, but I lost it." What specifically do those latter comments really mean?

That admission reveals that they understood the pointers offered during discussions dealing with the Consciousness and the Awareness and with the Absolute, only to soon revert back into their erroneous identification with body-mind-personality-beliefs because they did not grasp the ultimate understanding of the space…of the nothingness…of the null…of the void.

CHAPTER TWELVE

ZERO CONCEPTS

THE answer continued to the seeker who said: No identity at all? Everybody is SOMETHING, and whatever that SOMETHING is, is our identity.

Maharaj said, "This is all a big hoax, a big fraud, created out of nothingness." Ultimately, even "nothing" as a concept is abandoned.

He said, "The sum total of my spirituality now is nothing, even the word 'nothing' is not there, so there is no spirituality left." After reaching the point of zero concepts, how could there be such a thing as "spirituality"? It is just another concept, dreamed up by men. The Full Understanding lies far beyond the assumption of any spiritual or religious personas.

Maharaj also said, "The Absolute state cannot be explained by words." Of course, that pointer cannot be offered to beginners. The functioning of the totality must be understood before "the totality" can be dismissed as just another concept.

Ultimately, it can be asked, "So what is with all this talk—what is with all these words—about the 'anything'? About 'something'? About 'nothing'?" If one sees any part of this spontaneously-happening process as anything more than entertainment during the brief period of manifestation, then one has been fooled. Is this Advaita-heresy? Of course not. It is a pointer toward truth, but then, even "truth" is a concept, is it not?

Why cast aside all identities, concepts, ideas, emotions, attitudes, and beliefs? Because the consciousness, once conditioned, believes in the false. It becomes the supposed knower of concepts, the supposed thinker of ideas, the supposed emoter of emotions, the supposed believer of beliefs. All of that leads at least to unhappiness or to misery and to suffering in the extreme. Once even the consciousness is dismissed, what remains to sustain concepts? Nothing. In the absence of concepts, freedom can happen and peace can follow.

THE ADVANCED SEEKER'S SERIES

Every person, however, is trapped in the belief that his/her mind-flow and her/his thought-life is "the real." What nonsense. All is imagined or seen incorrectly; all concepts were dreamed up by ignorant, controlling men and passed down—generally without any questioning of those concepts at all—from one generation to the next.

Because that has been the case for generation after generation after generation, the planet is now dominated by non-Realized persons who are living their lives under the influence of the most ignorant concepts imaginable—ideas dreamed up millennia ago by men who had no understanding of facts and science and reality but who were driven by their superstitions and their ignorance instead.

Such remains the current status of the masses. To be free of a life driven by the influence of learned ignorance, one must abandon the belief in any belief ... including the belief that everything must be labeled ... including the labeling of whatever you think you are.

Advaita (at the purest and most advanced level of the Teachings) endorses zero concepts. It invites programmed and conditioned persons to be free of all beliefs and all ideas, recommending not that "minds" should be full but that all "minds" should be emptied, step-by-step, until no "mind" exists at all.

To assume no identity during the manifestation of consciousness will produce the exact same results as abiding as the Absolute or as the Awareness that is unaware of awareness. A relative existence marked by weariness and heaviness is steeped in concepts. A relative existence marked by lightness is burdened with few concepts. One in which total freedom is happening is marked by a belief in no concepts.

A relative existence characterized by complete freedom and peace is marked by emptiness. Meaning? Meaning it is not marked at all. A sense of heaviness results when identities are assumed. A sense of lightness happens when a minimum of identities are assumed. A sense of total freedom and a sense of peace (a sense of the unburdened emptiness) only happens when no identities are assumed.

Why are persons so opposed to these advanced teachings? Because they are driven by desires and fears. Because they have been programmed from early on to accept identities and to accumulate identities. Because they have been conditioned to "be somebody." Because they want to "be somebody" ... to really "be something."

Yet all of that is based in the duality of "loss-gain." There has never been any belief held by any person that did not have behind it a notion that some payoff would result from holding that belief. What nonsense when there is no WHO to gain and no WHO to lose…when there is nothing to gain and nothing to lose.

Nothing more is happening in this universe than a series of groupings and ungroupings, nothing more than being and not-being, nothing more than organizing and disorganizing and re-organizing and disorganizing again, nothing more than the supposed appearance of "something" from nothing.

To be free and at peace, understand Maharaj's pointer that, when persons are freed of ancient beliefs that are currently being accepted as truth, then "life ceases to be a task and becomes natural and simple, in itself an ecstasy."

If you study your relative existence as it is currently unfolding, is it natural, or supernatural, or unnatural? Is it simple…or complicated? Do you know the ecstasy of nothingness, or are you tolling for somethingness? Are you trapped in the illusions of the phenomenal, or have you reached the space?

Have you ever considered the possibility that "something" can manifest from nothing and can form groupings? Have you ever considered the possibility that "something" can ungroup and eventually be nothing again? Are you understanding how freeing it is—in the relative—to relate only to the nothingness rather than to identify with "something" … with "anything"?

CHAPTER THIRTEEN

From Nothingness
to the Absolute

A dedicated student of Advaita called "Sim from Kentucky"—upon hearing these Teaching on Nothingness for the first time—said: Now you are going to have to explain how we get from nothingness to the Absolute, which used to be the last stop on the train (or the first, depending upon your direction). A spark from the potentiality of the Absolute was the "old" starting point.

The reply was: an insightful remark at this juncture. It has been noted that the readiness is all. It may be that you are ready for the ultimate piece of the puzzle. It may be that you are ready to move beyond "kindergarten spirituality." It may be that you are ready to move beyond "high school and college physics and philosophy." You may be ready to receive your "Specialist Degree in Emptiness" and a "Doctorate in Nothingness."

You may be ready to understand that which is prior to Consciousness. You may be ready to understand that which is prior to Awareness. You may be ready to understand that which is prior to the current totality. You may be ready for the explanation of how it is that—from a state of non-existence and non-beingness and nothingness—everything in this universe (all all universes) came to be.

First, your inference is accurate: there is a process whereby, from the nothingness, a particle can manifest. This entire universe began with the instantaneous manifestation of an atom that split and fused and formed another atom. What is called "this universe" can be traced to an event that is similar to what is playing out continuously within what is called "the sun":

At the core of the sun, four hydrogen nuclei fuse together to form one helium nucleus, and that happens over and over. The part of the energy which that process releases as light travels in particle and wave form. After land plants evolved on earth (not 500 million years ago but closer to 700 million years ago), the stage was set for plants to convert energy that would not be usable by animals and humans into a form that could be usable. Plant photosynthesis, in turn, set the stage for the manifesting of energy-consciousness.

Understand, however, that prior to all that, it was from the nothingness that a manifestation happened spontaneously. Eventually, a manifestation of energy happened, and then even later a movement of energy from the "field" that would come to be referred to as "the Absolute" began happening. Via the development of land plants on planet earth, the stage would be set for the manifestation of consciousness. However, everything can be traced back to a void…to a vacuum.

It is necessary to pause and address a question that is often raised at this point during satsanga: "Does this mean that maybe Moses was 'right'? He wrote, 'In the beginning God created the heaven and the earth. And the earth was without form, and void; and darkness was upon the face of the deep'." No. It means that, as is often the case, someone took a philosophical fact from valid teachings and warped it into flawed religious dogma.

Had Moses been exposed to the Advaita teachings? Of course. Caravans carried teachings as well as goods between the MidEast and the Far East. It is known that Moses heard some of the Teachings because he plagiarized "I AM THAT; I AM" and put it in the supposed mouth of a burning plant.

(He had also heard of the pagan god in a tale that was 500 years old during his day. In one of the tales from that earlier religion, a captive people were freed by a god who lived underground. In the story, they wandered in the desert, received water when a magic rod was used to tap a rock, etc. Moses merely took that ancient tale, inserted himself in the god role, and now people today think that one million+ people really survived forty years of wandering through the desert.)

Do not draw the erroneous conclusion that his version of a "creator" had any validity just because he picked up a piece of this understanding and spoke of "the void" and spoke of that which was "without form" but later "assumed form." Two thousand years after Moses, a religion would evolve from the one rooted in the words of Abraham and reported by Moses. That teacher called "Jesus" would speak of the I AM, and the masses would also misunderstand the portion of the Advaita teachings that he referenced (and continue to do so to this day).

Here, instead, are the basic facts: a void did serve as "the launching space" for "this universe." Physicists who understand the null state can provide insight into the particulars, but the "advanced" Advaitin seeker need not understand all of the particulars to understand "how we got from nothingness to the Absolute," to use Sim's words.

CHAPTER FOURTEEN

A REVIEW OF KEY POINTERS

- Understand that everything which you take to be "spiritual" and "noumenal" is really nothing more than an accumulation of relative and phenomenal concepts.

- According to the earliest teachings shared among the Indigenous Peoples, that which is "true" is only the space between exhalation and inhalation. Close enough.

- "True Self" is not "God," though many who have morphed this philosophy into a religion will adopt and defend that Self-God, false-self concept as well.

- Ultimately, to try to support any "identity" alongside "the no-concept, non-dual Reality" is itself contradictory.

- At the "highest level" of understanding, any "identity" is seen to be conceptual.

- "Bliss" is merely an undisturbed, unconcerned vibration.

- The ultimate Advaita understanding is that there need not be any understanding. So relax.

- When a "state" of zero concepts is reached, it is understood that there is no "identity" at all. Nothing from nothing leaves...nothing, not "SOMETHING."

- "Absolute," "THAT," "Brahman," "God," "energy," "energy-matter," "Consciousness," "Awareness," and "SOMETHING" are still man-made labels generated by persons.

- Ultimately, to find out "who or what you are" is useless since there is no who to benefit, no user to use; on the other hand, finding out "who you are not" could eliminate unnatural and supernatural living and allow natural, AS IF living to happen throughout the remainder of the manifestation. That would also allow freedom to happen, and only if free can bliss happen.

- Only when the addiction to the sound and the fury ends can the joy and bliss of the silence begin.
- To look to the universe and to focus on the concept of "SOMETHING" prevents seeing "The Reality of the Emptiness," "The Reality of the Void," "The Reality of the Nothingness."
- Ego always wants more; freedom from the bondage of ego results in giving value to less.
- Ego is about going and doing and zooming in order to collect more; freedom from the love of more allows the non-doingness (the beingness only) to manifest, at least temporarily.
- Persons search for "the divine" and for an understanding of all that is "supernatural" when, in fact, there is nothing that is supernatural at all.
- The result of their having been fooled is an endless stream of desires and fears among persons. Those create a constant sense of longing, and longing generates a constant sense of dis-ease.
- The non-Realized never come to the understanding that it is only from a condition of emptiness (empty of concepts, of identities, of a "mind") that a sense of fulfillment can happen during the manifestation.
- The Realized can taste what the Italians call il dolce di fare niente—"the sweetness of doing nothing." The Fully Realized will shift even beyond that and will understand something even simpler than "the sweetness of doing nothing," namely, il dolce di Niente—"the sweetness of Nothing," period. Trace your roots. Go beyond self and Self, beyond Consciousness, beyond Awareness, and even beyond the Absolute to the seminal Nothingness. Abide as such.
- All identities are limiting. Limitations restrict freedom. Restrictions of freedom prevent the manifestation of happiness during the relative existence. Preoccupation with finding identities and assigning labels has the same effect.
- If you would be free, align with the nothingness. Reach the space.
- If you/You would be unconcerned, then all of your knowledge must go into liquidation. Has that happened? Have you reached the space?
- "The supreme Absolute…is only a name for communication purposes." (Maharaj)

- "This is all a big hoax, a big fraud, created out of nothingness." (Maharaj)
- Ultimately, even "nothing" as a concept is abandoned.
- Advaita (at the purest and most advanced level of the Teachings) endorses zero concepts. All of the mutated versions of Advaita, especially those which have been morphed into a religion by men with hidden agendas, are bastardizations … fabricated via the warped consciousness, accepted as truth by other specks of warped consciousness, and passed along now by such specks to other such specks.
- There is a process whereby, from the nothingness, a particle can manifest. This entire universe began with the instantaneous manifestation of an atom within a vacuum.
- It is from the nothingness that all manifestation happens spontaneously. After some groupings and ungroupings happen, the Nothingness will again prevail.
- Prior to "this universe," prior to Awareness, prior to Consciousness, and prior to manifestation, there was a "time" when only a vacuum was. Your "ultimate root" is even prior to time.
- If you're interested in oneness, understand that everything in this universe began as one, single atom that manifested within the emptiness of a vacuum.
- Purged of all identities, ideas, beliefs, and concepts, the consciousness can function as an empty vacuum. Originally, the empty vacuum was undisturbed, unconcerned…without burden, without activity, without any doings. The relative existence is miserable for those who are "full of it." If you would be undisturbed, unconcerned, without burden, without activity, without any doingness, be the emptiness. Reach the space and abide as such.
- Fear not…nothing is coming. No judgment…no endless punishment. Desire not…nothing is coming. No endless celestial caroling…no heavenly brothels and no extraterrestrial orgies…no endless reward. Nothing, so enjoy, NOW.

CHAPTER FIFTEEN

CONCLUSION

THE Direct Path Method of no-concept, non-dual Reality takes no prisoners; gives short shrift to those who want to fight to defend their ego-states; gives nothing to anyone; encourages de-accumulation rather than more accumulating; takes away all of the mirages that persons have attached to; eliminates the "mind"; and brings to an end the belief in all false personas and roles and phony images in order to put an end to disharmony-causing personality once and for all.

If one completes the entire "journey" to Full Realization, then what manifests afterwards, spontaneously and automatically, is the sweetness of the resulting Void … the peace that manifests when beingness happens from The Sweet Void of zero concepts.

Personas experience a constant state of flux, so happiness and unhappiness will constantly "come and go." Persons are caught up in a play in consciousness, and it has many characters…some of which they play and others which they take to be real. In that fictional play, there is no stability. Ultimately, of course, there is no stability, period. All is in a constant state of fluctuation.

Persons, taking the relative to be real, feel incomplete; they are trapped in the turmoil and flux. As a result of that constant fluctuation, their "relationships" will be marked by fluctuations as well; thus (in their "minds"), their favorite sinner will become an intolerable saint, or their beloved saint will become a much-despised sinner. They will constantly shift into and out of states of emotional intoxication, whether in traffic, at work, at home … wherever … whenever.

Such is the relative existence for those trapped in any identity and experiencing the fluctuations. In their attachment to the play and the drama and the roles, persons will walk the stage of the Drama of the Lie and will be the histrionic mouthpiece of "the something" and the "someones" and the "somebodies."

By contrast, what functions here is the consciousness which speaks as the mouth-piece of the Nothingness and the Void.

Whereas the Consciousness / Awareness is the Final Frontier of the understanding, the Nothingness was prior to the Frontier.

Seekers are only able to move to Stage Four and toward Stage Five when they truly grasp the simplicity of natural functioning. [See The Essence of the Teachings for an explanation of "The Five Stages" discussed by the early Advaitin sages, not to be confused with "The Seven Steps to Reality."] The relative is maddening to persons; abiding as the Absolute, madness cannot happen since there is no "mind."

Similarly, "something" can always be maddening to persons; the Nothingness, on the other hand, can have no effect at all…"good" or "bad." The Nothingness is the essence of AS IF living after Stage Five de-accumulation. The nothingness, and even the no-nothingness, are at the core of no-concept non-duality.

The ultimate freedom and independence can only happen if abiding as that Void. In that mode, abiding as that state of Nothingness with zero concepts, the relative existence happens naturally as the consciousness remains manifest but does not attach to any identities or ideas or beliefs or dogma or religious teachings or so-called "spirituality" or any other form of "learned ignorance." Functioning in that void, even the noble (and often ego-supporting) identity of THAT is of no concern.

The alternative to the peace of the Nothingness is that state of innumerable concepts in which most will live out the manifestation, trapped in personas, driven by fears and desires, imprisoned by attachments, never able to relax and take it easy, but convinced in that dream (or nightmare) state that they are free and happy. They will be in such denial that they will really believe, and enthusiastically proclaim, that they are not bored and that they are not depressed.

Yet they are not free, so they cannot possibly be happy. They are so bored that they can eventually develop an addiction to chaos in an effort to try to counteract their world-weariness (rather than seeing that "the world" is just another part of their dream—their Drama of the Lie). They are depressed, often on two levels: organic and situational. Why? They want to be "SOMEBODY" and they want to "be someone" significant or important or relevant or successful. Those aims will always be illusory and will generate desires that cannot be met, so frustration is guaranteed.

Happiness begins when the Stage One and Two search for more goes and when being content with less comes at Stage Five. Happiness becomes fixed when nothing is desired. It reaches a new height during AS IF living when the Void is enjoyed. It reaches the ultimate bliss after it is seen that, paradoxically, the Void is the fullness.

The re-purified consciousness will lead to de-accumulating, to understanding the bliss of the nothingness, to touching the validity of the void, and to being free of the effects of insanity and/or personality disorders that will otherwise dominate their relative existence.

To understand the sweetness of the Void does not prevent the happenings that will happen for the remainder of the manifestation. It will merely allow the arrogance that drives the seeking of significance to dissolve, will allow persons to stop thinking that everything matters so much, and will allow the end of making mountains out of proverbial molehills. That can bring to an end their living in the shadows of the valleys generated as a result of over-reacting and misperceiving.

The Full Understanding can end your attachment to illusions such as "this life"; such as, "my significance"; such as, "the great meaning that my life has"; such as "the need to cling to certain 'valuable' concepts, though they haven't provided the real answers even after thirty years or more"; ad infinitum. See, and then you can stop screaming for help and just…be.

Understand the Void. Rather than "having it all," go for "The Grand Prize": Nothing. When aligned with the nothingness, what needs to be said? Nothing. What needs to be heard? Nothing. In terms of noise, what is required? Nothing. What is there to be concerned about? Nothing. What is desired? Nothing. What is needed? Nothing. What can take away your independence? Nothing. What can take away your peace? Nothing. Via this understanding, what can happen in the relative existence that is not natural and peaceful? Nothing. What can move you from your position of neutrality and non-attachment? Nothing.

Will the elements still always return to the pool of universal elements? Yes. Will the air return to the pool of universal air? Yes. Will the energy return to the universal field of energy? Yes, but now, that which was before the elements, before the air, and before the manifestation of energy and matter, will be understood.

That which is beyond beingness and non-beingness will also be understood. That which was prior to either is understood. When that is understood, no desire for an identity manifests, and no fear of having "no identity" can manifest. What manifests is a position of zero concepts.

Zero concepts guarantees zero identities, zero fears, zero desires, zero unhappiness, zero anxiety, zero restlessness, zero conflict, zero attachments, zero imprisonment, zero…period.

Enjoy the Nothingness and even the No-Nothingness. Peace and Light

THE FINAL
UNDERSTANDING

by
floyd henderson

CHAPTER ONE

A series of books by the author offer the following:

1. An opportunity for seekers to be guided through the seven-step "journey" from identification with the false "I" (via the content of the book FROM THE I TO THE ABSOLUTE) and to move beyond The Seven Degrees of Separation from Reality";

2. An opportunity to understand the nature of Reality Beyond Self-Realization (with the content of the book CONSCIOUSNESS / AWARENESS); and

3. An opportunity to understand that which was prior to the Absolute, namely, The Void, the Nothingness.

To reach all three of those levels of understanding is to allow the seeker to grasp Sri Nisargadatta Maharaj's pointer that "wisdom is knowing that I am nothing."

For most seekers, the "journey" ends when they reach the third of seven steps as they move along the first-stage "path," specifically, the point at which they adopt a new persona ("The Spiritual One") and then never move any further.

There, Maharaj said, they engage in what he called "kindergarten-level spirituality" and they "mistake the dawn for the noonday sun." Only a few will truly understand the distinction between the consciousness and the awareness, and fewer still will be willing to abandon the notion that now they are Really Something and to consider the ultimate freedom of The Nothingness.

The book THE FINAL UNDERSTANDING is only for the few that are willing to consider that there is far more to grasp after having reached the third, spiritual step (which will only move them into the dim light of dawn"; for the few that have the slightest awareness that the brighter light of the full noonday sun awaits; and for the few that have some sense that the freedom and peace which come with abandonment of the notion that they are Really Something will allow for the full shift into the no-concept, no-identity, non-dual Reality.

In THE FINAL UNDERSTANDING, the author discusses:

A. The myths of a "Prior Me" and a "Post-Manifestation Me";

B. The myths of "You-ness," "Me-ness," and "Them-ness";

C. Krishna's pointers about that which is beyond the beingness and the non-beingness;

D. Abandonment of "the personal" and "The Personal" and an understanding of Presence instead;

E. The composite unity (elements, breath, conscious-energy);

F. The sixteen shifts in awareness which must happen in a step-wise fashion for misunderstandings to be abandoned and for the final understanding to manifest;

G. The pointers about religion and spirituality that were offered by Maharaj which allow seekers (who are trapped at the third step while playing their "new and improved persona or personas") to move along the entire "path" and then reach the final understanding;

H. A distinction between supernatural, unnatural, and nisarga (natural) living; and much more.

For those who have studied any of the various types of yoga and who have studied either Traditional Advaita Vedanta, Neo-Advaita, Neo-Vedanta, or Pseudo Advaita: the author of this book is a disciple of Sri Nisargadatta Maharaj so he uses the Direct Path Method of teaching along with the Nisarga (Natural) Yoga, all shared in simple, everyday English.

CHAPTER TWO

A visitor asked this when a pointer was offered that there was no pre-manifestation WHONESS: "No prior Me-ness? Surely there was something!"

Note that the pointers in the reply are not for the seeker that is on the early steps along the "path," nor for those attached to beliefs that are based on the content of supposedly "holy" texts.

The pointers that were offered in response were (as always) level-appropriate. Maharaj never offered a "gunpowder level" response to one whose words indicated that a seeker was still at "the wet charcoal stage." The same applies here.

Thus, these pointers are for those that have done it all, sought it all, "gotten" most of it, and yet realize that there is some "final piece" that is still missing; thus, these talks are for only those at the highest state of readiness.

That said, the response was as follows:

The only "prior something" in "your" case was a series of ancestors, and those ancestors were basically plant food. All who have been considered your "ancestors" and your so-called "parents" were nothing more than a conglomeration of food particles - just the essence of whatever was eaten. Those combined particles resulted in a form or space in which conscious-energy manifested for a spell and through which the air moved for a spell.

Seekers who have studied Traditional Advaita Vedanta - and some who have studied via the Direct Path Method here - want to be able to define some pre-manifestation "who-ness" or "what-ness" as well as some post-manifestation "who-ness" or "what-ness." At a certain level, fine.

With seekers at those certain levels, such talk of Self is level-appropriate. And yes, even Direct Path Method teachers will suggest that seekers at certain levels "find where they were days prior to conception," a consideration offered here on occasion.

But for the seekers moving farther along the "path," it is to be understood that at a certain point, even the egg and sperm did not exist as the forms that would later be involved in the impregnation that nine months later resulted in what was called "the birth" of what was called "you."

But here, at the ultimate level, the focus in the end is not on what is taught and learned (or un-taught and un-learned) via the Direct Path Method. Here, at the ultimate level, the focus is on that which can happen via an understanding of the Nisarga Yoga and the natural style in which the remainder of the relative existence can unfold when all notions of "who-ness" and "what-ness" dissolve.

The totally contented deer that live in the copses and smaller pockets of trees that surround the house are the model. The difference is, unlike programmed and conditioned persons, the deer do not have to go through the Direct Path Method steps as offered here in order to be prepared to understand the means to nisarga living as offered here.

They go straight to it, automatically ... spontaneously. They enter into a style of natural living and are never "diverted" from the path they travel. That only happens to humans. So let the discussion move forward in order for the diversions to be dissolved and in order for the natural, free, blissful, non-dual, no-concept, no-beingness, and no non-beingness abidance to begin and to be enjoyed ... NOW.

Thus, the invitation is (to those ready, and only for those ready) to receive the final understanding. With that prerequisite, consider: how could any "you" have existed "prior to" if even the food (which would be converted to an egg cell and a sperm cell that would unite and result in an impregnation) had not even been eaten in those days prior to conception and if - even earlier - the food that would become an egg cell and a sperm cell did not yet even exist in its edible form?

Go back - follow the trail in order to trace what you think yourself to be. Move back from (8) the conception to (7) a sperm set into motion to spontaneously seek an egg to (6) an act of friction to (5) plant food cells being transformed into sperm and egg cells to (4) plant food being prepared and eaten to (3) plant food being acquired to (2) plants growing to (1) the elements.

Where in that chain - which can be traced back and can be seen to have been repeated for trillions upon trillions of times for millions upon millions of years on this planet - could you possibly claim the existence of any "you-ness" or "You-ness"?

WHO would want to make such a claim? Only the one motivated by arrogance, as is a woman in Louisiana who is totally pre-occupied with "her genealogy." Only one so trapped in one or more ego-states and in so much egotism that one would want to trace his or her lineage back to some "famous, big name people" and beyond that to "God" or "a god" or "a goddess" or some "Supreme Self."

All of that talk is fine along the way, but at the end of all of the talk, is one merely attached to newly-acquired Advaita concepts or is one free to abide naturally? The end game here is not to allow a new ego-state to emerge, namely, "The Advaita Vedanta Expert"; the end game here lies not in the teaching method but in the yoga ... not in acquiring new knowledge but in being free of all knowledge and living as naturally as everything else on the planet except humans.

The option should be clear: (A) the "personal- you, persona-game" will trap you for the entirety of the manifestation in the fluctuations between gladness and sadness, between efforts to generate chaos out of boredom or efforts to control in order to eliminate chaos; or (B) the "end-game" will allow for the freedom to merely witness persons as they try to control and as they generate chaos or as they react to chaos and try to eliminate it.

CHAPTER THREE

THE farther removed You become from your "Me-ness" and their "They-ness," the smaller everything that is witnessed will become. This final understanding allows you to turn around the telescope that you have been using to witness what you witness - exaggerating its size and significance - and allows you to look at all through the reversed telescope and witness everything in a far more accurate view:

by turning the telescope around, all that is witnessed appears to be small and insignificant. That is as it should be. Then, you will function as the doe that was witnessed one morning while coasting by her during the morning bicycle ride.

She lay at the edge of the road in the cool blue shade. She watched "the approach" and "the passing by" but her two huge eyes revealed a totally detached expression - a totally detached demeanor - and it was clear that neither "floyd" nor the bike nor "the coming" nor "the going" meant a damn thing to her.

With the final understanding, you can live as sanely as she. You will not be attached to, nor pre-occupied with, "the apparent coming" or with "the inevitable going." That will leave you free of the misery and suffering that are generated by the desires and the fears of personality and personal identity (or, more typically, multiple identities).

The invitation here is to be as free of the concepts of "Me-ness" and "Them-ness" as she and to then abide as she abides: with total independence, with total freedom from cares and concerns, with an ability to do what must be done to allow the manifestation to continue for now but to simultaneously abide in a fashion that allows the manifestation to continue in a natural - rather than in some phony, supernatural or some debilitating, unnatural - manner.

[Again, please note that the pointers in this reply are not for the seeker that is early along the "path," nor for those attached to beliefs that are based on the content of supposedly "holy" texts, nor for Spiritual Giants, next to whom I am a mere pygmy. One recently leveled the charge, "This is not spiritual awakening."

The reply: "Exactly! This is many steps beyond that level! You pegged Me spot on!"

And again, these pointers are for those that have done it all, sought it all, "gotten" most of it, and yet realize that there is some "final piece" that is still missing; thus, these talks are for only those at the highest state of readiness, those that have transcended all role-playing, including playing religious or spiritual roles.]

So, the response continues:

This final understanding is outright rejected prior to consideration by most on "the journey," truly despised by others. Many who claim to be totally Realized - which would require that they presently abide in a no-concept, no-identity, non-dual manner - nevertheless cling to their Advaita or Hindu or Vedanta concepts and cling to an identity, identifying "with" something Supreme or "as" something Supreme. So much for no-concept, no-identity abidance. So much for ego-less-ness and for egotism-less-ness.

Ego (whether the term refers to "identity" or "selfness" or "Selfness") is still identity, no matter its mind-and-persona-assigned "rank." If Krishna was pointing to truth when he reported that what follows the manifestation is beyond being and even beyond non-beingness, then Personal Identification is as big a hoax as personal identification.

And if Krishna was pointing to truth when he reported that what follows the manifestation is beyond being and even beyond non-beingness, then whatever preceded the manifestation also has nothing to do with beingness or even non-beingness (because whatever is real is unchanging, "then," "now," or "later").

Next, to WHOM could Personal Identification be important? To WHOM could Personal Identification be special? To WHOM could Personal Identification be noble? WHO is claiming "spiritual awakening" while denying others are awakened? WHO is "This Special Knower"?

Furthermore, WHO that looks objectively and clearly at the consequences of this manifested consciousness would give it any value? WHO - except those so attached to body and mind and personality (and to the perpetuation of this consciousness) - would accept it, if an option had been offered?

WHO - other than those desiring such perpetuation - would think it sane to desire multiple cycles in multiple "lesser" forms leading, supposedly, to some "greater" forms, all believed in with a willingness to experience cycle after cycle of misery and suffering and all satisfied with the prospect of having happiness eventually rather than grasping the bliss at the only time it can be known, which is right now?

WHO believes that there can be a knower and knowingness in the Absolute when no such thing is possible? Those who normalize suffering "here" and "now" in order to receive some reward "there" and "later"? Those who have assumed some spiritual or special identification now?

Maharaj's advice to one could apply to all: "I advise you to give up spirituality and follow your vocation."

and this:

Visitor: "The scriptures say that we have our karma and ours sins and that is why we are here."

Maharaj: "That is for the ignorant masses. One who has realized the Self-Knowledge 'I Am,' for him these stories are of no use."

See, your stories, all of them, are of no use; thus, you are invited to re-consider the biological, scientific facts introduced yesterday that can lead to this final understanding: for the seekers moving farther along the "path," it is to be understood that even the egg and sperm did not exist that would later be involved in the impregnation that nine months later resulted in what was called "the birth" of what was called "you."

You were also invited to:

Go back - trace what you think yourself to be. Move back from (7) the conception to (6) a sperm set into motion to spontaneously seek an egg to (5) an act of friction to (4) plant food cells being transformed into sperm and egg cells to (3) plant food being prepared and eaten to (2) plant food being acquired to (1) plants being grown.

CHAPTER FOUR

TO review, you were invited additionally to consider this: the end game here lies not in the teaching method but in the yoga ... not in acquiring new knowledge but in being free of all knowledge and living as naturally as everything else on the planet lives ... except humans. So, to continue with the process of debunking your belief about a "prior Me-ness":

The food particles / cells within two humans which would combine with each other through an act of friction - entered into for their pleasure and not at all with "you" in mind - began a process that would someday be called "you"; however, those particles / cells did not even exist until a few days prior to conception. How could "you" have been "prior to" when the plant food elements that would form the space that they would call "you" had not even been consumed, much less transformed yet into eggs and sperm?

At times, "Presence" and "the Composite Unity" are discussed when seekers come here for Advaita retreats. You can speak of being the consciousness or the conscious-energy, but here, what registers is not even that. Here, what registers is a feeling only, and that feeling is not "I am present" but is "I am Presence."

[Notice: To emphasize for the "advanced" seeker, understand that the message is not "You are present and she is present and I am present." Most accurately, the statement is, "I am Presence." That alone do I feel.]

On the patio one morning, a bird was sitting on the edge of the table. After preparing a cup of breve and then going outside and approaching the table, the bird flew away. Why? Did it have "a thought?" No. Was it conscious of some verbalized lesson taught? No.

It moved away merely because the manifested consciousness allowed it to sense its Presence. Combine that with the desire of the manifested consciousness to extend itself and voilà - the movement away. If talk of the presence of consciousness fits more with the understanding you have at this point, fine, use that for now.

At some point, though, if You reach the final understanding that is being pointed to here, You will allow Me to pour into You the Ultimate Medicine that acts as what is called here "a type of dissolving agent." (Again, this talk too is only for those at the highest state of readiness.)

Then, all of your sense of Me-ness and a prior Me and a post-manifestation Me will dissolve into nothingness. There will be no you ... no You ... no individual ...nothing personal ... nothing Personal ... and, in the end ... not even the consciousness of "being present."

Want peace? There it is. In sleep, there is no sense of being present that is being registered. Prior to, as the Absolute, there was no "being present" that was registering. Post to, as the Absolute, there will be no "being present" that will register.

If there is a WHO involved, "being present" will register and you'll fly about as the bird did that morning when it became disturbed because it wanted its "being present" to continue.

The bird that morning had no choice, but you might. If you become free of being driven by personas, (especially your "good" spiritual persona vs. your former "bad" roles that you have supposedly abandoned), which would you choose?

Presence and peace, or "being present" and fluctuating between peace and disturbance? Playing spiritual roles for the next forty years, or living naturally and joyfully now, day by day?

Strutting about in a fine cloak of spirituality that requires constant maintenance, or moving through this relative existence in a low-maintenance garb (as is the case with the one here that is admittedly a tiny pygmy when next to the Spiritual Giants who occasionally approach and hover overhead and look down at this tiny speck)?

CHAPTER FIVE

I N the undertaking for You to be free of all beliefs - including the belief in a "prior Me" - then You must reach the next level of understanding.

That means You must abandon belief in "a present Me" - understanding that what You are taking to be "a Me" is not that at all - in order to be free of belief in "a prior Me" and also belief in a "later Me" that will exist post-manifestation.

All sense of "personal" and / or "Personal" must be abandoned in order to reach the no-concept, no-identity state; thus, the next transition is this: to make the gradual move away from such talk as "I am present, she is present, he is present," You were invited to use "I am Presence" instead; now, even that must be transitioned because "am" is to be followed by nothing.

So, now the shift will be away from "It is not that I am present but that I am Presence" to ... "Presence Is." That can be witnessed by the unobstructed consciousness if all of the obstacles that were set into place by programming and conditioning and acculturation and domestication have been removed.

Understand that Me-ness is as conceptualized as Is-ness, Am-ness, and being-ness. To attach to such concepts will be to block any chance to "see" the Absolute (and that which is beyond, neither of which can be expressed in words because Truth can be known - at least while the pure consciousness is manifested - but not stated).

This subject matter is covered in the "Advanced Seekers' Trilogy" of books but this is not told to novices or to "Spiritual Giants" or even to those at steps one through seven on the seven step "journey" from the "I" to the Absolute.

If you would abide as the Absolute, as that unmanifested Awareness, then you must understand the pointers offered in the second book in that series, a book intended to be read after reading FROM THE "I" TO THE ABSOLUTE: namely, "Consciousness / Awareness." It is explained there that ...

... "in" the Absolute realm, there is awareness but no aware-of-ness, but what I speak of here - if I am speaking of the final understanding - is even beyond the Absolute. That is why the third book in the "Advanced Seekers' Series" deals with the final "shift" <u>From the Absolute to the Nothingness</u>.

For now, understand this: prior to conception, which was a spontaneous act with no single cause, there was no You. At best all that can be said accurately is what Maharaj notes, that there was what he called a "you-are-not state." The elements were. Then the elements were eaten. Then cell transformations happened. Then an act of friction happened.

Nine months later there was the composite unity of elements, breath, and conscious-energy, but what could you take to exist as "You-ness" prior to the act of conception when the egg and sperm involved did not exist until shortly prior to the conception after plant food was consumed and plant cells transformed - spontaneously - into sperm and egg cells?

Furthermore, understand that in all of that, there was no "creation." Neither energy nor matter can be created. What was, was, but what was, was not "you" or "You" in any way. Understand that and then expand the point to include the "world" so that You understand that no world was created; from that, know that there was no one or One who created a world ... or anything else. Just as the composite unity that would be called "you" came about spontaneously, so too did what is called "the world" arise spontaneously. More significantly, understand that both "you" and "the world" are illusions.

CHAPTER SIX

HOW it is that what is called "floyd" is so completely free of all of the "stuff" of this relative existence though enjoying the bliss of the Absolute having been overlaid upon the relative? Having understood the impersonal consciousness, then it was a tiny step farther to reach an understanding of the present state of impersonal Presence. (This pointer too is only for those at the highest state of readiness.)

In order for the ultimate understanding to happen, however, it is not only necessary to understand that there was no "you" or "You" prior to manifestation and that there will be no "you" or "You" post-manifestation; it is also necessary to know that there is no "you" or "You" now. The composite unity involves no "Me-ness," no "You-ness," no "Them-ness." Such personalized, individualized identities - no matter how noble they seem - would have to be dualistic by their very subject-object nature, the belief in those concepts allowing only lip service to be given to the unicity ... to truly understanding the Oneness.

Yes, the Direct Path pointers that guide seekers along the later steps of the seven-step "journey" from identification with the false "I" to abidance as the Absolute most assuredly discuss "You-ness" / the True Self / the Pure Witnessing Consciousness.

Thorns all, however, to be discarded at the level of the final understanding. So many take their favorite teaching method and its teachings as the final step, adopting a religious or spiritual persona and fixating in that role for the remainder of the manifestation ... doin spiritual stuff and eating spiritual stuff and wearing spiritual stuff and - in all of their spiritual doingness - living in what they take to be a most non-natural, supernatural, "elevated," "higher" (and, yes, "separate and different") manner.

Here, the Direct Path Method can be considered the vehicle by which the "journey" happens along the "path" and the Nisarga Yoga can be considered the map; however, neither is the destination. The destination is nisarga (natural) living.

It has been witnessed that far too often, "The Spiritual Ones" (who are full of Self) feel separate and different from "the non-spiritual ones" who are full of self (or selves). Yet the ego-state of "The Spiritual One Full of Self" exhibits as much arrogance - and often more - than those persons who are trapped in their own assumed ego-states and who are embroiled in self.

How to be free of the persona that is Full of Self as well as the personas that are full of self? How to be free of belief in a "Prior Me," a "Present Me," and a "post-manifestation Me"? Simple: understand the stages that are involved.

CHAPTER SEVEN

THOUGH the stages have been discussed time and again on this site, many in recently-received e-mails have requested that the series of shifts be delineated exactly because some seem contradictory to others. At some point, they are. They have been offered in the step-wise fashion required for the shifts to occur (each movement to the next understanding predicated on previous shifts that must happen in as exact an order as the seven steps to Realization).

Thus, the stages of the shifts shall be delineated exactly in order as requested.

Understand first that these stages lay out the shifts involved in the movement from the no perception, no you, no-perceiver state to the misperceiving state to the perception state to the clarity and understanding state to the Final understanding state. The stages - and the ever-continuing cycles - unfold in this manner:

I. The no-you state, the you-are-not state, the no-beingness and no non-beingness state

II. The manifested consciousness state, the "I am" state

III. The "I am this" and "I am that" state

IV. The "I am present but no longer believe that I am limited to the formerly-assumed 'this' or a 'that' " state

V. Though I do not believe that I am "this" or "that," I do believe that I am Something - and even "Something Special" - that shall be forever (So all beliefs have not yet been discarded)

VI. "I am Presence" (That understanding allows for at least some distance to manifest between the "I" and the notions of "materiality and physicality")

VII. "Presence is" (That understanding takes the "I" out of the picture completely)

VIII. "No presence is" (That removes from the picture the concepts of the limited "Is-ness," the "Am-ness," the "Beingness," and even the "Non-Beingness")

IX. "I am nothing" (The "wisdom manifested" state as the pointer "Wisdom is knowing that I am nothing" is understood)

X. "There is no one to be wise, to know, to understand" state

XI. The "Neti-neti" state

XII. The "I am the Absolute Awareness with no aware-of-ness" state

XIII. The "Rather than, 'I am nothing,' the Nothingness is" state

XIV. Then, the "nothing is" state, including nothing and no one to believe, conceptualize, learn, perceive, know, understand, do, or assume anything (At this point, Reality has been overlaid upon the relative and abidance can happen in the deer-like mode with the limitless freedom of nothingness: no concepts, no beliefs, no duality

XV. The Unmanifestation stage

XVI. The cycle is complete with there once again being the no-you state, the you-are-not state, the no-beingness state, the no non-beingness state

The I Am-ness allowed for only the most limited degrees of understanding, necessarily based as the beingness is in a sense of something existing that could have multiple identities (or one "Super Identity"). Because of programming, conditioning, acculturation and domestication, it is not possible to leap from "I am" to "Void-ness." Shifting by stages is required until the limited knows that which is limitless.

CHAPTER EIGHT

TO ease the movement through stages I - XVI, an understanding of the composite unity often facilitates the process.

It must be understood that all of the things that one took himself / herself to be in the past - including any and all personalized and individualized ego-states, roles, selves, identities, stage characters, personas, personalities, etc. - were nothing more than misperceptions.

Specifically, this must be seen: that which is nothing more than a composite of elements, breath, and conscious-energy was mistakenly assumed to be something "personal." Of those three, which part could be considered "personal"? No part. Not the elements. Not the breath. Not the conscious-energy.

Additionally, to be free of feeling offended or threatened or hurt, see that none of those three could ever possibly take anything "personally" (or "persona-ly").

Having transcended the I-Amness, in fact, no part of the composite unity can know itself (some will prefer "ItSelf") as "I am." Even that Am-ness has been left behind, having been recognized as just another concept to be discarded on the final leg of the "path."

Maharaj: "The 'state' of 'beingness' is clearly an incomplete, provisional state of understanding. The sages and prophets recognized the sense of 'being' initially. Then they meditated and abided in it and finally transitioned it, resulting in their Ultimate Realization."

After the Final Understanding manifests, then abidance happens spontaneously, not as the "I am" but as the Absolute Awareness - awareness that is not aware of - and there is no registration even of the "I am" anymore.

There is in the Absolute (or as the Absolute) no "one" to know or to recognize beingness or Am-ness. Most assuredly, therefore, there is no "one" abiding in the Nothingness (or as nothing ... as no thing) that can register any sense of "I Am." All happens spontaneously with no sense that there is some "one" making it happen or some "one" doing anything.

All of that was filtered out when the "veil" was passed through when the movement from the illusory "here" and the misperceived "this" to the Reality of the nothingness happened. Wherefore any sense of a "prior Me" if not even a sense of a "present Me" is registering?

To speak of a "prior Me," you must have missed the point of the talk on the Presence and the composite unity in the post you referenced. Now, the invitation is to consider both. Then the case with you can be the same as the case here: the I-Amness state has been transcended, and You too can transcend the state if you but understand.

Maharaj taught that the Presence (the I-Amness) should not even be here: "The non-'I-Am-ness' only can meet that nothingness."

Does the deer sit in the cool blue shade and mentally repeat, "I Am, I Am, I Am"? Practice that mantra in the early steps along the "path" in order to end once and for all the habit of following "I am" with any personifying noun or adjective, but at some point, please! Stop it. Stop the mental machinations and sink into the bliss of nothingness.

Maharaj advised seekers to move "up to the precipice of consciousness" and to then fall "into the abysmal depth." Everything experienced, he said, is non-eternal. His invitation was to "experience" the eternal and to "experience" the Void, even as it is understood that there is no "experiencer" at all.

Transcend the I-Amness and only then will you know total independence and total freedom, and only with the manifestation of total independence and total freedom can the complete bliss then manifest; yet even the bliss can only happen now, not "later," not post-manifestation. Bliss is now or never, and bliss is only available consistently when abidance happens naturally.

To delusionally try to live "supernaturally" - in either a super-spiritual or super-religious style that stops the movement along the seven-step "path" at the third step - will actually result in living unnaturally (knelling, rising, pleading, attending, chanting, dunking, sprinkling, burning this, ringing that, etc.).

Maharaj reflected on a visit to the loft by two college students and how he advised them to "forget spirituality." He invited them to follow "their normal inclinations" - that is, their natural tendencies - and to "do your normal duties" and "just give up spirituality."

That advice was rooted in his own experience that had bogged him down. He was trying to spare them years or decades of being similarly bogged down. He said:

"I got involved in spirituality, in the business of spirituality, [but] finally I lost that love of the Self also. I have no more love for the Self."

What an otherwise-warped manner of thinking, as if loving the Self is less selfish and less self-centered than loving the self (or selves). To be preoccupied with Self as opposed to being preoccupied with self still results in preoccupation and in the busy-ness of occupation with Self.

Only those who ...

... love the doingness of religion and

... love the going and the doing and zooming involved with spiritual exercises and

... who are too bored to be able to sit quietly in the solitude and

... who unconsciously prefer chaos over calm and
... who find natural living to be "less noble" and

... who think that they require love from the masses or admiration from the crowds in order to feel full inside

would take a busy religious life or a busy spiritual life over a simple, relaxing, quiet, natural existence. And that option is not a "no-brainer."

It is a "no-minder."

Maharaj: "So long as one depends on the mind, the mind will always make us unhappy. What is suffering really? Suffering is only something which has been engendered by a thought or a word - [by] the mind."

Nothingness. Mindlessness. Doing-less-ness. Ahhhh.

CHAPTER NINE

AGAIN, these posts have been for those that have reached the end of the "path" and are now ready to fall "into the abysmal depth" and be totally free. That means the points in this book:

A. have not been for the masses who are living lives in which they are playing a variety of characters on a stage in their "Theatre of the Lie";

B. have not been for those who identify with the body-mind-personality triad instead of understanding the composite unity of elements-breath-conscious-energy;

C. have not been for those who have stopped playing their earlier "lesser roles" but who have now adopted "higher personas" (either "The Religious One" or "The Spiritual Giant") and are subsumed in the activities of those ego-states and in the egotism that both engender; and

D. have not been for those who have discarded their "love of self" but have replaced that with the equally egocentric "love of Self."

Here, there is neither any subject-object "I love self" (as happened in "the old days") nor any "I love Self" (as happened at the midpoint on the "path" to Realization when the focus was on trying to live "religiously" and "spiritu-ally" and before Full Realization resulted in a natural, no-role manner of living instead).

All of that adoption of "new and improve roles" happens at step three of the seven steps on the "path" to Realization where the playing of "good" roles replaces the playing of "bad" roles. That phase was eventually seen for what it really is: just arrogance-generating nonsense where new roles replace old roles and where seekers become convinced, delusionally, that they are free of their false identities.

It became understood that a naturally-abiding deer loves neither self nor Self nor consciousness, though it will respond in the fashion that the consciousness always responds in order to try to extend the length of its manifestation.

But what did the one called here, affectionately, "The Maverick Master of Mumbai" offer in terms of the final understanding about religion and spirituality and why one or both must be played for a time but must be transcended eventually if the full understanding is to come?

CHAPTER TEN

MAHARAJ ON RELIGION

MAHARAJ: "Thousands of organizations have come and gone, thousands are yet to come. All of them are based on a certain concept" so " ... none of these organizations have any use; the ultimate thing is to find out about one's true nature. In this, organizations can do nothing because they are all based on a certain concept."

F.: Religions are the key source and key disseminator of dualistic concepts, focusing as they do on good vs. bad, right vs. wrong, moral vs. immoral, heaven vs. hell, reward vs. punishment, higher vs. lower, ad infinitum.

Maharaj: "Once the knowledge of the Self dawns, there is no longer any question of good or bad, suffering or not suffering, happiness vs. unhappiness; the question just does not arise."

CHAPTER ELEVEN

MAHARAJ ON SPIRITUALITY

MAHARAJ: "In the true state, nothing is. All this spiritual talk is spiritual jargon. You can talk in the world to the ignorant masses; you can convey any number of concepts to them" but " ... such concepts are for the ignorant people."

He asked: "Ultimately, what are these spiritual talks? They are meant for so long as ignorance prevails. To remove the ignorance, so-called knowledge is necessary. The knowledge removes the ignorance and then itself also goes"; then, he said, "both knowledge and ignorance are thrown overboard."

Also, he addressed the very reason that "Spiritual Giants" come here and criticize these pointers, as they did during the days he shared:

"I will not talk about what is being generally talked about elsewhere on the mistaken notion that they are discussing 'spiritual knowledge.' Parroting the opinions of others, that is not knowledge." He added, "Whatever knowledge you have is hearsay."

He taught: "Don't be led astray by all the so-called spiritual disciplines and rigmaroles."

Maharaj: "If you think you are interested in spirituality, I am dissuading you," advising, "Don't jump into this spiritual thing."

Instead, his invitation was to fall into "the abysmal depth" of the nothing-ness, to garner the wisdom that will make clear that "You are nothing." Then, the no-knowing, no-knower, no-concept abidance as the Awareness state can happen.

As that state, there is no aware-of-ness. The precipitating understandings that allow for abidance as the Absolute (and as that "depth" which is beyond) include the following:

1. Nothing is as it appears;
2. This beingness - by its very nature - is a culprit, engendering a limited sense of understanding and a sense of separate identity;
3. The "I-Am-ness" is worn by all but a few as a shroud of illusion, typically blocking the view of the Absolute and most definitely blocking the enjoyment of the bliss of the Nothingness;
4. Even identification with the consciousness, the Absolute, and the Nothingness must be transcended, allowing the remaining abidance to happen as the no-concept, no-belief, non-dual, no-identity Reality;
5. There was no "Prior Me or You" and there shall be nothing remaining with any sense of a post-manifestation "Me or You";
6. As the Void, there is also no "Present Me," no "Present You," and no "Present Them."

Floyd: Inquiries continue to be received that ask for a clarification of the terms frequently mentioned here, namely, natural living, unnatural living, and supernatural living. Some pointers offered in the past will be shared for more recent visitors to the site.

The relative existence will unfold in one of three ways: either in a (Nisarga) natural manner; in a supposedly (super) natural manner; or in a most (un) natural manner. Just as oil and water cannot mix, there can be no sane existence that can happen in a "partly this style" and "partly that style."

For example, there can be no sane existence that can happen in a partly unnatural and partly natural manner; furthermore, there can be no sane existence that can involve living in any combination of styles because that will preempt abidance as the unicity and will support the illusion of duality. Some trying to live in all three styles are lost in triplicity and are trapped in the misery of their multiple personality disorder.

CHAPTER TWELVE

(SUPER) NATURAL LIVING

SUPERNATURAL living preempts natural living. To believe that one is living in a supernatural fashion is to believe that one is accessing a super-power. Supernatural beliefs are supported by magical thinking, and all magical, erroneous thinking is supported by the concepts and falsehoods that are stored in what is called "the mind."

The basic, supernatural belief is that the natural existence cannot happen effectively without being in a close relationship with an other-world power who lives not in close proximity but who lives in a place that is very far away in a location that is always "up there" (no matter where on the globe such a believer might be standing while pointing upward).

(NOTE: For many, the belief is that there is not a single, other-world power but that there are multiple gods assuming hundreds of forms, a belief that is no different at all from the beliefs held by ancient Greeks and Romans who thought that their myth-based stories were true).

However, for most of the 14.5 million years that humans or human-like beings walked the planet, they lived in a natural, non-supernatural manner because there was no language by which they could be taught that myths and superstitions are true.

Written language developed a little more than 5000 years ago, at which time the dreamed-up tales of gods began to be recorded in texts that would someday be considered "holy." So out of the 14.5 million years that humans have walked the planet, all but the last few thousand years were lived quite naturally and quite successfully without any holy texts discussing supernatural beings and teaching supernatural concepts.

Additionally, all 14.5 million years were lived (with the possible exception of the last 100,000 years of that span) without any oral tales being told and circulated about supernatural concepts and supernatural beings. How can that be known? Science proves without a doubt that it was only about 100,000 years ago that, anatomically, humans developed hominid vocal tracts that were of a shape that would permit a range of speech sounds.

Even then, it would have required thousands of years for the development of vocabulary and thousands more to develop supernatural concepts that could be verbalized. So natural living prevailed for millions of years whereas the human effort to try to live supernaturally is a recent phenomenon in terms of the overall human experience; moreover, the relative existence was a fairly simple existence prior to efforts by controlling men and women to overlay supernatural concepts onto the previously all-natural existence. That complicating factor and the roots of distortion and delusion were discussed in 2008 in this passage:

Note the loss of simplicity when the first medicine man dreamed up not just a rain god but an angry rain god. Before that point, humankind would have witnessed and accepted the fact that when it rains, it rains; when it does not rain, it does not rain; when it is hot, it is hot; and when it is cold, it is cold.

After that god was dreamed up, note how complicated things became during the relative: parents had to offer up a daughter to have sex with a medicine man claiming to be "god's representative on earth"; to be killed; to have her heart cut out; and to participate as all passed the heart about and ate the body and drank the blood in a service that provided the chance to "commune" with the rain god and please him with sex and sacrifice.

Those early "worshipers" who engaged in the first communion services began to define morality and then inventoried what is "good" behavior and what is "bad" behavior so as not to anger the rain god any further; they codified their beliefs in "holy" books; they began to engage in preemptive strikes, sacrificing in advance rather than after the rain had stopped.

Now, when humans behave in the natural ways that humans engaged in for millions of years, other complicating concepts are added to the mix from the storehouse of supernatural beliefs: guilt, shame, rejection, disgrace, and fear, including the fear of not being rewarded now, the fear of not earning an eternal reward but of suffering eternal punishment instead, and the fear that if they don't give money or gifts and hours of "service," they will not get rewards both now and forevermore.

So the notion of trying to live supernaturally likely took a foothold 5000 or so years ago and certainly not more than 100,000 years ago. Compared to the natural way that humans lived for the other 14.4 million years, supernatural living is "the new kid on the block" in terms of the way that some humans try to live. It is not natural.

CHAPTER THIRTEEN

(UN) NATURAL LIVING

NEXT, unnatural living is an even "newer kid on the block." Unnatural living began when persons developed a section of the brain that is capable of storing and retrieving information. The storage part is commonly referred to as "the mind."

Again, the "thinking part" of the brain did not start processing ideas and concepts and beliefs until language developed. Nor did personality or personalities develop; therefore, the assumption of personas as identities did not happen except at the very end of the total human experience that has gone on for 14.5 million years.

Unnatural living only resulted after languages developed and after cultures developed and after those cultures began teaching their false concepts about multiple "identities." The subsequent unnatural way of living began when persons became so fooled that they (a) began to think that they are what they are not and (b) eventually ended up not having even the slightest clue about Who / What They Truly Are.

As a result, if persons today do not complete the seven-step "journey" to Reality, then they will never know Who/What They Truly Are. What hampers most seekers is not a lack of willingness to seek but their inability to find a teacher who can say, "You are right here on the 'path.' The next step is specifically this and then your final steps after that are these, specifically."

CHAPTER FOURTEEN

NISARGA, NATURAL LIVING

ABIDANCE with a lightness of being is natural living, not unnatural living and not supernatural living.

The pointer was offered that there can be no sane existence that can happen in a "partly this style" and "partly that style." That would be "dualistic living," and after he was taught the Advaitin understanding, Christ reportedly offered the pointer that "a dual-minded person is unstable in all ways."

Peace and freedom come when the Realized know that what some take to be "the supreme state" is really just the natural state, but that understanding can only come from beyond "the mind." Maharaj said, "Just live your life as it comes, but alertly, watchfully, allowing everything to happen as it happens, doing the natural things the natural way ...."

Then pure and natural beingness, free of body and <u>mind</u> states, would happen from the platform of abidance as the original, natural state.

If a nisarga, natural fashion of living were to happen, then the remainder of the beingness would happen effortlessly. Of course employment could continue, but it would happen effortlessly; of course "relationships" could continue, but they would happen effortlessly; and of course all that is required to nurture the beingness for the remainder of the manifestation would also happen, but it would happen effortlessly.

And <u>Love</u>, which few will ever understand but which most seek, would also happen quite effortlessly and most blissfully.

You may visit
FloydHenderson.com
or
Amazon.com
or
Amazon.co.uk
or
Amazon.de
for other titles by Floyd Henderson
PEACE, LOVE, LIGHT